THE STRUGGLE FOR
EUROPE'S CONSTITUTION

ANDREW DUFF

FEDERAL TRUST

For Dermot Coleman

1956–2004

Contents

Glossary

CAP	Common Agricultural Policy
CBI	Confederation of British Industry
CFP	Common Fisheries Policy
CFSP	Common Foreign and Security Policy
COREPER	Committee of Permanent Representatives
ECHR	European Convention for the Protection of Human Rights and Fundamental Freedoms
EEC	European Economic Community
GDP	Gross Domestic Product
GNI	Gross National Income
IGC	Intergovernmental Conference
NATO	North Atlantic Treaty Organization
OECD	Organization for Economic Co-operation and Development
OSCE	Organization for Security and Co-operation in Europe
QMV	Qualified Majority Vote
WEU	Western European Union
WTO	World Trade Organization

Preface

This is a book about the European Union's new Constitution that was signed by twenty-five national leaders in Rome on 29 October 2004. The Constitution was intended to come into force on 1 November 2006, once duly ratified by all member states.

That will not be. In May and June 2005 France and the Netherlands rejected the Constitution in referendums. All other things being equal, there is now no possibility that a promised referendum in the United Kingdom would give a positive answer. Accordingly, the ratification process elsewhere is grinding to a halt.

The rejection of the Constitution poses huge problems for the European Union at home and abroad. The political class in Europe generally, but in France, the Netherlands and Britain in particular, must ask itself some searching questions about how and why it failed to carry the Constitution. The European Council has ordained a 'period of reflection' on the Constitution. I examine the various options available and conclude that the reflection exercise should be used to prepare for a judicious renegotiation of the Constitution. If the EU could manage to recast the Constitution successfully, it will emerge from the crisis greatly strengthened.

If on the other hand nothing concrete comes out of the period of reflection, the EU will be much debilitated. There are certainly those in these circumstances, not least in Britain, who will prefer to drop the constitutional project. But ditching the Constitution would not mean that the problems it is designed to address will go away, or that the dissenters will suddenly be satisfied.

If the newly enlarged Union is to prosper it needs to be reformed. The reforms prescribed in the Constitution were arrived at after the long, innovative and highly legitimate process of the European Convention. A large consensus was formed around the Constitution of the EU institutions, national governments and parliaments (including the French, Dutch and British). It would be odd now entirely to surrender the Constitution to the historical archives. The Constitution is very good; but it is not perfect, and can be improved: it should therefore be salvaged if possible.

This book explains why the drafting of the Constitution is such an important episode in the history of the Union, and why its ultimate fate will so directly affect the future of Europe and its place in the world. I hope the book may help the reader decide whether or not to support the Constitution, and its renegotiation.

STRUCTURE OF THE BOOK

The book begins with the story of how and why the Constitution came to be written (chapters 1 and 2). The narrative of the main part of the book (chapters 3 to 19) broadly follows the logic of the structure of the Constitution itself. I describe what the Constitution says, why it says it, how it compares with the existing Treaties, and what it might mean if and when it enters into force. Chapter 20 looks at the failure to secure ratification and at the options now available to the Union as to what to do next. I argue that the Constitution can and should be rescued, and suggest, in chapters 21 and 22, some policy and institutional topics for renegotiation, as well as a process by which this hazardous task might be undertaken.

The Constitution – officially the *Treaty establishing a Constitution for Europe* – has a preamble, four parts, thirty-six protocols, two annexes and fifty declarations. There are 448 articles of the Constitution proper: only twenty-six articles are cited here in full, though numerous others are in part. Those who wish to access the whole text and have a computer can find it easily via the Europa site on europa.eu.int. Those who do not have access to the web should demand a (free) copy of the Constitution from their own government. It is also published at €25 by the EU Publications Office at publications.eu.int.

The articles of the Constitution are numbered sequentially. In common usage the articles are often prefixed by a Roman numeral to indicate to which of the four parts of the Constitution they belong. I adopt this system in the footnotes, but not in the text itself, which flows more smoothly when the prefixes are dropped (as they surely will be if and when we ever become more accustomed to the text).

Part One (Articles I–1 to I–60) contains the main provisions of the Constitution. Part Two (Articles II–61 to II–114) comprises the Charter of Fundamental Rights. Part Three (Articles III–115 to III–436) deals with the policies and functioning of the Union. Part Four (Articles IV–437 to IV–448) contains the general and final provisions.

ACKNOWLEDGMENTS

As far as secondary publications on the Constitution in English are concerned, there are as yet few. One expects more. Peter Norman has written the classical chronicle of the Convention: *The Accidental Constitution: the making of Europe's constitutional treaty*, EuroComment, Brussels (new & revised edition), 2005. Also interesting is Guy Milton and Jacques Keller-Noëllet, *The European Constitution: its origins, negotiation and meaning*, John Harper, London, 2005. Peter Ludlow's EuroComment series on each meeting of the European Council is informed and provocative.

The team at the Federal Trust has continued to surpass itself in commenting on the constitutional project. My special thanks are due to Brendan Donnelly and John Pinder. FT.com – the website of a truly European newspaper – gives me a monthly slot to rehearse my views. Other bodies – notably, the Trans-European Policy Studies Association (TEPSA), the European Policy Centre (EPC) and the Centre for European Policy Studies (CEPS) – have been useful sounding boards and networks.

I have written the book because I would like to live in a united Europe that is a constitutional democracy. I also want to share something of my own experience as a Member of the European Parliament who is privileged to have served in both the Convention on the Charter of Fundamental Rights (1999–2000) and in the Convention on the Future of Europe (2002–03). If there is another Convention, I would also like to serve in that.

Inevitably, my views are flavoured by my way of being a federalist by philosophy, a Liberal in politics, a Briton by nationality and a European by vocation. My views will not be shared by all those who, wittingly and unwittingly, have stimulated them. The Brussels press corps seldom ceases to amaze. Officials of the Parliament, Commission and Council are unfailingly polite even when exasperated. It continues to be an honour to work with many MEPs from all parties on the constitutional project. From my time in the Convention I am especially grateful to Pat Cox, Lamberto Dini, Lone Dybkjaer, Robert Maclennan and Wim Vanden Broucke.

My assistants during these years have been David Charlesworth and Tim Huggan in Cambridge, and Bernardo Costa Pereira, Roland Fleig, Rafael Jiménez-Aybar in Brussels. Most of all, my thanks go to Guillaume McLaughlin who makes me act as well as think.

Andrew Duff
Brussels and Cambridge
August 2005

CHAPTER 1

Europe's constitutional story

Europe's states and their peoples are more united today than at any time in history. Sixty years on from the end of the Second World War, the bonds that bring Europeans together in an economic, monetary and political Union of 455 million citizens and twenty-five member states are impressive and unprecedented. Yet powerful and successful though it undoubtedly is the European Union remains unfinished. European integration by peaceful and democratic means is still experimental. Those who wish the experiment well see the need for change and consolidation. Being in the majority, they have been able in recent years to pursue an ambitious programme of political and institutional reform which culminated in the signing of a new Treaty establishing a Constitution for Europe in Rome on 29 October 2004.

The Constitution was planned to enter into force two years later, once it had been ratified by all its member states. At the time of writing, thirteen states have completed their own ratification procedures; two have not, and ratification in the rest has stalled. Rejection of the Constitution in the French referendum on 29 May 2005 and in the Dutch referendum three days later has pitched Europe forward into a new and rather unexpected chapter in its constitutional story.

Although the Constitution in exactly its present form is unlikely to come into force, it is far from being dead and buried. The problems that the Constitution was designed to address are still with us. Too much has been invested in the writing of the Constitution and in securing its support by the governments of the twenty-five member states for it to be consigned casually to the historical archives. While there is certainly a crisis over its ratification, the basic consensus that was built into its drafting seems robust and the arguments behind it are sound. The need for the Union to reach a durable constitutional settlement is still pressing, indeed even the more so now that public opinion is shown to be sceptical. Nobody argues that the Constitution in its present form is perfect, or that in changed circumstances it could not be improved. But the options for redrafting the political choices are already well rehearsed. Whatever happens now in the immediate aftermath of the French and Dutch No votes, it is likely that many if not most of the provisions of this constitutional text will become part of the Union's constitutional order in due course.

Whether the eventual constitutionalisation of the Union results from a short and sweet renegotiation of the present text or more gradually by way of piecemeal, incremental change is a matter for debate. For reasons which will be explained in this book, we favour renegotiation now as more conducive to public opinion and more likely to complete satisfactorily the political processes that are already well underway. Once the arguments for the Constitution have been capably put, and the alternatives properly assessed, some sensible modifications can be made with every expectation that popular consent can be secured across Europe, including that of the most sceptical of countries, the United Kingdom.

Whether the fate of the present Constitution is to be a good first draft of a renegotiated text or a guide for future reforms, it is important to understand it well if we are to do better next time. So this book explains how the Treaty establishing a Constitution for Europe came to be written. It describes what the Constitution says, explains why it says it, and discusses what it might mean for Europe and the world. It examines why the ratification process of the Constitution has stumbled. It argues that the present, enforced period of reflection on the future of the Constitution should result in its careful renegotiation leading to its acceptance not only by Europe's states but also by its citizens. We suggest how this might be done.

ORDER OUT OF DISORDER

The European Union can ride a crisis. It was born out of the wreckage of war and was crafted to cope with a generally disorderly continent whose history is more war than peace, as much barbarism as chivalry, and much poverty and social instability amid rising wealth and social cohesion. Throughout its many centuries of general political disorder, however, Europe has been a place of enormous creativity in the arts and sciences, of enterprise in commerce, of faith and humanity. It is where the idea of democratic citizenship was born and took hold, and where a yearning for liberty and equality became prevailing driving forces. Europeans have always engaged themselves deeply in how to organise political society. They have been hugely inventive in statecraft. City states, theocracies, nation states, empires, despotism (enlightened and otherwise), fascist and communist dictatorships, constitutional monarchies, unitary republics, federal republics, even federal monarchies: all have been tried within a few miles and years of each other. It is as if Europe has forever been conducting a vast and continual political experiment on itself.

The common religious, cultural and philosophical heritage of Europe means that at one level the constitutional experiment has been collective and pan-European. Yet the political tests have taken place in different and often rival national laboratories. Results of the individual trials have not been well co-ordinated; many have not achieved ripe constitutional formulation. Indeed, throughout this foment of political change in Europe, there has been very little sense of durable constitutional settlement. (For this, we look to America.) Since the French Revolution in 1789 France has had sixteen different constitutions. Most of mainland Europe has suffered regularly from war, civil strife or revolution. Even Great Britain, that most stable and evolutive of European countries, has had periods of social unrest and political conflict, not least in relation to its neighbouring island of Ireland. Most European countries have some painful history of anti-semitism. All European countries, and not least those with a recent colonial past, are experiencing difficulties today in integrating significant numbers of ethnic minorities.

A recurrent theme of the story told in this book is Britain's peculiarly difficult relationship with the continental mainland. But Britain is not the only country for which European integration creates difficulties. Both Jean Monnet and Charles de Gaulle were Frenchmen, and an unresolved tension between them about the role of national sovereignty continues to cause trouble at the heart of French European policy. Two powerful Frenchmen exemplify this confusion today. Jacques Delors, President of the European Commission from 1985 to 1995 and chief author of the single market, calls ambiguously for a 'federation of nation states'. Jacques Chirac, President of the French Republic since 1995, wants united Europe to be a world power at the same time as he seeks to preserve scope for independent national action. Typical French ambivalence towards European federalism is not confined to the Republic. It is shared to a very large extent by Great Britain, which makes the volatile relationship between the French and British so ironic.

No doubt because of these historic national doubts and ideological quarrels, there has never been a simple, steady improvement in the way Europe has chosen to govern itself. Reformation has been followed by reaction. The advances of the eighteenth century Enlightenment and nineteenth century industrial revolution did not prevent Europe from slipping into its worst possible disorder in the first half of the twentieth century. After 1914 Europe's political and religious leaders lost their moral compass. European democracy was insufficiently mature and liberalism too weak to prevent the descent into war and genocide. The collapse of the old autocracies and the rise of fascism and communism proved to be a fatal combination – quite literally so for upwards of 100 million Europeans between the outbreak of the First World

War and the death of Stalin in 1953. Europe's civil war left it wounded and exhausted, and divided along the Iron Curtain. After 1945, world leadership passed to the United States of America.

During the last fifty years, however, firstly under American guardianship, the European Union has succeeded against the odds in bringing some order out of that chaos. European unification was demanded by a popular movement in the aftermath of the Second World War. The democratic leaders who emerged from the collapse of the French Third Republic, German Third Reich and Italian Fascism seized their own constitutional moment. It is right to attribute to Jean Monnet, Robert Schuman, Konrad Adenauer and Alcide De Gasperi the honorific title of 'founding fathers'. So, too, to Winston Churchill, who, while wishing to keep Britain somewhat apart, had the wisdom to encourage mainland Europeans to gather themselves together in the face of the Soviet threat. All the former belligerents, including the UK, were moved to establish a fresh form of intergovernmental co-operation in the Council of Europe as early as 1949. Shortly afterwards, the European Union, involving its members in the pooling of national sovereignty, was given its first form. France, Germany and Italy along with Belgium, the Netherlands and Luxembourg came together to create the European Coal and Steel Community in 1951. The original Six, who managed, despite difficulties, to continue along the path to economic and political integration, were eventually joined by the United Kingdom in 1973. By the time the Berlin Wall fell in November 1989, the European Union had grown to twelve member states. Five years later, the neutral countries of Austria, Finland and Sweden had joined up. And on 1 May 2004 ten more states joined, mainly from the former Soviet bloc.

At the time of writing, four more states are at various stages of their accession processes, while yet others are lining themselves up to apply for candidacy. The earliest possible date for the entry of Bulgaria and Romania is 2007. Turkey cannot expect entry until 2014. Croatia is keen to get in before Turkey. Apart from the Ukraine and the countries of the Western Balkans (with Macedonia in the lead), Norway may make its third application to join – in which case, Iceland may follow suit. Even without the curiosity of Switzerland, the Union is likely to have over thirty member states by 2020, with a population of nearly 600 million.

The EU is a strong pole of attraction to outsiders, but its internal evolution has been far from smooth. The agreement in principle to pool sovereignty proved difficult to apply in practice once the first, and easiest, phase of integration, involving the removal of national barriers, was succeeded by the inherently more complex stage of trying to fashion common policies across a wide spectrum. An early failure was the collapse of the European Defence Community in 1954. The UK first declined to join in the European Economic

Community and then, once it had changed its mind about membership, had its application twice rejected by France. At the same time, President de Gaulle also provoked the most serious attack on the emerging supranational authority of the EU by adopting an 'empty chair' policy in the Council. The UK, for its part, as soon as it had been let inside embarked on an effort to re-negotiate its terms of membership. The European Court of Justice and the European Parliament (directly elected since 1979) grew to be more powerful institutions. As the stakes were raised, the institutional dialectic became very much more complex. Decision making was slow and could be agonising. 'Euro-sclerosis' came to threaten the good functioning of the institutions and the good name of the Union.

BUILDING A CONSTITUTIONAL ORDER

How should one characterise the European Union? It is a peace project, placating once bitter enemies. It is a form of functional collaboration between governments, the scope of which has continued to grow from its initial focus in the 1950s on coal and steel towards a wider common market and customs union in the 1960s, to a fully fledged single market from the 1980s, to an economic and monetary union in the 1990s and, today, to common internal and external security policies. The European Union invokes the social and political integration of its peoples, initially, with the involvement of the social partners, in the field of labour policy, and later, with the participation of political parties, towards the development of the concept of EU citizenship, a common corpus of fundamental rights and a distinct common European polity. It is an internationally recognised legal entity above and beyond its member states within its own areas of competence, with a home-grown system of justice to settle its disputes.

Being quintessentially European, of course, the European Union cannot quite bring itself to agree about what it is. It has a continuing identity crisis, and worries a lot about its legitimacy and direction. But it has become clear that whatever the European Union is, it is not just one thing – not just a federal state, or just another international organisation, or just a common market, or just a supranational constitutional order. It has elements of all those four things, and its purpose too is fourfold: peace, prosperity, justice and security.

Europe's constitutional experiment has not taken place in isolation. In fact, had it not been for the perils of the Cold War or for the help and encouragement of the US the indigenous efforts at European unification might have stalled quickly. Interdependence among European states took on a new urgency once the phenomenon of globalisation became both self-evident and unstoppable.

Europe united could help to shape its response to globalisation politically: Europe disunited would not. When the Soviet empire collapsed, largely under the weight of its own contradictions, the peoples of Central and Eastern Europe demanded their rightful place in the Western unification process. At the same time, Europe's partnership with America changed forever. US hegemony began to be more resented than admired in Europe, and serious problems arose in EU–US relations with respect to trade, science, climate change, ethics, human rights, the future of Nato and, most dramatically, over what strategies to pursue in the Persian Gulf and the Middle East. With a wide new enlargement now pending and the external challenge to the EU more acute, the inevitable question was posed: could the European Union both expand and continue to integrate? One school of thought hoped that Europe would be able to widen and deepen at the same time. Another, epitomised by Margaret Thatcher, British prime minister from 1979 to 1990, believed happily that enlargement would lead ineluctably to a looser and less integrated Union. Was she right?

In June 1993 the leaders of the then twelve member states met in the European Council and agreed to lay down terms that would govern their future approach to the challenge of enlargement. The Copenhagen criteria determined that:

'Membership requires that the candidate country has achieved stability of institutions guaranteeing democracy, the rule of law, human rights and respect for and protection of minorities, the existence of a functioning market economy as well as the capacity to cope with competitive pressure and market forces within the Union. Membership presupposes the candidate's ability to take on the obligations of membership including adherence to the aims of political, economic and monetary union'.

'The Union's capacity to absorb new members, while maintaining the momentum of European integration, is also an important consideration in the general interest of both the Union and the candidate countries.'

In the event, Central and East European countries discovered that their transition from communism would be more problematical and protracted than had been foreseen. Meanwhile, the existing member states of the European Union stumbled through three difficult Intergovernmental Conferences of their own – at Maastricht in 1991, Amsterdam in 1996 and Nice in 2000 – before reaching the conclusion that if the momentum of European integration were to be maintained in the teeth of enlargement, more radical constitutional change would be necessary. The Intergovernmental Conference (IGC) is the Union's traditional way, prescribed in the Treaties, of revising its system of governance. Member state representatives – first diplomats, then junior ministers followed by heads of government – meet over several months in closed session to thrash out package deals between themselves. Only the fittest survive. The Commission participates but does not vote. The European Parliament has over the years acquired observer status at IGCs, but enjoys the power neither of initiative nor of assent.

During the 1990s, each reform of the Treaties was worse than the last. The scope of the package slimmed and the quality of the deal deteriorated. At the end of the long and fractious IGC that culminated in the Treaty of Nice in December 2000, the leaders had to agree on a Declaration that committed them to a 'deeper and wider debate about the future of the European Union' and to making a more considered declaration in one year's time on the 'continuation of this process'.[1] Already at Nice four items were picked out for special treatment:

- 'how to establish and monitor a more precise delimitation of powers between the European Union and the Member States, reflecting the principle of subsidiarity;'
- 'the status of the Charter of Fundamental Rights, proclaimed in Nice, in accordance with the conclusions of the European Council in Cologne;'[2]
- 'a simplification of the Treaties with a view to making them clearer and better understood without changing their meaning;'
- 'the role of national parliaments in the European architecture'.

The Declaration of the Nice Treaty also agreed that a new IGC would be convened in 2004. Frustration with the IGC process was voiced more widely, not least in the European Parliament, which had called for the establishment of a proper constitutional convention even before the debacle of Nice.[3] After Nice it fell to the Swedish presidency of the Council to pick up the pieces. The European Council, meeting in Göteborg in June 2001, agreed to broaden participation in the preparation of the next IGC and even to consider the creation of what it called an 'open forum'. The Swedes included as one option for this open forum the Parliament's idea of a convention, modelled on one that had drawn up a Charter of Fundamental Rights in 1999–2000.

'HOW TO ORGANISE POLITICS': THE LAEKEN DECLARATION

On 14–15 December 2001 Europe's heads of government met up to consider all these questions afresh. Present were the heads of state or government of the

---

[1] Declaration No. 23 of the Treaty of Nice.
[2] The Cologne European Council in June 1999 had established the Convention on the Charter of Fundamental Rights.
[3] European Parliament Resolution (Duhamel Report) on Constitutionalisation of the Treaties, 25 October 2000, A5–0289/2000.

fifteen member states of the European Union, the twelve 'accession states', and the 'candidate' state of Turkey. The meeting of the European Council took place in the exotic surroundings of King Leopold II's glasshouses at the Palace of Laeken, in a suburb of Brussels. It discussed, amended and published an eight page Laeken Declaration on the Future of the European Union. This had been drawn up by the Belgians with the advice of a group of supposedly wise men.[4] Although somewhat wordy, the Declaration eventually reaches its destination: a decision to set up a special Convention 'composed of the main parties involved in the debate on the future of the Union' whose task was to 'consider the key issues arising for the Union's future development and try to identify the various possible responses'.

The Laeken Declaration identified three basic challenges:

'How to bring citizens, and primarily the young, closer to the European design and the European institutions, how to organise politics and the European political area in an enlarged Union and how to develop the Union into a stabilising factor and a model in the new, multipolar world'.

Specifically, the Declaration wanted the Convention to 'clarify, simplify and adjust' the division of competence between the Union and its member states.

'This can lead both to restoring tasks to the Member States and to assigning new missions to the Union, or to the extension of existing powers, while constantly bearing in mind the equality of the Member States and their mutual solidarity.'

It was suggested that there should be a clearer distinction made between the exclusive competences of the EU on the one hand and of the member states on the other, as well as a better definition of the area of competence that is shared between the Union and its states. How could these spheres of competence be protected against 'creeping expansion' of EU competence? How could they be reorganised? 'What amendments should be made to the Treaty on the various policies?' In this context, the Declaration mentioned a 'more coherent common foreign policy and defence policy', a 'more integrated approach to police and criminal law co-operation', intensified co-ordination of economic policy and 'co-operation in the field of social inclusion, the environment, health and food safety'. No specific suggestions were made of policies that could be repatriated to member states, although the question was posed as to whether the 'day-to-day administration and implementation of the Union's policy [should] be left more emphatically to the Member States and, where their constitutions so provide, to the regions?'.

[4] Giuliano Amato, Jean-Luc Dehaene, Jacques Delors, Bronislaw Geremek and David Miliband.

The Declaration went on to propose a simplification and reduction of the Union's instruments. It suggested introducing a distinction between executive and legislative measures, a return to the framework nature of the EU Directive as originally intended – establishing common aims but leaving it to member states to find the ways and means – and a clarification of when non-legislative, looser methods of policy co-ordination would be most appropriate. This 'open method of co-ordination' had been introduced to the Amsterdam Treaty, under Swedish influence, at a time of more than usual weakness of the Commission. Its aim was to increase peer pressure among the member states to achieve voluntary bench-marks or targets particularly, but not exclusively, in the field of economic policy.

Turning to the institutions, the Laeken Declaration asked a lot of radical questions in a rather breathless way. It is worth citing these in full because they were to be trodden over both by the Convention and by the Convention's critics. Concerning the democratic legitimacy and transparency of the institutions, the Declaration fired the following volley:

'How can the authority and efficiency of the European Commission be enhanced? How should the President of the Commission be appointed: by the European Council, by the European Parliament or should he be directly elected by the citizens? Should the role of the European Parliament be strengthened? Should we extend the right of codecision or not? Should the way in which we elect the members of the European Parliament be reviewed? Should a European electoral constituency be created, or should constituencies continue to be determined nationally? Can the two systems be combined? Should the role of the Council be strengthened? Should the Council act in the same manner in its legislative and its executive capacities? With a view to greater transparency, should the meetings of the Council, at least in its legislative capacity, be public? Should citizens have more access to Council documents? How, finally, should the balance and reciprocal control between the institutions be ensured?'.

With respect to the role of national parliaments, the Declaration asked:

'Should they be represented in a new institution, alongside the Council and the European Parliament? Should they have a role in areas of European action in which the European Parliament has no competence? Should they focus on the division of competence between Union and member states, for example through preliminary checking of compliance with the principle of subsidiarity?'.

Worried about the efficiency of decision making in a Union of thirty states, the Declaration asked:

'How could the Union set its objectives and priorities more effectively and ensure better implementation? Is there a need for more decisions by a qualified majority? How is the codecision procedure between the Council and the European Parliament to be simplified and speeded up? What of the six-monthly rotation of the Presidency of the Union? What is the future role of the European Parliament? What of the future role and structure of the various Council formations? How should the coherence of European foreign policy be enhanced? How is synergy between the High Representative and the competent Commissioner to be reinforced? Should the external representation of the Union in international fora be extended further?'.

'TOWARDS A CONSTITUTION FOR EUROPEAN CITIZENS'

Trying to sum up, the leaders committed the Convention to four fundamental reforms of the current EU Treaties. First was 'simplifying the existing Treaties without changing their content'. Here it was suggested that the current distinction between the European 'Union' and the European 'Communities' should be reviewed, along with the division into the 'three pillars'. The pillars were the legacy of the Treaty of Maastricht (1992) which had superimposed the 'Union' on the 'Communities' without abolishing the latter and, moreover, had created three distinct ways of doing things in the Union depending on whether they fell broadly into the area of economic affairs, foreign and security policy or co-operation in justice and home affairs. Nevertheless, to invite simplification without a change of meaning was asking for trouble, and fairly obviously contradicted the earlier injunction to consider 'amendments ... to the Treaty on the various policies'. Laeken failed in this respect to improve on the Declaration of the Treaty of Nice that had summarily called for 'a simplification of the Treaties with a view to making them clearer and better understood without changing their meaning'. The European Council seemed to want easy constitutional answers to difficult political questions without daring to broach a debate about a reform of the common policies of the Union. It was a conceit with which the Convention was never quite able to come to terms.

The second basic reform mooted by Laeken was the possibility of making a distinction between a basic treaty and the other treaty provisions, possibly with different amendment and ratification procedures. That was a sensible suggestion, not least because the current rules forbade any treaty revision whatsoever unless and until all member states had agreed to it and ratified it according to their own, disparate constitutional requirements.

Thirdly, the Declaration raised again the thorny question of the status of the Charter of Fundamental Rights which had been drafted by the earlier Convention but had been accepted by the European Council at Nice, only one year previously, as a mere code of conduct, without mandatory effect:

'Thought would also have to be given as to whether the Charter of Fundamental Rights should be included in the basic treaty and to whether the European Community should accede to the European Convention on Human Rights.'

Fourth and lastly, the heads of government steeled themselves to declare, albeit somewhat querulously:

'The question ultimately arises as to whether this simplification and reorganisation might not lead in the long run to the adoption of a constitutional text in the Union. What might the basic features of such a constitution be? The values which the Union cherishes, the fundamental rights and obligations of its citizens, the relationship between Member States in the Union?'

As a mandate to the Convention the Laeken Declaration was hugely tempting. It barely concealed divisions of opinion among heads of government as to the scope and purpose of the Convention. It invited the Convention both to 'identify the various possible responses' to a lot of questions – some of which were self-evident – and also to consider 'in the long run ... the adoption of a constitutional text'. To hedge its bets, therefore, the European Council concluded that what it sought from the Convention was a 'final document':

'The Convention will consider the various issues. It will draw up a final document which may comprise either different options, indicating the degree of support which they received, or recommendations if consensus is achieved.

'Together with the outcome of national debates on the future of the Union, the final document will provide a starting point for discussions in the Intergovernmental Conference, which will take the ultimate decisions.'

THE ROLE OF THE INTERGOVERNMENTAL CONFERENCE

Reference in the Laeken Declaration to an Intergovernmental Conference was essential. Whatever the Convention came up with it would not itself have the constituent power to change the EU Treaties. Article 48 of the Treaty on European Union, essentially unchanged from Article 236 of the Treaty of Rome (1957), insists that a 'conference of representatives of the governments of the Member States' shall be convened 'for the purpose of determining by common accord' any amendment to the Treaties. Many of the prime ministers gathered in the Laeken greenhouse took comfort from the surety of the prospect of an eventual IGC that would verify or reject the proposals from the Convention. Others, with longer experience, were less attracted by the prospect of another IGC. After all, it was precisely because previous IGCs had failed so obviously to equip the EU with the tools it needed to cope with enlargement that a constitutional Convention was now being proposed. The Laeken Declaration owed its very existence to the relative failure of the Treaty of Nice. As Maastricht begat Amsterdam and Amsterdam begat Nice, so Nice begat Laeken. A Protocol to the Treaty of Amsterdam (1997) had laid down that 'at least one year before the membership of the European Union exceeds twenty', an IGC should be convened 'to carry out a comprehensive review of the provisions of the Treaties on the composition and functioning of the institutions'.[5] To reinforce the point, the governments of Belgium, France and Italy had appended a Declaration to the Treaty of Amsterdam asserting that the Treaty 'does not meet the need ... for substantial progress towards reinforcing the institutions'.[6] In its turn, Amsterdam had been conceived by the Treaty of Maastricht, which actually provided for a new IGC to be convened in 1996.[7] Even the Single European Act (1986) had provided that revisions to the Treaty should be considered in respect of foreign policy five years after its coming into force.[8] This series of legal commitments to making future constitutional progress bears witness to the strength of the perennial goals of integration as well as to the frustrations experienced in reaching them. Would the Convention relieve the frustration?

THE CONSTITUTIVE PROCESS

Prior to the European Council at Laeken there had been endless speculation about the identity of the person who would be chosen to chair the Convention. The names of various grandees were mooted. In the end it was by a process of natural selection that Valéry Giscard d'Estaing emerged. Former President of France, former MEP, former President of the European Movement, and at the time President of the Conseil Régional of the Auvergne, Giscard had the experience and authority necessary for the job. He also wanted it. Giscard was not an uncontroversial choice, however, especially among federalists, who feared he leant to the intergovernmentalist side of the argument, and among socialists, who disliked his liberal tendencies. In a clever move, the European Council appointed Giuliano Amato, former socialist prime minister of Italy, and Jean-Luc Dehaene, former Christian democrat prime minister of Belgium, as Vice-Presidents. Guy Verhofstadt, the Belgian prime minister who chaired the European Council and who was the principal author of the Laeken Declaration, declared himself satisfied that VGE would be 'bien entouré' by Amato and Dehaene. This proved a correct judgement.

---

[5]   Article 2, Protocol on the institutions with the prospect of enlargement.
[6]   Declaration No. 57 of the Treaty of Amsterdam.
[7]   Article N.2 (later Article 48) of the Treaty on European Union.
[8]   Article 30.12, Single European Act.

In addition to its President and two Vice-Presidents, the Convention was composed of representatives of the heads of the governments of the fifteen member states and thirteen candidate states, two national parliamentarians from each of the twenty-eight countries, sixteen representatives of the European Parliament, and two members of the European Commission – making 105 full members in total. Every ordinary member of the Convention had an alternate member. With official observers, secretariat and assistants, there could be up to 400 people present at plenary sessions of the Convention.[9] The Laeken Declaration provided for the candidate member states to play a full part in proceedings without, however, being able to prevent the formation of a consensus among the *conventionnels* from the fifteen member states.

A Praesidium, or steering committee of the Convention, was established of the presidency and nine others drawn from the Convention: two each representing the European Parliament, national parliaments and the Commission and one representative of each of the governments whose turn it would be to chair the Council during the life of the Convention (Spain, Denmark and Greece). The Convention's proceedings were ordained to be completed 'after a year' in time for the last European Council of the Greek presidency.

THE CONVENTION ASSEMBLES

Whatever misgivings there had been at Giscard's appointment were quickly dispelled by his display of formidable intellect and seemingly tireless energy. Only occasionally would he depart from studied politeness in the chair – and then never by accident. His opening speech, on 28 February 2002, adorned the Laeken Declaration with an interpretation that most of his audience (José Maria Aznar apart) was pleased to hear.

The Convention viewed the Laeken Declaration with mixed feelings. It was fairly obvious that the Convention could have descended into theological debate about how literally it was to receive the scripture from Laeken. That would have been a pity because there were some silly bits of the Declaration, a good deal of repetition, and some poorly edited clauses inserted at the last minute under pressure from Tony Blair, the British prime minister. Zealots for the Convention (including this author) took comfort from Guy Verhofstadt's insistence on 'no taboos'. They were keen to seize the day, and did so. Some even contributed their own self-sacrificial 'martyr texts' to show a way forward

[9] Official observer status was given to representatives of the Economic and Social Committee, the Committee of the Regions, the social partners and the Ombudsman.

and to provoke reaction.[10] There were others who argued that the Convention should produce a choice of texts from which the impending IGC could choose, but the presidency sensibly forbore to publish its own skeleton draft of the Constitution until quite late on in the proceedings, thereby foreclosing the option of a lengthy deliberation around alternatives.

The early months were dubbed 'the listening phase', in which all members of the Convention were invited to expostulate on the state of the Union and the future of Europe. This was a protracted but useful stage, especially for the representatives of the new member states and for national parliamentarians of existing member states, many of whom needed time to brief themselves about the state of the Union and to catch up with the latest developments.

President Giscard, who had left the Elysée Palace a full twenty years beforehand, was not alone in learning a lot about the contemporary European Union from the first phase of the Convention. Even hardened insiders were impressed at the rigour of the analysis, at the increasingly informed nature of the debate, and about the breadth of interesting proposals advanced. The listening phase also succeeded in identifying those who would play leading roles in the latter stages of the Convention, and in quelling suspicion about the working methods. Draft rules of procedure, published in March 2002, had antagonised many ordinary members of the Convention because they threatened to put too much power in the hands of the Praesidium and also to marginalise the alternate members. In practice, these regulations were hardly referred to again: the presidency adopted pragmatism as the best way forward, and, as a result, gained the trust of the bulk of the Convention. The alternates, too, were kept busy as the scale of the work confronting the Convention was realised.

Several working groups were set up to debate in detail and in more privacy (but not complete seclusion) some of the most problematical issues. These included the role of national parliaments, subsidiarity, the Charter of Fundamental Rights, legal personality, external action, defence, economic governance and the complementary competences of the Union. One of the most important of such groups, chaired by the agile Giuliano Amato, was tasked with 'simplification'. Later, under pressure from the left wing in the Convention, a group was added to discuss social policy. To relieve pressure in the plenary, the working groups were supplemented by 'discussion circles': essentially more private forums in which real rows could be had (and were) about the reform of

---

[10]   The first martyr text was my own: *Model Constitution for a Federal Union of Europe*, CONV 234/02, 3 September 2002. This had only 19 articles: the Charter is made a Protocol and the policy chapters are published separately in a revised Treaty of Rome. Organic laws are created at the top of the hierarchy for quasi-constitutional matters, such as the financial system or the codecision procedure.

the judicial and financial systems of the Union. Important as these inner circles were, it was only at the reception of their conclusions on the floor of the plenary that the presidency could divine whether or not a sufficient consensus had been reached. Often it was not. The Convention should be judged not only on the quality of the consensus achieved but on the raft of diagnoses and prescriptions it discarded. Not everything that was said and done in the Convention was entirely appropriate for posting on the excellent website.[11]

Beyond the formal structures of the Convention itself were the party political formations that coagulated inside it and a wide range of fringe events from militant federalist to diehard nationalist, meeting regularly for breakfast, lunch and dinner – or just drinks – throughout the duration. NGOs, think-tanks and pressure groups of one sort and another, the social partners and the churches gathered in Brussels and trooped through corridors and meeting rooms. Some structure was implanted into the way the Convention consulted civil society. The Economic and Social Committee and the Committee of the Regions, consultative bodies of the EU, played a useful role. A youth forum was established. Academic colloquia sprang up around and about the Convention, and have since spawned a large corpus of scholarly analysis. The press struggled with the complexity and the length of the argument, but some of the most astute commentaries were made by jobbing members of the Brussels press corps who were the first to recognise that the Convention, whatever it was, was not routine.

What made the Convention so special in terms of the constitutional development of the European Union, apart from the eclectic mix of personalities assembled therein, was the predominant parliamentary nature of the beast. The Convention surely contained many features of the classical intergovernmental diplomacy that Europe has loved at least since the days of the Congress of Vienna. But it had a wider, democratic legitimacy because its major component was members of parliament, both national and European. Some ninety political parties were represented in the Convention. Critics of the Convention (and there are some) must at least concede that its make-up faithfully reflected the current composition of Europe's parliaments. Its parliamentary nature made it rather exciting. At first, it was thought likely that national and European parliamentarians would be ranged against each other. It was a wise French Senator, Hubert Haenel, who remarked that it was a myth that all good Europeans lived in Brussels and all bad Europeans lived in the national capitals. 'Yes', agreed Giscard, 'the truth is that there are good and bad Europeans in both'. By the time the Convention closed its doors on 10 July 2003 there were more 'good Europeans' all round.

[11] http://european-convention.eu.int

Chronology of European Union Treaties

Title	Signatories	Signature	Entry into force
Treaty establishing the European Coal and Steel Community (ECSC) ("The Six")	Belgium, France, Germany, Italy, Luxembourg	Paris, April 18th 1951	July 25th 1952 (expired on July 23rd 2002)
Treaty establishing the European Economic Community (EEC)	The Six	Capitol Hill, Rome, March 25th 1957	January 1st 1958
European Atomic Energy Community (EURATOM)	The Six	Capitol Hill, Rome, March 25th 1957	January 1st 1958
Treaty establishing a single European Council and Commission of the European Communities	The Six	Brussels, April 8th 1965	1 July 1966
Treaty amending Certain Budgetary Provisions of the Treaties establishing the European Communities	The Six	April 22nd 1970	January 1st 1971
Act concerning the Accession to the European Communities of the Kingdom of Denmark, Ireland and the United Kingdom of Great Britain and Northern Ireland	The Six + Denmark, Ireland, Norway, United Kingdom (Norway's accession stopped by referendum)	Brussels, January 22nd 1972	January 1st 1973
Treaty amending Certain Provisions of the Protocol on the Statute of the European Investment Bank	The Nine	Brussels, July 10th 1975	6 April 1978
Treaty amending Certain Financial Provisions of the Treaty establishing the European Communities	The Nine	July 22nd 1975	June 1st 1977
Act concerning the Accession to the European Communities of the Hellenic Republic	The Nine + Greece	Athens, May 28th 1979	January 1st 1981
Treaty amending, with regard to Greenland, the Treaties establishing the European Communities	The Ten + Denmark + Government of Greenland	Brussels, March 13, 1984	February 1, 1985

Act concerning the Accession to the European Communities of the Kingdom of Spain and the Portuguese Republic	The Ten + Portugal, Spain	Lisbon/Madrid, June 12th 1985	January 1st 1986
Single European Act (SEA)	The Twelve	Luxembourg, February 17th 1986; The Hague, February 28th 1986	July 1st 1987
Treaty on European Union (TEU)	The Twelve	Maastricht, February 7th 1992	November 1st 1993
Act concerning the Accession to the European Union of the Republic of Austria, the Republic of Finland and the Kingdom of Sweden	The Twelve + Austria, Finland, Sweden	Corfu, June 24th 1994	January 1st 1995
Treaty of Amsterdam amending the Treaty on European Union, the Treaties establishing the European Communities	The Fifteen	Amsterdam, October 2nd 1997	May 1st 1999
Treaty of Nice amending the Treaty on European Union, the Treaties establishing the European Communities	The Fifteen	Nice, February 26th 2001	January 1st 2003
Act concerning the conditions of accession of the Czech Republic, the Republic of Estonia, the Republic of Cyprus, the Republic of Latvia, the Republic of Lithuania, the Republic of Hungary, the Republic of Malta, the Republic of Poland, the Republic of Slovenia and the Slovak Republic and the adjustments to the Treaties on which the European Union is founded	The Fifteen + Cyprus, Czech Republic, Estonia, Hungary, Latvia, Lithuania, Malta, Poland, Slovakia, Slovenia	Athens, April 16th 2003	May 1st 2004
Treaty establishing a Constitution for Europe	The Twenty Five	Rome, October 29th 2004	[November 1st 2006]

CHAPTER 2

Writing the Constitution

It is quite difficult to write a good constitution. Talleyrand, following Napoleon Bonaparte, said that a good constitution should be short and obscure. Those of us who gathered in Brussels at the end of February 2002 to write Europe's new constitution were attempting a difficult task of potential historic importance. Could we capture for Europe the first major constitutional moment in its post-national era? We were charged with simplification of the pile of international treaties that had developed as the rule book for European integration over the previous half century. We doubted whether we could be short. In these democratic times, we knew we must not be obscure.

Again unlike Napoleon, whose regime was quickly deluged, all of us in the Convention, radicals and conservatives alike, were committed to trying to achieve a sense of constitutional settlement. We tried not only to seize the moment but also to prepare the EU for a long constitutional future. Indeed, the official name of what came to be known simply as the European Convention was the 'Convention on the Future of Europe'. The Convention's chairman, Valéry Giscard d'Estaing, said that he wanted the Constitution to last for fifty years. His was a bold claim, but a necessary message for the Convention to hear. In addition to setting high goals for the Convention, Giscard obliged its members to face up to the reality of the current situation of the Union in which the pace of integration had reached a high pitch.

During the last decade, the European Union had experienced three major treaty revisions that had hugely expanded its political competence and legal stretch; it had established an economic and monetary union; it was about to take in ten new member states, most of which were in any case themselves exhausted by their tricky transition from communism; it faced a gravely deteriorating international situation. Europe's public opinion, however, was in an unsettled mood, finding it worrisome to keep abreast of such massive change. The European voter clearly enjoyed the fruits of globalisation but appeared to resent being out of control of the process of globalisation. Most Europeans seemed to tolerate the European Union rather than love it;

some loathed it as the embodiment of the loss of national power; many were wholly unclear about where European unification was now headed, and, more dramatically, where it would stop. The lack of a genuine popular legitimacy for the European project haunted the Convention. Could we possibly invent or discover the *demos europeo*, that elusive polity of European citizens?

French constitutional history was not the only ghost in town. Many British press and politicians alike fondly believed that, as they had no written constitution of their own, neither did they need one: and, moreover, any European constitution would be bound to be a Bonapartist entrapment. Those, like the Spanish and Irish, with experience in modern times of writing their own constitutions were wary. Representatives from former communist states, like the Polish, were likewise marked by their all-too-recent experience of constitutional abuse.

Only the American experience of writing a constitution seemed to offer an unalloyed source of joy and inspiration. But was this really Europe's Philadelphia moment? Valéry Giscard d'Estaing fitted well into the part of George Washington. The former French President had clearly read his Federalist Papers and Benjamin Franklin as well as Talleyrand and Lafayette, and he actively promoted the analogy with the Philadelphia Convention of 1787. But where were the Madisons and Jeffersons? Were the rest of us up to it? In fact, could we do better than the American Founding Fathers? Could we avoid the bloody civil war that had eventually engulfed America over the same, vexed federal questions that we ourselves now confronted?

DECLARATION OF INTERDEPENDENCE

Tempting as it was to have turned up to Convention meetings in eighteenth century fancy dress, the Convention was rather a sober affair. As the Convention's serious work got underway, the historical analogy with 1787 became less obvious. Perhaps the closer parallel was the Declaration of Independence in 1776, the first but inconclusive step towards the building of the American federal state. The Convention's Constitution certainly turned out to be an assertion of constitutional autonomy by the Union – perhaps a Declaration of *Interdependence*. Very few voices were heard in the Convention arguing for the immediate formation of a European federal state. Equally few were openly in favour of dismantling the Union and retreating to full national independence for its component states. In later chapters we examine the outcome in detail, but it is worth noting here, in a first assessment, that it came to be generally accepted in the Convention that through its work the paradigm of a united Europe was being shifted in a federalist direction.

Whatever the eventual fate of the 2004 Constitution, all twenty-five member states that signed it were voluntarily accepting new supranational constraints on the exercise of their individual national sovereignties. Under the Constitution, compared with the Treaty of Nice, it would be very much more difficult, if not impossible, for individual member states to go their own way whilst wilfully disregarding the interests of their partners. Every signatory state is agreed to rely on each other and on the joint supranational institutions for mutual support and common discipline. Each member state is committed to addressing common problems together and to seeking shared solutions. All agreed to pool their sovereignty to a very significant degree, albeit while insisting on residuary safeguards. They bestowed upon EU citizenship the garb of a Bill of Rights. They gave the Union greater, if limited competence. They reinforced the parliamentary and judicial powers of the Union institutions. They subscribed to the theory of constitutional fidelity. Although few European leaders will as yet openly disavow national patriotism in favour of a European constitutional patriotism, it is also true that those who accepted the Constitution must have anticipated that the values of mutual loyalty and solidarity as enshrined in it could be expected to mature.

These are the reasons why most federalists are enthusiastic supporters of the Constitution. The European Parliament, where federalists are well represented, backed the Constitution with a majority of over two-thirds, and many MEPs have been campaigning for its entry into force. For them, as for this author, the Constitution is a good and wholly necessary step forward in the direction of a stronger and more federal Union. And it is not only the outcome that is largely welcomed, but also the process of the Convention itself, which has been praised quite rightly as being more open and pluralistic than the traditional Intergovernmental Conferences. The Constitution, if ratified, would have signalled progress in the search for the European Union's elusive popular legitimacy. A successful constitutional settlement would have been seen as the crowning achievement of the recent years that witnessed the successful introduction of the euro as well as the historic enlargement to Central and Eastern Europe.

A CONSERVATIVE EXERCISE

Of course not all members of the Convention, still less national leaders, would agree with such a federalist assessment of the Constitution. It is not necessary for them to do so. The fact is that there is also a respectable conservative argument to be made in favour of the Constitution. Whereas Philadelphia had worked in a revolutionary climate, the European Convention worked to refine and consolidate what already existed in the EU treaties, and to codify the fifty years' case law of the European Court of Justice. As Laeken had indeed commanded, the Convention successfully delimited the powers of the Union. In so far as the Convention could write down and relate the origins and clarify the future purpose of the Union, it did so. The Constitution entrenches existing safeguards and reinforces checks and balances. It spells out how competences are only conferred upon the Union by a unanimous decision of the member states. It reduces the danger of subversive or creeping federalism by illuminating clearly who does what.

Because European integration is an inherently complex process, it did not prove possible for the Convention to simplify the EU's system of governance as much as some would have wished. No doubt the text itself should have been shorter. But little credence should be given to those ardent critics who claim that the Constitution is unreadable: gentle inquiry usually reveals that they have scarcely tried to read it. The Constitution is much clearer than the pile of existing EU treaties. As a tidying-up exercise, the Constitution was something of a success. Any numerate and literate (and committed) reader can pick up the Preamble and Part One of the Constitution (Articles 1 to 60) and learn how he or she is governed from Europe, by whom and in what way. Anyone who perseveres to Part Two (Articles 61 to 114) will see how their rights are protected from abuse by the supranational authorities of the Union, as well as how he or she, as a European Union citizen, has a duty to respect the fundamental rights of all fellow citizens. The yet more avid reader will find in Part Three (Articles 115 to 436) a better description of the common policies of the EU than has ever been made available before. Part Four (Articles 437 to 448) contains some fairly straightforward general provisions and describes how the Constitution may be revised in the future.

A EUROSCEPTIC VIEW

Even those who truly dislike the European Union could find comfort in several provisions of the Constitution. There is the new clause that allows a member state to secede from the Union.[1] It remains the fact that, as under the present EU treaties, all major amendments to the Constitution will have to be carried unanimously and ratified by all member states according to their own constitutional requirements.[2] Eurosceptics tend to see the European Council, which is the collective body of national heads of state or government, as the necessary and desirable counterweight to the integrationist forces ranged against them in the European Commission, European Parliament and Court

---

[1]   Article I–59.
[2]   Article IV–443.3.

of Justice. Supporters of that viewpoint, like the British government, claim that one of the major successes of the Constitution is precisely that it strengthens the European Council. Jack Straw, the British foreign secretary, believes that the President of the European Council will be in a strong position to control the Commission. He and others take comfort from the thought that, according to the Constitution, the new President of the Commission cannot become entirely the creature of the Parliament, but will still be nominated by the European Council. Such interpretations of the Constitution provoke sharp reactions from federalist *militanti* – but they also go to show why the Constitution can command support from those of a conservative hue, and why the bitterly hostile reaction to the Constitution by rightwing nationalists is an absurd exaggeration.

Confronted by populist nonsense, however, it is important to get the story right. The Convention has had a mixed review from early academic critics. A fashionable school of 'liberal intergovernmentalists' tends to downplay the significance of the Convention and therefore to be quite sanguine about the defeat of the Constitution.[3] National governments act in an informed and rational manner to pursue self-interests. By contrast, it is said, the supranational institutions are destined to remain reactive and fairly weak – although they may play a useful role in engaging transnational interests behind the project of integration. According to the intergovernmentalist school, the Convention was a useful but cosmetic exercise, with the real constitutional bargains being struck between governments once the Convention was safely out of the way. It is alleged that whatever successes that can be accredited to the Convention were the result of crafty behind-the-scenes bargaining by Giscard to secure the compliance of key national leaders. The Intergovernmental Conference which followed the Convention is regarded as being scarcely different to its predecessors. Neither the Commission nor the Parliament is deemed to have played any significant role in the IGC.

THE CONVENTION'S LIMITS

This book does not share that particular critical analysis. Nevertheless, successful as the Convention undoubtedly was, it would be a mistake not to acknowledge that it had certain limitations. Naturally, the Convention was not a substitute for the Intergovernmental Conference. For one thing, as we have already noted, all treaty revision has to accord with the provisions of the present Treaty on European Union which prescribes an IGC to change it. For

---

[3] See, for example, Andrew Moravscik and others in *Prospect*, No. 112, July 2005.

another, the Convention was rather experimental. It took place in controversial circumstances. Not everybody had been convinced the Convention was either necessary or desirable. The British, in particular, remained hostile to the notion of a second Convention until the al'Qaeda strike at the USA on 11 September 2001 served to change the context in which European integration was regarded in London, as elsewhere. Even then, the UK government, having sought in the first instance to prevent the Convention taking place, tried continually to undermine it and, subsequently, to reduce the force of its proposals.[4]

It was not only the British government which perceived its own immersion in the politics of the Convention as high risk. The Convention was too large, too open and pluralistic to be capable of being controlled by governments. Only the formidable chairmanship of Giscard d'Estaing and his two Vice-Presidents Giuliano Amato and Jean-Luc Dehaene, coupled with the management skills of Secretary-General John Kerr, were able to steer the body home more or less within the agreed timetable. But the Convention was never condemned to succeed: failure was always an option right up to and beyond the Thessaloniki European Council in June 2003. And there were several participants and many close observers who would have been none too sorry to see the experiment stumble.

In such trying circumstances, advocates of the Convention needed much collective wisdom to ensure its success. One of the most necessary attributes was self-restraint. The Convention could – and did – stretch the mandate from Laeken, but there were clear limits to what it could do. Notably, it could not re-write the common policies of the Union, tempting though that was. It had to stick to its constitutional brief, which meant clarifying and refining political objectives, setting the legal framework, codifying jurisprudence, cataloguing competences, streamlining decision making and rationalising instruments – and writing it all down as well as possible. The Convention quickly learned that there were politically controversial areas in which the discovery of consensus would be well nigh impossible. That is, for example, why the Convention made no important proposals for the strengthening of the economic governance of the Union.

THE GREAT PATRIOTIC ISSUES

The Convention recognised that there were issues of sovereign importance to member states that were not susceptible to the new style of discourse

---

[4] Alain Lamassoure MEP told the Convention that the difference between it and Philadelphia was that the Americans had solved the British problem *before* they began to draft their constitution.

established in the Convention. These related not so much to the balance of power between the member states and the Union level of government but to that between the member states themselves. The IGC ended as all previous IGCs have ended with a jostling among national leaders for advantage based on relative size, wealth and esteem.

The weighting of votes in the Council, the distribution of seats in the Parliament, and status of nationality within the Commission are all inter-related questions that the Convention could not have resolved even if it had had the temerity to try. However federal the Union becomes, the pecking order among states will continue to matter. Indeed, the more powerful the Union gets to be, the more the member state governments will wish to be seen to be punching their weight, especially in the Council. Occasionally, a display of machismo may cloud judgement.

By their behaviour at the IGC and, indeed, during the latter stages of the Convention, the governments of Spain and Poland showed how easy it was to exaggerate the importance of the competition league between member states. In defence of the advantageous positions they had gained at Nice, the Spanish and Polish prime ministers became truculent, even unreasonable, until they were both toppled by domestic crises early in 2004. But Spain and Poland were by no means the only countries to concern themselves with the repercussions of enlargement and constitutional reform on their relative positions in the league table. Many of the leaders who participated at the close of the IGC in June 2004 had also been at Nice in December 2000, and were still suffering from the hangover they had acquired during that terrible night in Nice when Council voting weights and Parliamentary seats had been traded like chips in the casino at Cannes. It was never going to be easy for those leaders to admit their past mistakes, and for none more difficult than Jacques Chirac.

The Nice IGC had been badly destabilised by France's decision to concede a loss of parity with Germany in the Council. The voting formula invented at Nice had three elements to reaching the qualified majority: 71.3 per cent of the votes cast by two-thirds of the member states representing at least 62 per cent of the population of the Union. The introduction of the population key puts Germany into an unrivalled position. President Chirac was still sorely embarrassed by the memory of the Nice debacle (for which, it must be admitted, he was largely and personally responsible). That Germany and France should be equal powers in the European Community had been established by Monnet and Schuman in the 1950s, endorsed by Adenauer and De Gaulle in the 1960s, and confirmed by Giscard and Schmidt in the 1970s. During the negotiations on the Maastricht Treaty in December 1991, François Mitterrand had conceded that Germany should have more MEPs than France. But that deal was part of the package which gained for France German commitment to the single currency. Jacques Chirac, at Nice, had less to show for his trouble and, in any case, loss of standing in the Council was always going to be very much more painful for France than the earlier but comparable slip down the European Parliamentary stakes.

A RITE OF PASSAGE FOR THE EUROPEAN PARLIAMENT

It is, of course, possible to exaggerate the role of the European Parliament in the Convention. Numerically, there were only thirty-two MEPs out of a total membership of 207, and none from the candidate countries. But its influence spread quite remarkably across the Convention, largely through the formation inside the Convention of the party political groups, but also as a result of the relative activism of MEP *conventionnels* with respect to civil society and the media, as well as their high attendance record at Convention meetings. Outside the official component from the Parliament, there were many other members of the Convention with first-hand experience of the institution. Half the members of the Praesidium, including Giscard, were or had been Members of the European Parliament.[5] The Parliament also scored because all meetings of the Convention were held on its premises. One British minister was heard to complain that MEPs had the unfair advantage of 'playing at home'.

One could not assess the Parliament's growing influence in the constitutional debate without judging the final outcome of the IGC against the comprehensive catalogue of priorities and objectives established, with some consistency over time, in various parliamentary resolutions. When others – notably, heads of government – were lauding the results of the Amsterdam and Nice IGCs, the Parliament had been highly critical. Having participated successfully in the Convention which drafted the Charter of Fundamental Rights in 1999–2000, MEPs were the first to call for a second Convention to formulate more comprehensive and radical revisions to the EU Treaties. The Parliament actively supported the Belgian presidency of the Council in the drafting of the Laeken Declaration. It was quick to appoint and organise its own delegation to the Convention, as well as deciding to act as host for all the meetings of the Convention itself. It acted throughout in an entrepreneurial manner.

The European Parliament's greatest contribution to the success of the Convention, however, was to accept Giscard's injunction to compromise. The

---

[5]   Giscard d'Estaing, Hänsch, Katifioris, Mendez de Vigo, Palacio Vallelersundi and Vitorino. Alojz Peterle was an Observer MEP from May 2002. Jean-Luc Dehaene became an MEP in 2004.

capacity to compromise comes more easily to European Parliamentarians than it often does to their national colleagues, for whom a simple majority decision is usually the order of the day. MEPs are elected without the formal manifesto commitments and strict party discipline of their national counterparts. They need to be both agile and creative in the formulation of policy. The European Parliament is well used to building cross-party and, perforce, transnational majorities in the course of its everyday legislative work.[6] Despite the vigour of their criticisms of the Convention's working methods in the initial phase of the Convention's life, as soon as the substantive debate began Parliament's representatives showed themselves in a new – and to some surprising – constructive light. MEPs in the Praesidium and the numerous working groups and circles of reflection that were created to tackle some specific problematic questions proved themselves adept at proposing and supporting compromises. Some of the most obstinate members of the Convention were national MPs whose opposition had to be defeated by blunt expressions of majority opinion.

At the outset, there were many participants and observers of the Convention who expected that the Parliament would be out-manoeuvred by national governments as the negotiations reached their climax and the hard bargains had to be struck. This did not happen. In fact, if anything the role of the MEPs became more vital in the last weeks of the Convention when the Praesidium began to be less than the sum of its parts and crucial coalitions had to be formed on the floor of the plenary and in delegation meetings. It was the self-conscious alliance of pro-integration national MPs with like-minded European parliamentarians which, in the end, allowed the presidency to find and articulate the final product. In June and July 2003, a number of joint meetings between MPs and MEPs were held to draft a short-list of final demands. This list was then negotiated by the leaders of the parliamentary groups with Giscard himself, largely by-passing the Praesidium.

The performance of the parliamentary contingent shone by comparison to that of the representatives of the national leaders who, true to IGC form, were unable to agree among themselves when left to their own devices. Government delegations in the Convention frequently appeared to be badly prepared, ill focussed and poorly co-ordinated at the national level. Whereas such shortcomings can be fairly well concealed in the closed confines of a classical Intergovernmental Conference, they all became cruelly exposed in the open forum of the Convention. To make a point effectively a member of the

---

[6]   The Parliament has to get a majority of all its members (in other words, 367 votes out of 732 Members) to amend draft legislation at the crucial second reading stage of the codecision procedure. The largest single group (EPP-ED) has only 267 members, making coalitions with other groups essential.

Convention had to be able to justify it against possible attack under the 'blue card' system whereby short interventions could be made to challenge a previous speaker and to provoke real debate. Some found it difficult to adjust to the novel mix of diplomatic and parliamentary style. MEPs, on the whole, enjoyed themselves immensely.

It was the parliamentary ingredient which saved the Convention. While Valéry Giscard d'Estaing was understandably anxious to secure the consent of the national leaders (especially from the larger member states), he also knew that no consensus would be possible in the Convention without the active collusion of Members of the European Parliament. From the outset Giscard and the European Parliament delegation were united in their hostility to producing a mere options paper for the IGC. They both wanted, and eventually got, a single draft constitution against the expectations of most member state representatives and many national parliamentarians. (In the event, there was only a fairly inconsequential 'minority report' drafted by a very small number of eurosceptics of both Thatcherite and Muscovite tendencies, led by David Heathcote-Amory MP and Jens-Peter Bonde MEP.) The presidency and the European Parliament shared a common interest in maximising publicity for the work of the Convention and in insisting on transparency of discourse. Neither party wanted it to be possible for national representatives to be able to say one thing inside the Convention and another outside. Transparency was vital to ensure coherence. Both Giscard and the MEPs had a clear vested interest in making a success of the enterprise. Despite quarrelsome moments, the two parties quickly learned to respect and to listen to each other.

The role of the European Parliament did not end with the close of the Convention in July 2003. The Italian presidency decided that the Parliament should be 'closely associated and involved' in the work of the IGC, and have an upgraded status from that which its observers enjoyed at Nice, Amsterdam and Maastricht. Pat Cox, President of the Parliament from January 2002 until July 2004, played a full part in the IGC at summit level. Inigo Mendez de Vigo followed by Elmar Brok (both of the European People's Party) and Klaus Hänsch (Socialist) were appointed Parliament's representatives at the ministerial level of the IGC. Mendez de Vigo is the elegant and agile spokesman of the EPP on constitutional affairs. He chaired the European Parliamentary delegation to the Convention, and served on the Praesidium. Brok is the formidable and long-serving chairman of the Parliament's Foreign Affairs Committee, and chaired the EPP caucus in the Convention. Hänsch, a distinguished former President of the Parliament, was a Vice-President of the Parliament's delegation to the Convention. Several of the Parliament's administrators were fully involved in the IGC's official working groups. The boost given to the transnational political parties by their work in the Convention was carried through to the IGC. The European People's Party, the Party of European Socialists and the European Liberal, Democrat and Reform Party functioned well throughout the whole constitutional process, and matured as a result of it.

Comparing input to output, too, the European Parliament has reason to be well satisfied. In so far as the Parliament's main objectives were achieved, MEPs can be said to have set the political agenda for the Convention and the IGC. The normalisation of the legislative procedure, the effective abolition of the three pillars of the Maastricht Treaty, the widening of budgetary competence, the Charter of Fundamental Rights made binding – all these have appeared as the top priorities in each and every European Parliamentary resolution on constitutional matters for several years. The common adoption of the term 'constitution', albeit informally, was peddled by Parliament precisely in order to change the political discourse that surrounded treaty revision. The large majority accorded by MEPs to the endorsement of the results of the IGC is a measure of Parliament's satisfaction in both the process and the outcome of the Convention. The European Parliament seems content to have been recruited as a constitutional player, joining the European Commission, national governments and national parliaments as capable of being held to account for the future drift and direction of European Union affairs. With the greater responsibility accorded Parliament in the two Conventions between 1999 and 2004 has come greater respectability. The European Parliament has matured through this constituent process, becoming a more sophisticated and effective institution internally as well as externally. (Its decision to block the appointment of the incoming Commission of José Manuel Durao Barroso in the autumn of 2004 would surely have been unthinkable in pre-Convention days.)

THE GOVERNMENTS CLOSE THE DEAL

As planned, Valéry Giscard d'Estaing presented the Convention's preliminary draft of Parts One and Two of the Constitution to the European Council at Thessaloniki on 20 June 2003. The leaders received him politely, if nervously. They accepted the draft as 'a good basis' for starting the Intergovernmental Conference, and hoped the final Constitutional Treaty could be signed 'as soon as possible and in time for it to become known to European citizens before the June 2004 elections for the European Parliament'. The ten acceding states would participate fully in the IGC on an equal footing with the current member states. 'The Parliament will be closely associated and involved in the work of the Conference.'

The IGC opened with a formal session in Rome on 4 October 2003, but the bizarre chairmanship of Silvio Berlusconi caused it to flounder at the European Council meeting in Brussels in December. Only the ingenuity and tenacity of the Irish presidency that took over from the Italians saved the negotiations. The Taoiseach, Bertie Ahern, insisted that the failure of the IGC would have grave consequences for Europe at home and abroad. He made all sides in the negotiation move, skilfully adjusting the stance of his own government on one or two sensitive points in the process and facing up to British obduracy on a number of their tedious 'red lines'. He reminded his colleagues of the need to bring a European dimension to policy making by broadening the scope of qualified majority voting (QMV) in the Council. But he added that there would be little point in having more Council decisions subject to QMV if it were too difficult to reach the qualified majority threshold. Everyone was made aware of the danger of failing to complete the IGC under the Irish presidency. Ireland would be succeeded in July by the Dutch who were likely to become submerged in arguments over the opening of accession negotiations with Turkey and the review of the medium term financial perspectives of the Union. After the Luxembourg presidency in January 2005, the incoming UK presidency in July, if it had been served up an unfinished IGC, would have been more than pleased to consign the whole constitutional project into the deep-freezer.

Fear of potential hazards in the future was heightened by current calamity. On 11 March al'Qaeda bombed Madrid, causing many deaths. The crisis galvanised a rare moment of European solidarity, as well as triggering the fall of the government of José Maria Aznar and its replacement by the distinctly more pro-European socialist government led by José Luis Rodriguez Zapatero. Not only the Spanish but also the Polish prime minister, Leslek Miller, was dispatched from office by a domestic crisis with a European flavour. Both were largely unlamented departures that greatly eased the task of the Irish presidency in bringing the IGC to a successful conclusion. This happened at the Brussels meeting of the European Council on 18 June 2004. The final text, polished by the linguists and lawyers, was signed in an elaborate ceremony in the Campidoglio in Rome on 29 October.[7] It was a very much more crowded room than it had been some forty-seven years previously for the signing of the original Treaty of Rome – and, under the direction of Berlusconi's chum Franco Zeffirelli, infinitely more kitsch.

---

[7]   The text was published in the EU Official Journal C 310 on 16 December 2004.

CHAPTER 3

The Preamble

Having examined the context in which the Constitution was written, we turn now to the text.

The beginning is important. A useful requirement of any successful constitution is that it is immediately approachable to the interested citizen. All previous EU Treaties had begun with a lengthy list of the heads of state whose plenipotentiaries, being found in good and due order, then append their signatures. Some in the Convention wanted to stick to the traditional formulary because it served to reinforce the idea that the Constitution was merely an international treaty between sovereign states. Others yearned for the greater resonance as well as the brevity and simplicity of the US Constitution which begins, famously:

'We the People of the United States, in Order to form a more perfect Union, establish Justice, insure domestic Tranquility, provide for the common defence, promote the general Welfare, and secure the Blessings of Liberty to ourselves and our Posterity, do ordain and establish this Constitution for the United States of America'.

HIS MAJESTY THE KING OF THE BELGIANS ...

Back in Brussels, as the debate deepened it became clear that few representatives of national governments were prepared to agree a comparable self-assertion of European popular sovereignty implicit in the American phrase 'We the People'. A compromise was reached whereby the idea that the European Union drew its inspiration and legitimacy from both its states and its peoples was relegated to Article 1 of the Constitution. The Preamble would be restricted to historical and cultural references.

So it was that Albert II, 'His Majesty the King of the Belgians', by virtue of the alphabet rather than his glasshouses, remains the first citizen to be mentioned in the Constitution. Queen Elizabeth II of the United Kingdom brings up the rear.

Whether or not to call the new treaty a constitution gave rise to much, mostly sterile discussion. Both supporters and opponents of the Constitution have been divided about what to call it. What is beyond dispute is that states have constitutions; clubs have constitutions: the European Union, as a stately club, can have a constitution if it so chooses. In practice, the phrasing of the Preamble would make no difference to the status of the Constitution. Technically speaking, the 'Treaty establishing a Constitution for Europe' is a 'constituent instrument of an international organisation' according to Article 5 of the Vienna Convention on the Law of Treaties. By repealing previous EU treaties, the new Treaty re-founds the existing European Union and Communities on a constitutive basis. 'We the People' would have helped to assert its constitutional character. King Albert will do.

Curiously, the Preamble also expresses gratitude to the members of the Convention for having drafted the Constitution. It is no accident in this respect that the chief author of the Preamble was Valéry Giscard d'Estaing, the proud chairman of the Convention, who worked hard at its drafting, and who, shortly afterwards, was to be elevated to the ranks of Immortals by being elected a member of the Académie Française. Notwithstanding Giscard's literary skills, there were several other drafts of the Preamble submitted by the Convention that may have better passed the tests of elegance and pithiness. What survived, however, was Giscard's insistence on emphasising the values of the Enlightenment as the source of inspiration for the European Union, along with his tone of unabashed confidence.

EVER CLOSER UNION?

King Albert was not the only controversial point. Could the Convention claim to be working on behalf of all 'Europe' or just for the European Union? To what extent should the Preamble reflect the Preambles of the previous treaties? How would the Preamble to the whole Constitution sit with the Preamble to the Charter of Fundamental Rights that would now be inserted as Part Two of the Constitution? There were even those, fearing drafting infelicities, who questioned the need for a Preamble in the first place.

A particular problem arose over the time-honoured phrase 'ever closer union among the peoples of Europe'. The idea of permanent revolution rather clashed with Giscard's insistence on durability. But this was a tricky issue also for the British, for whom 'ever closer union', first appearing in the Treaty of Rome (1957), now carried dangerous overtones of unrelenting federalism.[1] A rather

---

[1] The phrase is particularly alarming in the French version, which speaks of 'une union sans cesse plus étroite'. Ironically, however, it was British premier John Major who insisted on its retention in the Treaty of Maastricht as being better than a proposed explicit reference to federalism.

academic solution was found: 'reunited after bitter experiences, … united ever more closely, to forge a common destiny' – which also has the advantage of being somewhat redolent of the Preamble to the original Treaty of Paris (1951) that established the European Coal and Steel Community. The Treaty of Paris boasted the most concise and eloquent of Preambles, as follows:

'RESOLVED to substitute for age old rivalries the merging of their essential interests; to create, by establishing an economic community, the basis for a broader and deeper community among peoples long divided by bloody conflicts; and to lay the foundations for institutions which will give direction to a destiny henceforward shared, …..'.

GOD

A difficult decision for the Convention and the IGC was whether or not to invoke God as the source, or even a source, of European unification. In their time, the founding fathers of post-war Europe, good Roman Catholics to a man, had not done so. They intended to build a modern, secular European Union free from the ideological ties that had so recently compromised the dignity of their societies and risked the survival of their states. It remained – and remains – the case, however, that many of the member states of the European Union are bound constitutionally to the Church. In some countries, such as Ireland and Greece, the evocation of the power of the Church hierarchy in the national constitution and the role of the clergy in education runs counter to the trends of liberal modernity. In others, such as the UK, the continued official establishment of the state Church is being contested. In Greece and Spain the legacy of civil war still divides society with respect to Church allegiance. But in Central Europe the Church intervened actively, even boldly to support the transition from communism. Pope John Paul II, formerly Bishop of Krakow, was a powerful advocate of the idea that European integration is liberation from communism.

The hierarchy of the Roman Catholic Church became engaged in the work of the Convention. Poles, Austrians, Bavarians, Slovaks and Italians pushed hard for the inclusion in the Constitution's Preamble of an *invocatio Dei*. Clergy of all denominations, including Orthodox, lobbied heavily to have a specific Preamble reference to Christendom or to Christianity as the main religion of Europe. Faced with these demands, the Convention was naturally concerned to avoid causing offence to Europe's many millions of Jews, Muslims, Buddhists and Hindus. The humanists lobbied in a contrary direction. Liberals argued that while God had brought mankind the means of grace and the hope of glory, the fundamental values of the European Union were man-made. It became clear that, had Christianity been specifically mentioned, the Preamble would have had to grow into a lengthy historical essay in order to quantify also the contribution to Europe's heritage of other religions, notably Islam. The presence in the Convention of the Muslim democrats from the Turkish governing party AKP helped to steady the debate. Giscard, although no lover of Turkey's EU membership aspirations, remained faithful to the laic tradition of the French Republic (and of Kemal Atatürk).

Constant pressure from the churches, however, drove a fairly reluctant Convention to grant them a privileged status in the Constitution's chapter on the democratic life of the Union.[2] While this was enough to satisfy moderate Catholics and the Protestants, the Vatican continued to press for the insertion of the *invocatio Dei* in the Preamble. The hapless Polish prime minister continued to threaten to block the whole Constitution on this one point, even in the closing moments of the IGC in Brussels on the night of 18 June 2004. Only the noise of the champagne corks popping and an acerbic rebuke from the chairman, Irish prime minister Bertie Ahern, stopped him in his tracks. The Taoiseach was later vindicated by the Pope, who invoked a blessing on all those dignitaries who gathered in Rome on 29 October 2004 to sign the Constitution.

Also at the insistence of Ahern, the IGC dropped a cryptic quote from Thucydides, beloved by Giscard.[3] It accepted from the Irish presidency a shorter, less flowery (and, frankly, better) version of Giscard's original text, as follows:

> Drawing inspiration from the cultural, religious and humanist inheritance of Europe, from which have developed the universal values of the inviolable and inalienable rights of the human person, democracy, equality, freedom and the rule of law,
> Believing that Europe, reunited after bitter experiences, intends to continue along the path of civilisation, progress and prosperity, for the good of all its inhabitants, including the weakest and most deprived; that it wishes to remain a continent open to culture, learning and social progress; and that it wishes to deepen the democratic and transparent nature of its public life, and to strive for peace, justice and solidarity throughout the world,
> Convinced that, while remaining proud of their own national identities and history, the peoples of Europe are determined to transcend their

---

[2] Article I–51.

[3] *'Our Constitution ... is called a democracy because power is in the hands not of a minority but of the greatest number'*, from the funeral oration of Pericles, Thucydides II, 37.

ancient divisions and, united ever more closely, to forge a common destiny,
Convinced that, thus 'united in its diversity', Europe offers them the
best chance of pursuing, with due regard for the rights of each
individual and in awareness of their responsibilities towards future
generations and the Earth, the great venture which makes of it a special
area of human hope,
Determined to continue the work accomplished within the framework
of the Treaties establishing the European Communities and the Treaty
on European Union, by ensuring the continuity of the Community
acquis,
Grateful to the members of the European Convention for having
prepared the draft of this Constitution on behalf of the citizens and
States of Europe,
Have designated as their plenipotentiaries: .....
Who, having exchanged their full powers, found in good and due form,
have agreed as follows: .....'

CHAPTER 4

Defining principles and objectives

The unexpectedly lively argument over the Preamble prepared the ground in the Convention for the debate about what the Union stands for and where it is going. Laeken required the Convention to give systematic answers to some basic questions about definition. Without such an existential debate it would have been impossible for the Convention to claim to have re-founded the Union on a constitutional basis. It was indeed a solid achievement of the Convention that it could settle on a sharper definition of the purpose of the European Union and a clearer articulation of political objectives than can be found in the existing EU treaties. In the aftermath of the referendum setbacks for the Constitution, it is ironic to hear the sudden call by British and other ministers and their friends in national media for a profound debate about the nature and purpose of the Union. One may wonder why those same people contributed but lamely to that very same debate in the Convention on the Future of Europe.

The Convention found the first Article tortuous to negotiate. To achieve consensus, it had to combine three elements: the Union's dual legitimacy drawn from citizens and states, the constitutional re-foundation of the Union, and, lastly, the principle of conferral under which it is the member states that confer competences on the Union and not the other way around.

There were many, especially from the ranks of the European People's Party, who would have preferred to use the term 'peoples' to 'citizens'. Others, however, feared that 'peoples' would serve to dilute the constitutional standing of European citizenship. In any case, the peoples of Europe, including non-citizens or nationals of member states, were both addressed and to some extent protected by the Charter of Fundamental Rights in Part Two of the Constitution.

A second sentence was added to Article 1.1 to provide for the facts, first, that wherever competence is conferred on the EU by member states, the Union co-ordinates the policies of its member states, and, second, that the Union exercises those competences 'on a Community basis'. That last phrase gave rise to difficulties of comprehension in that it refers elliptically to the very European

Communities that this Constitution seeks to abolish. 'Community basis' means the classical decision-making process whereby the European Commission proposes draft law which is then disposed by the legislator composed jointly of the Council, representing the states, and the Parliament, representing the people.[1] 'Community basis' is the supranational order of EU institutions – Commission, Council, Parliament and Court of Justice – whose job it is to guarantee respect for the Treaties, to pursue their objectives and to enjoy law-making powers that have primacy over the laws of individual member states. In other words, 'Community basis' means the federal powers of the Union, and the method by which they are exercised.

It is a shame that the (mainly) British terror of speaking about federalism obliged the Constitution to take refuge in a euphemism precisely when it needed to be at its most forthright. It was a pity to be cryptic. For the uninitiated reader the only clue as to what 'Community basis' might mean lies in the fifth paragraph of the Preamble, which speaks of the debt owed by the Union to the former European Communities and to the Community's 'acquis' (expropriated into English). The 'acquis communautaire' is both the corpus of law, policy and jurisprudence developed over the last half century by the supranational institutions, but it is also the style of working within them. It is what must be assimilated by an accession state.

EUROPEAN IDENTITY

No other clause of the Constitution was trodden over with such laboriousness as Article 1.1. It is something of a relief, then, to turn to Article 1.2 which says simply enough that any European country that subscribes to promoting the Union's values is eligible for accession. There are no membership qualifications concerning size, demography, religion or spheres of influence, although the criterion of having to be 'European' should not go unremarked. The Convention did not try to define what it is to be European. Perhaps because of its own intensely pluralistic character, the Convention was fairly sanguine about acknowledging Europe's plural identity, in part geographic, in part cultural.

Europe as an intellectual concept has global reach. Values which we have now come to think of as universal were inspired originally by Europe's Enlightenment and articulated first by Western politicians and philosophers, mostly but by no means exclusively Christian. Capitalism and the regulated

---

[1]   The Convention had the marginally better 'in the Community way', although common usage is 'the Community method'.

market economy are European exports. In a world so deeply shaped by European history and culture, it would be rather conceited for Europeans to be narrowly prescriptive about what it is to belong to Europe.

Geography is not much help. Geographical Europe lies between the Atlantic and the Urals, in the south tucked between the Straits of Gibraltar and the Bosphorus. Anatolia is Asia Minor. Cyprus, to the east of Ankara and to the south of Tunis, also lies beyond Europe's geographical frontiers. Yet Cyprus, part Hellenic and Christian and part Turkish and Muslim, tells us more about Europe's cultural locus. It is undeniably European in the same way that one speaks of the USA or Australia or Argentina as being European. Cyprus is markedly more European than, say, India or South Africa, although both those countries have strong European characteristics. Cyprus was part of the Ottoman Empire for 300 years and then a British colony from 1878 to 1960. Both Cyprus and Malta, the other Mediterranean island that joined the EU in 2004, are Europe's frontier with the Arab world beyond. They share that distinction, and much else besides, with Turkey.

The question of Europe's definition of itself is of most immediate concern to Turkey, a member of the Council of Europe since 1951 and a long-standing member of Nato. Turkey was granted a unique association agreement with the EU in 1963, and full candidate status at the Helsinki European Council meeting in December 1999. As such, Turkish representatives took part in the Convention. Since its general election in November 2002, Turkey has made rapid progress towards becoming the world's first successful Muslim democracy, in itself a distinctly European concept. Its eligibility for EU membership was confirmed by the European Commission, European Parliament and European Council during 2004, with accession negotiations due to begin on 3 October 2005. Turkish efforts to reform its own constitution and to meet the Copenhagen criteria as well as settle its outstanding differences with Greece and Cyprus have coincided with the EU's own constitutional exercise. Europe's Turkey question is as intrinsic a part of the Union's current efforts to identify itself as is the debate on the Constitution. The Turkish question played heavily during the Convention. We have already seen how it shaped the drafting of the Preamble. It recurred in the negotiations over the Constitution's first article. And hostility to Turkish membership played an important part in boosting the No vote in both the French and Dutch referendums. The two issues are linked, not least because for most Turkophiles Turkish membership is inconceivable unless the Union can first be reinforced by providing itself with a proper Constitution. Only the British Conservatives adopt a position which is at once pro-Turk but anti-Constitution, while the far right and far left across Europe is anti-Turk and anti-Constitution.

It must be admitted that the Constitution was not designed by the Convention to satisfy anyone with a yearning to know exactly where the frontiers of Europe lay. Differences of opinion within the Convention about Turkish accession were known to exist – not least because Giscard was outspokenly hostile. Yet because there was no appetite for dividing the Convention unnecessarily, it was agreed to retain in the Constitution the ambiguity of the existing EU treaties on the question of boundaries. It was felt that there was no need to be more specific about Turkey at that stage when the ultimate decision about whether it should join the Union was certain to be at least a decade away. The issue was therefore neatly ducked. Perhaps that was a mistake. Any radical effort to renegotiate the text might be minded to revisit the question of enlargement. We will return to it ourselves in chapter 16.

The first article of the Constitution, in its final version, reads in full as follows:

Article 1

Establishment of the Union

1. Reflecting the will of the citizens and States of Europe to build a common future, this Constitution establishes the European Union, on which the Member States confer competences to attain objectives they have in common. The Union shall co-ordinate the policies by which the Member States aim to achieve these objectives, and shall exercise on a Community basis the competences they confer on it.

2. The Union shall be open to all European States which respect its values and are committed to promoting them together.

It was logical, therefore, though far from simple, for the second article of the Constitution to lay down the Union's values. A fierce argument developed about both content and precedence. In the end, the Convention settled for 'human dignity, liberty, democracy, equality, the rule of law and respect for human rights', in that order, and relegated 'pluralism, tolerance, justice, solidarity and non-discrimination' to a second sentence. The debate was far from academic, because it is Article 2 which establishes the values which, if breached, can provoke the suspension of a member state from the Union. The precedence established between these values would surely be relevant in litigation against a member state in those circumstances.[2]

The Convention failed to resolve two disputes about values. The first, raised most often in the Convention by Hungarians worried about their diaspora,

[2]   Article I–58.

concerned respect for the rights of minorities. The Convention had preferred to deal with minority rights in the context of the Charter in Part Two of the Constitution, where it followed the first Convention in choosing to focus on individual and not collective rights. But the IGC decided to give the group rights of minorities top billing in Part One. The second issue, raised most often by women, concerned gender equality. The dissenters argued that equality between the sexes should be valued on a par with equality between persons. In the end, the IGC included the concept in the second sentence. The final Article 2 reads as follows:

Article 2

The Union's values
The Union is founded on the values of respect for human dignity,
freedom, democracy, equality, the rule of law and respect for human
rights, including the rights of persons belonging to minorities. These
values are common to the Member States in a society in which
pluralism, non-discrimination, tolerance, justice, solidarity and equality
between women and men prevail.

It would be easy to scoff at the minutiae of these quarrels about values. But it was genuinely difficult to reflect in constitutional language the diversity of contemporary European society with its rich variety of anxieties and aspirations. And the setting of hierarchies matters in a new legal order.

No less difficult was the formulation of the catalogue of Union objectives. Here, more starkly than with values, partisan preferences between left and right were in evidence. Having been patched together fairly unsystematically, the existing Treaties offered no more than a jumbled check list of competing objectives. It was an essential test for the Convention that it would succeed in rationalising as well as modernising the provisions about what the Union seeks to achieve, and in making them readable. The Convention passed that test. Article 3 sets out the Union's objectives in a clear and relatively succinct fashion, and achieves the balance necessary to accommodate in constitutional form the various economic models on offer in Europe.

Convention members had to work particularly to get the three ingredients of integrated 'sustainable development' into the Constitution: economic growth, social progress and environmental improvement. Business leaders lobbied hard to install the idea of Europe's competitiveness and to insist, with the help of the European Central Bank, on the retention of price stability. The rights of the child appear in a draft EU treaty for the first time. Again, hierarchy is important. The promotion of peace appears as the primordial objective of the Union, rather than as a value, which suggests that non-peaceful means might be applied in order to further the Union's objectives: the EU is not pacifist, then. In the external field, moreover, the EU must work not only to observe international law, but to develop it. It is noteworthy that these clauses were being drafted in the middle of the poignant circumstances surrounding the invasion of Iraq. The final version of Article 3, tweaked editorially by the IGC, reads as follows:

Article 3

The Union's objectives
1. The Union's aim is to promote peace, its values and the well-being of its peoples.
2. The Union shall offer its citizens an area of freedom, security and justice without internal frontiers, and an internal market where competition is free and undistorted.
3. The Union shall work for the sustainable development of Europe based on balanced economic growth and price stability, a highly competitive social market economy, aiming at full employment and social progress, and a high level of protection and improvement of the quality of the environment. It shall promote scientific and technological advance.
It shall combat social exclusion and discrimination, and shall promote social justice and protection, equality between women and men, solidarity between generations and protection of the rights of the child.
It shall promote economic, social and territorial cohesion, and solidarity among Member States.
It shall respect its rich cultural and linguistic diversity, and shall ensure that Europe's cultural heritage is safeguarded and enhanced.
4. In its relations with the wider world, the Union shall uphold and promote its values and interests. It shall contribute to peace, security, the sustainable development of the Earth, solidarity and mutual respect among peoples, free and fair trade, eradication of poverty and the protection of human rights, in particular the rights of the child, as well as to the strict observance and the development of international law, including respect for the principles of the United Nations Charter.
5. The Union shall pursue its objectives by appropriate means commensurate with the competences which are conferred upon it in the Constitution.

GUIDING PRINCIPLES

Before the Constitution moved on to lay down the competences of the Union, it was necessary to reaffirm some cardinal principles that since the inception of the Union have moulded the acquis communautaire and gradually shaped its system of governance. The first concerned the basic freedoms of movement of people, goods, services and money on which the single market is built. These four freedoms are not just to be respected, but guaranteed by the Union. The second long-standing, core principle of the Union outlaws discrimination on the grounds of nationality. On Article 4 hangs all the law of the European Union, as follows:

Article 4

Fundamental freedoms and non-discrimination
1. The free movement of persons, services, goods and capital, and freedom of establishment shall be guaranteed within and by the Union, in accordance with the Constitution.
2. Within the scope of the Constitution, and without prejudice to any of its specific provisions, any discrimination on grounds of nationality shall be prohibited.

As a direct counter-balance to the requirement for member states to obey the EU regime of the single market and non-discrimination on the grounds of nationality, an article is then inserted to establish states' rights. The Union explicitly recognises that it must not intrude into the national 'no go' areas, the 'essential state functions' concerning security, law and order and territorial integrity.

Article 5 breaks new ground by insisting that the EU institutions must respect the domestic constitutional structures of the member states – including their variable systems of regional and local self-government. In the English version of the Constitution, the clause provides for respect of the 'national identities' of the member states, 'political and constitutional'. This may or may not be taken to refer to the pluralist nature of many member states within which there is no longer a single identifiable nationality (as opposed to citizenship) exclusive to the confines of the state.[3]

Previous EU treaties had restrained member states from impeding the

---

[3] Potentially, many English, Irish, Scottish and Welsh would find comfort from this provision, as would Basques, Catalans, Corsicans, Flemish and Walloons – and, potentially, Kurds. However, the existence of plural identities is only recognised in the English version of the Constitution: other language versions refer only to a singular national 'identity'.

successful accomplishment of the Union's objectives and had enjoined them to show mutual solidarity. In response to case law, a more concise articulation was made by the Convention of the need for member states to help each other meet the demands and obligations of Union membership. The need for 'sincere co-operation' among member states on the one hand, and between them and the Union on the other, became an express, guiding principle of the Constitution. Member states thereby recognise explicitly their mutual duty towards each other. In the Convention's debates about loyalty, several of its members were at pains to resist a move by the British to accentuate the distinction between the Union on the one side and its member states on the other. Too sharp a separation between the Union's different parts could have damaged the integrity of the federal system. Sincere co-operation between all parties is particularly important – and for the UK sensitive – in the field of foreign and security policy. An important provision, therefore, containing constitutional innovation, Article 5 reads as follows:

Article 5

Relations between the Union and the Member States
1. The Union shall respect the equality of Member States before the Constitution as well as their national identities, inherent in their fundamental structures, political and constitutional, inclusive of regional and local self-government. It shall respect their essential State functions, including ensuring the territorial integrity of the State, maintaining law and order and safeguarding national security.
2. Pursuant to the principle of sincere co-operation, the Union and the Member States shall, in full mutual respect, assist each other in carrying out tasks which flow from the Constitution.
The Member States shall take any appropriate measure, general or particular, to ensure fulfilment of the obligations arising out of the Constitution or resulting from the acts of the institutions of the Union. The Member States shall facilitate the achievement of the Union's tasks and refrain from any measure which could jeopardise the attainment of the Union's objectives.

LEGAL PRIMACY

A key element in the relationship between the European Union and its member states is the principle of the primacy of Union law. Although the principle had been established by jurisprudence of the Court of Justice from the earliest years of the EEC and subsequently affirmed by successive British governments, its existence seemed to take Peter Hain, Tony Blair's distinguished representative in the Convention, by surprise.[4] Hain's embarrassment served to demonstrate the perfect wisdom of codifying the case law of the Court. There is shock value in stating the blindingly obvious about legal precedence in constitutional terms, especially for those countries, such as the UK, where sentimental attachment to old-fashioned notions of national parliamentary sovereignty can impair full comprehension of and loyalty to the supranational system of governance of the European Union.

Article 6 of the Constitution states the guiding principle of European Union constitutional law as simply as possible, as follows:

Article 6

> Union law
> The Constitution and law adopted by the institutions of the Union in exercising competences conferred on it shall have primacy over the law of the member states.

To underline the point a Declaration was added by the IGC which notes that Article 6 'reflects existing case law' of the EU Courts. This was the first of thirty Declarations annexed to various Articles of the Constitution by the IGC. Declarations are non-binding in legal terms. They are usually intended to help one or two member states justify themselves back home, as indeed does Declaration No. 1, on codifying the primacy of EU law, for the British government at Westminster.[5]

What is meant by the primacy of EU law? The principle was most clearly established in an early judgment of the Court of Justice. In Costa v. ENEL (1964) the Court found that, in contrast to ordinary international treaties, the European Community created its own legal system which became an integral and binding part of the national legal systems of member states.

'The transfer by the States from their domestic legal systems to the Community legal systems of the rights and obligations arising under the Treaty carries with it a permanent limitation of their sovereign rights, against which a subsequent unilateral act incompatible with the concept of the Community prevails.

---

[4] The best official explanation of the legal and constitutional impact of EU membership on the UK was a White Paper published by the Labour Government in May 1967 (Cmnd 3301).
[5] In addition to the Declarations to thirty Articles of the Constitution, there are Declarations to eleven of the Constitution's Protocols and another seven Declarations made unilaterally by member states.

'By creating a Community of unlimited duration, having its own institutions, its own personality, its own legal capacity and capacity of representation on the international plane and, more particularly, real powers stemming from a limitation of sovereignty or a transfer of powers from the States to the Community, the Member States have limited their sovereign rights, albeit within limited fields, and have thus created a body of law which binds both their nationals and themselves.'[6]

EU law is directly applicable within member states. It is interpreted uniformly across the whole of the Union. It has direct effect, which means that it is applicable directly by national courts. EU law confers rights and obligations on citizens which national jurisdictions must seek to uphold. Extensive use has been made of the facility by which national judges can refer to the European Court of Justice for a preliminary ruling on questions of EU law. Accession to the Union means that a member state accepts not only all current EU law but also all future EU law. National parliaments may not legislate to cause conflicts, intentional or not, with EU law. Member states are liable for breaches of EU law within their own national jurisdictions. It is the job of the Court of Justice to see that the law of the Union is observed and to rule on incompatibilities between EU and national law.

National courts have grown to be fairly receptive to the precedence they must give to EU law. Although the concept of EU supremacy over national constitutions has not been universally acknowledged by rulings of the constitutional courts of every member state, national jurisdictions have been careful to avoid confrontation on this issue with the Court of Justice. Different member states have adapted their own constitutions to reflect these realities in a number of ways. Dutch basic law is very precise about the precedence that must be given to the EU legal order; the German and Italian constitutions, by contrast, are rather vague on the matter. The relevant UK statute is the 1972 European Communities Act which gives legal effect to EU law. In the course of ratification, a number of member states are having to consider whether, and if so how best to re-align their national constitutions with that of the EU.

To summarise, therefore, primacy of EU law means that wherever there is a conflict between an EU and a national law, it is the EU law that prevails to the extent necessary and the national law shall not apply. The abolition of the Maastricht three pillars has the important, perhaps dramatic, effect of extending EU primacy to justice and home affairs. The implications for the

---

[6] Case 6/64 *Costa v. ENEL*, ECR 585. Subsequent jurisprudence has upheld and reinforced the precedence of EU law, notably *Internationale Handelsgesellschaft* (1970), *Simmenthal* (1978), *Factortame* (1990) and *Francovich* (1991).

former second pillar are less far-reaching partly because there is much less legislation in the field of foreign and security policy but also because the Constitution deliberately limits the involvement of the Court of Justice in this area.

LEGAL ENTITY

It follows from the fact that the Union enjoys an autonomous legal order that it is an entity to be acknowledged in its own right on the international stage. Article 7 of the Constitution, simply enough, would acquire for the Union a legal personality. Previously only the European Communities have enjoyed a *persona* in international law. The European Commission therefore negotiates international trade treaties under a mandate received from the Council. The abolition of the three pillars would require this practice to be extended across the whole policy spectrum of the Union's competence. With the Constitution in force, the Commission will be able to negotiate and sign treaties on behalf of the Union as a whole in many more areas, including international conventions on the environment and aspects of external and internal security policy. The EU will be able to join international organisations in its own right. There will be an end to the confusion whereby the EU has had to be represented both by the Commission and by its member states at the same international conferences. This will aid both legal certainty and political transparency. The Union cannot be expected to stand on its own two feet in world affairs unless it is a fully recognised legal entity in its own right. Exercised well, the Union's legal personality would enable it to become a more coherent global player in the context of the United Nations. It does not mean that the UK and France would have to give up their separate seats on the UN Security Council. But it does mean that it would be easier for them to act as a single entity on behalf of the EU in circumstances where they and the other EU member states can manage to agree on a common foreign and security policy.

One of the first practical results of the acquisition of legal personality would be an EU application to accede to the European Convention for the Protection of Human Rights and Fundamental Freedoms (ECHR), a question to which we return in the next chapter.

Nevertheless, all risk of legal uncertainty is not quite removed by Article 7. Because the Constitution envisages a restricted role of the European Court of Justice in common foreign, security and defence policy, there is always the possibility that member states might try to shelter from judicial review for their actions in foreign affairs behind the anonymity of the Union's legal personality.

The first section or Title of the Constitution concludes by recognising certain symbols of the Union. Article 8 provides that these are the flag (twelve gold stars on blue background), the anthem (Beethoven's Ode to Joy), the motto 'Unity in Diversity', and the currency (the euro). 9 May, the day of the Schuman Declaration in 1950, is to be the annual 'Europe Day', celebrated, as the Constitution says, ' ... throughout the Union'.

CHAPTER 5

European Union citizenship: rights and duties

Citizenship of the European Union was formally created by the Treaty of Maastricht (1992), largely at German and Spanish insistence, in order to give practical expression to the right of the individual to move freely around the single market. Practical benefits of EU citizenship were limited at first to an extension of the franchise for local authority and European Parliamentary elections in member states other than one's own, and to a widening of mutual diplomatic protection. The right to petition the Parliament as well as to approach the Parliamentary Ombudsman in cases of maladministration by one of the EU institutions were also introduced. Citizenship began to acquire more salience once the Treaty of Amsterdam (1997) expanded the Union's ambitions in the field of internal security policy. Amsterdam also installed an important extension to the competence of the EU, enabling it to 'combat discrimination based on sex, racial or ethnic origin, religion or belief, disability, age or sexual orientation'.[1]

Concerns that the fast pace of European integration was running too far ahead of the languid emergence of EU citizenship prompted the powerful German Constitutional Court in Karlsruhe to warn against any further transfer of competence in this field to the EU level without a concomitant strengthening of fundamental rights protection. The German government used its term of office as president of the Council to propose the setting up of an EU-wide Convention to draft a Charter of Fundamental Rights. This innovative proposal was accepted by the European Council at Cologne in July 1999, and the sage Dr Roman Herzog, the former German Federal President, was appointed chairman of the Convention.

The sixty-two strong Convention, made up of representatives of the heads of government, the Commission, and MEPs as well as national MPs, set to work.[2]

---

[1] Article 13 TEC.

[2] The Charter Convention comprised 15 representatives of heads of government, 30 national MPs, 16 MEPs and one Commissioner (Antonio Vitorino), along with official observers from the Court of Justice and the Council of Europe.

It succeeded, beyond the expectations of many, to draft by consensus. The result was a modern catalogue of the classical fundamental rights as well as the principles which have guided the development of EU law and policy over the years. Its express purpose was to protect the citizen from any abuse by the EU of the power it exercises. The draft Charter of Fundamental Rights of the European Union, agreed on 2 October 2000, comprised fifty substantive articles, divided into chapters on dignity, freedoms, equality, solidarity, citizens' rights and justice. These were followed by four horizontal articles that set out the scope of the Charter, the limitations and level of protection of the rights, and prohibition of their abuse.

During the drafting of the Charter, particular controversies arose over the 'post-modern' provisions, such as eugenics and human cloning. Most difficult of all were the rights in the field of social policy, where the Charter had to avoid giving the impression that anyone without a job or a house could obtain one or the other merely by application to the EU courts. In general, the self-image of European society formulated in the Charter is one of liberty and pluralism. Restrictions on freedom, for example in the area of data protection, have to be prescribed by laws that are to be enforced by an independent authority. Freedom of thought, conscience and religion is emphasised, as is the right to free expression. Frequent reference is made to the principle of subsidiarity, and the need for the EU institutions to respect national laws and practices. Throughout the Charter it is the right of the individual person that is articulated. The onus falls on each individual to respect the rights of others. Collective rights as such are eschewed in order to avoid treading upon the collective rights of other groups.

The draft Charter was presented by the Convention to the leaders at their meeting in Biarritz later in October. It was accepted, although not without demur, especially from prime minister Blair who felt himself boxed into a corner. Two months later, at Nice, the Charter was 'solemnly proclaimed' by the Council, Commission and Parliament. A majority in the European Council would have preferred at that stage to have given the Charter the status of a justiciable document, with mandatory effect. On the instructions of President Herzog, the Convention had drafted the Charter as if it were to become mandatory. The Charter's focus, therefore, was deliberately limited to the European Union institutions and agencies, at home and abroad, including member state governments when and in so far as they carry out EU law and policy. But desperate to avoid creating new legal obligations at European level, and fearful of nationalist reaction back home, the United Kingdom continued to insist that the Charter should be left out of the Treaty of Nice and kept merely as a political code of conduct.

Even the Charter's political proclamation at Nice was in itself something of an achievement as the UK had been clearly most apprehensive about the whole project since its inception, and had at first threatened to block it outright. Tony Blair realised, however, that to have continued to oppose the Charter would have left Britain isolated (except, that is, for Ireland, whose own opposition melted once London's objections had been lifted). Concurrent developments with respect of the rise of the far right across the Union, not least in Austria, had raised the stakes. Moreover, the imminence of enlargement heightened the salience of fundamental rights. It was difficult for Britain – a strong supporter of enlargement – to counter the argument that the impending admission to the European Union of states with only a limited experience of liberal democracy, many of them with large national or ethnic minorities within their own borders, necessitated a Charter of Fundamental Rights.

British antipathy to the whole Charter project was and is difficult for its partners to understand. In mainland Europe it is accepted that respect for fundamental rights requires not only parliamentary and judicial legitimacy but also wide social consensus. The Charter Convention dealt with British objections seriously but firmly. While it squarely addressed social and economic matters, it cast them more as principles to guide the good government of the Union rather than as fundamental rights that could be guaranteed by way of a remedy delivered by the EU institutions. The result is that within the Charter some clauses enjoy more judicial automaticity than others. Clarity as to which is which became an obsession of the British government.

Yet the British success at Nice in preventing the installation of the Charter within the Treaty backfired. Its status as a proclamation was ambiguous in terms of EU law, and actually served to invoke the very legal confusion that the British government claimed it was so anxious to avoid. Despite the fact that the UK government insisted that the Charter created no new legal obligations, the Prodi Commission and European Parliament both undertook to be bound by its provisions.

As the Laeken Declaration suggested, it was clear that the Treaty of Nice had left an unstable situation with respect to the Charter. The constitutional Convention knew that a crucial test of its credibility was how it would deal with the instability. A way had to be found to install the Charter within the Constitution with mandatory effect on EU institutions and their agencies, including member state governments, when and in so far as they were implementing EU law and policy. Once they had more or less accommodated the constitutional purpose of the Convention, the British were led to accept that a Bill of Rights was a necessary prerequisite of the emerging Constitution. By that stage, however, Britain's eurosceptic politicians and media had developed a phobia about the Charter which proved to be very difficult for Blair's government to face down. Fuelling this mistrust of the Charter was the CBI, the British employers' federation, who claimed that a binding Charter would undo Margaret Thatcher's legislation which had famously restricted trade union power. However, contrary to what the CBI and the Conservative Party were claiming, the Charter would not give the EU carte blanche to dismantle Thatcherite labour laws. The Constitution makes it quite clear that the Charter's field of application is restricted to the existing powers and tasks of the Union.[3] In so far as the provisions of the Charter that contain principles are concerned, its judicial scope is limited to laws and executive acts of the EU and to acts of member states when implementing EU law.[4] The right to strike is recognised 'in accordance with Union law and national laws and practices'.[5] The Union is competent only to 'support and complement the activities of the Member States' in the field of industrial relations.[6] And, in any case, EU legislation in this area has to be adopted by unanimity in the Council.[7]

BRITISH OBSTACLE OVERCOME

Eventually, under intense pressure from the Convention, but not without internal government divisions at home, Tony Blair conceded. He instructed his representatives to accept that the Charter would become binding, but invited them to do all in their power to limit the damage. Accordingly, the UK government fought a rearguard action to dilute the legal force of the Charter. The horizontal clauses were adjusted by the Convention to make clearer the difference between classic rights (for a breach of which the courts have to seek direct remedies) and fundamental principles (which inform the formulation, enactment and implementation of EU law). The IGC added a clause to say that the courts should give 'due regard' to the explanatory memorandum drawn up by the Praesidium of the Charter Convention.[8] In the House of Commons, on the BBC and in the British tabloid press, the UK government proclaimed a great victory against the

---

[3]   Article II–111.2.
[4]   Article II–112.5.
[5]   Article II–88.
[6]   Article III–210.1.
[7]   Article III–210.3.
[8]   Article II–112.7.

alleged overweening activism of the Court of Justice. In practice, the government's achievements are more modest. Greater clarification of the distinction between rights and principles, which shall be differently interpreted, is to be welcomed. However, complete separation between the two would be against the spirit of the Charter which aims to be a single and comprehensive catalogue of modern rights. It is obvious that some provisions defy strict categorisation: for example, that on equality between men and women, and those on legal, economic and social protection contain both rights and principles.[9] Even the greater prominence accorded the explanatory memorandum gives rise to no substantive change. The explanations are not in themselves justiciable, and would have been one tool of interpretation used by the courts in any case, regardless of where and how they were published. Of academic interest, the explanations describe the sources of each provision of the Charter in terms of jurisprudence, general principles of EU law, specific EU legislation, the EU Treaties and the Constitution itself, as well as relevant statutes of international law.

AVOIDING COMPETING RIGHTS REGIMES

Where the UK government managed to attract sympathy, however, was in its argument that the EU's Charter of Fundamental Rights should not be set up in competition with the 1950 European Convention for the Protection of Human Rights and Fundamental Freedoms (ECHR). It was fully agreed that consistency and conformity between the Charter and the ECHR were essential if legal uncertainty was to be avoided. But members of the Charter Convention insisted that the scope of the Charter should be broader and its thrust more modern than that of the older document. The draftsmen of the Charter, in the first instance, and, then, of the Constitution could see no good reason why the Union should not gradually develop over time a superior fundamental rights regime to that of the member states of the Council of Europe. That conclusion was reflected in one of the horizontal clauses, Article 112.3, which reads:

> Insofar as this Charter contains rights which correspond to rights guaranteed by the Convention for the Protection of Human Rights and Fundamental Freedoms, the meaning and scope of those rights shall be the same as those laid down by the said Convention. This provision shall not prevent Union law providing more extensive protection.

[9] Articles II–83, 93 and 94, respectively.

As long as the Charter remains a voluntary code of conduct, the extent of EU law making in the field of fundamental rights as well as the role of the European Court of Justice will remain marginal. However, if and when the Charter acquires binding effect, the Court of Justice can be expected to develop rapidly its own case law in the field of human rights. The Strasbourg European Court of Human Rights will in any event remain the external supervisor of the EU Courts in Luxembourg, just as it is for the national courts of the member states.

Coupled with the decision of the Convention and the IGC to install the Charter with binding effect at the heart of the Constitution was the agreement to commit the European Union, equipped with its newly comprehensive legal personality, to seek accession to the ECHR. It has been a curious anomaly that although every member state is and has to be a signatory to the ECHR, the Union itself has not been. In reaction to an approach by the German Constitutional Court in 1994, the European Court of Justice had concluded that the EU lacked the competence to accede in its own right to the ECHR.[10] The Constitution creates a way for this to be rectified. Under the Constitution, the EU would negotiate to become the forty–sixth signatory of the ECHR, with the beneficial result that the EU institutions and their officials would henceforward be subject to exactly the same discipline as member state governments and civil services.

CITIZENSHIP COMES OF AGE?

Overall, the Charter adds up to a coherent and reasonably concise catalogue of fundamental rights. Its visibility is greatly heightened by the belated but nevertheless welcome decision to install it at the centre of the integration process and at the heart of the Constitution. The Constitution would allow European Union citizenship to come of age.

The Charter becomes Part Two of the Constitution. No special revision procedure was invented for the Charter, so any amendment to its provisions, however minor, would be subject to the same dual key of unanimity both of governments and of national parliaments or referendums as Part One. Such a ponderous process might discourage sensible amendments from being attempted, with the attendant risk that the Charter fails to keep pace with social, cultural and scientific developments and becomes an archaic nuisance. A prospective renegotiation of the Constitution, therefore, would be wise to consider introducing softer ways of amending the Charter.

[10] Opinion 2/94, concerning a case brought in the Bundesverfassungsgericht by Manfred Brunner against the Treaty of Maastricht. 1996 ECR 1–1759.

At the IGC the Charter's explanatory memorandum, so beloved of the British, became Declaration No. 12. The table below summarises the contents of the Charter as it was installed eventually in the Constitution.

PART TWO

THE CHARTER OF FUNDAMENTAL RIGHTS OF THE UNION

Preamble

TITLE I: DIGNITY

Article II–61	Human dignity
Article II–62	Right to life
Article II–63	Right to the integrity of the person
Article II–64	Prohibition of torture and inhuman or degrading treatment or punishment
Article II–65	Prohibition of slavery and forced labour

TITLE II: FREEDOMS

Article II–66	Right to liberty and security
Article II–67	Respect for private and family life
Article II–68	Protection of personal data
Article II–69	Right to marry and right to found a family
Article II–70	Freedom of thought, conscience and religion
Article II–71	Freedom of expression and information
Article II–72	Freedom of assembly and of association
Article II–73	Freedom of the arts and sciences
Article II–74	Right to education
Article II–75	Freedom to choose an occupation and right to engage in work
Article II–76	Freedom to conduct a business
Article II–77	Right to property
Article II–78	Right to asylum
Article II–79	Protection in the event of removal, expulsion or extradition

TITLE III: EQUALITY

Article II–80	Equality before the law
Article II–81	Non-discrimination
Article II–82	Cultural, religious and linguistic diversity
Article II–83	Equality between women and men

TITLE VII: GENERAL PROVISIONS GOVERNING THE INTERPRETATION AND APPLICATION OF THE CHARTER

Article II–111   Field of application
Article II–112   Scope and interpretation of rights and principles
Article II–113   Level of protection
Article II–114   Prohibition of abuse of rights

The Charter is given mandatory status under the provisions of Article 9 of Part One of the Constitution. The same clause provides for the Union's accession to the ECHR. It also repeats the earlier Treaty formulation that respect for fundamental rights constitutes a general principle of Union law. Article 9 reads as follows:

Article 9

Fundamental rights
1. The Union shall recognise the rights, freedoms and principles set out in the Charter of Fundamental Rights which constitutes Part II.
2. The Union shall accede to the European Convention for the Protection of Human Rights and Fundamental Freedoms. Such accession shall not affect the Union's competences as defined in the Constitution.[11]
3. Fundamental rights, as guaranteed by the European Convention for the Protection of Human Rights and Fundamental Freedoms and as they result from the constitutional traditions common to the Member States, shall constitute general principles of the Union's law.

The unexpected obstacles to the successful ratification of the Constitution leave the Charter for the time being as a political code of conduct in legal limbo. Without the Constitution in place, no progress can be made by the Union in signing up to the ECHR. In anticipation of the Constitution coming into force, the European Commission has already taken steps to tighten up its own methodology in relation to the Charter, with the aim of ensuring that a culture of fundamental rights is locked into EU legislation. Every draft law will be screened to see that it fully takes into account classic civil rights like those guaranteeing freedom of expression and those protecting citizens from the intrusive powers of the state. It is to be hoped that the Council and Parliament will be just as observant, especially where there is a variance with the general principles of equality before the law and non-discrimination, or where a law implies a limitation of a fundamental right which must be justified under

---

[11] Article I–9.2 carries both a Protocol (no. 32) and a Declaration (no. 2) designed to facilitate the process of accession to the ECHR.

Article 52 of the Charter.[12] But the fact that the Charter will remain, at least
for the moment, without mandatory effect presents the institutions which seek
in good faith to deploy it with a potential problem.

There will be problems for the Court of Justice, too, in the non-ratification of
the Constitution. Several Advocates-General and the Court of First Instance have
already shown themselves willing to exploit the Charter as an interpretative tool;
and recent judgments of the Court have been far-reaching in bolstering the rights
of citizens in residency cases. It will be interesting to see how the Courts now react
to the actuality of constitutional failure in these sensitive fields. In anticipation,
however, of an eventual settlement of the crisis, we should note that Article 10 of
the Constitution sets out the rights and duties of the EU citizen, as follows:

Article 10

Citizenship of the Union

1. Every national of a Member State shall be a citizen of the Union.
Citizenship of the Union shall be additional to national citizenship and
shall not replace it.

2. Citizens of the Union shall enjoy the rights and be subject to the
duties provided for in the Constitution. They shall have:

(a) the right to move and reside freely within the territory of the
Member States;

(b) the right to vote and to stand as candidates in elections to the
European Parliament and in municipal elections in their Member State
of residence, under the same conditions as nationals of that State;

(c) the right to enjoy, in the territory of a third country in which the
Member State of which they are nationals is not represented, the
protection of the diplomatic and consular authorities of any Member
State on the same conditions as the nationals of that State;

(d) the right to petition the European Parliament, to apply to the
European Ombudsman, and to address the institutions and advisory
bodies of the Union in any of the Constitution's languages and to obtain
a reply in the same language.

These rights shall be exercised in accordance with the conditions and limits
defined by the Constitution and by the measures adopted thereunder.

The rider in Article 10.1 that EU citizenship is a supplement to and not a
substitute for national citizenship was included, cleverly, to mollify
conservative eurosceptic opinion.

---

[12] Article II–112.

CHAPTER 6

What the Union can and cannot do

Having established the values and principles that motivate the purposes of the Union, and having installed a regime of fundamental rights, the first part of the Constitution proceeds to lay down the competences of the Union and the principles which govern their use. The Preamble already introduces us to the concept of competences conferred on the Union by the member states and its corollary that competences not so conferred remain with the states. The principle of conferral is re-stated more fully in Article 11 of the Constitution. This helps our understanding of the European Union in two respects. First, it combats the suspicion – hard to prove but widely shared – that the EU level simply acquires competences almost subversively by dint of Commission aggrandisement or by inference of the judgments of the Court. Insistence on conferred competence in the Constitution puts an end to any possibility of inferred competence. Second, the fact that competences are explicitly conferred on the Union to achieve specific objectives makes it easier to interpret the principle of subsidiarity, whereby competences should be exercised at the lowest possible level of government compatible with efficacy.

Subsidiarity is itself redefined in the Constitution to embrace the regional and local levels of governance. Concomitant to subsidiarity is the key principle of proportionality, whereby EU action should be proportionate to the scale of the problem that it seeks to address. The tendency of past Commissions to use a large hammer to crack small nuts has to be avoided if the EU is to become identified with better law-making. Applying the principle of proportionality features prominently in the jurisprudence of the Court of Justice, whereas the judges have tended to regard subsidiarity as a political device requiring political rather than judicial solutions. Article 11 reads as follows:

Article 11

Fundamental principles
1. The limits of Union competences are governed by the principle of

conferral. The use of Union competences is governed by the principles of subsidiarity and proportionality.

2. Under the principle of conferral, the Union shall act within the limits of the competences conferred upon it by the Member States in the Constitution to attain the objectives set out in the Constitution. Competences not conferred upon the Union in the Constitution remain with the Member States.

3. Under the principle of subsidiarity, in areas which do not fall within its exclusive competence, the Union shall act only if and insofar as the objectives of the proposed action cannot be sufficiently achieved by the Member States, either at central level or at regional and local level, but can rather, by reason of the scale or effects of the proposed action, be better achieved at Union level.

The institutions of the Union shall apply the principle of subsidiarity as laid down in the Protocol on the application of the principles of subsidiarity and proportionality. National Parliaments shall ensure compliance with that principle in accordance with the procedure set out in that Protocol.

4. Under the principle of proportionality, the content and form of Union action shall not exceed what is necessary to achieve the objectives of the Constitution.

The institutions of the Union shall apply the principle of proportionality as laid down in the Protocol on the application of the principles of subsidiarity and proportionality.

There was a long debate in the Convention about how to classify competences. Nobody argued for a power of general competence to be given to the European Union (that is, an autonomous 'competence competence'). Some who hailed from a classical federalist background, notably representatives of the German Bundesrat, argued at first that the Convention should draw up a complete catalogue of detailed vertical competences – that is, how functions were to be divided between multi-layered governance in each relevant policy sector. This approach implied a need for an article spelling out member states' residuary competences, the drafting of which would have been no simple task. Others in the Convention, including the Commission, would have chosen to set out competences in a way that demonstrated more directly the intensity of EU level action in each field. Most, however, preferred to settle for a definition based on the existing treaties and jurisprudence, designed to assist comprehension and interpretation, but leaving a degree of flexibility in the arrangements to allow both for national diversity and for the present (still formative) state of integration. Representatives of the European Parliament were adamant in pushing to get real innovation in this area so as to avoid the current necessity to engage in an archaeological dig through the treaties to unearth the facts about what the Union can and cannot do.

Three classes of functional competence were therefore established by the Convention: exclusive, shared and complementary. Their characteristics are set out as follows:

Article 12

Categories of competence
1. When the Constitution confers on the Union exclusive competence in a specific area, only the Union may legislate and adopt legally binding acts, the Member States being able to do so themselves only if so empowered by the Union or for the implementation of Union acts.
2. When the Constitution confers on the Union a competence shared with the Member States in a specific area, the Union and the Member States may legislate and adopt legally binding acts in that area. The Member States shall exercise their competence to the extent that the Union has not exercised, or has decided to cease exercising, its competence.
3. The Member States shall co-ordinate their economic and employment policies within arrangements as determined by Part III, which the Union shall have competence to provide.
4. The Union shall have competence to define and implement a common foreign and security policy, including the progressive framing of a common defence policy.
5. In certain areas and under the conditions laid down in the Constitution, the Union shall have competence to carry out actions to support, co-ordinate or supplement the actions of the Member States, without thereby superseding their competence in these areas.
Legally binding acts of the Union adopted on the basis of the provisions in Part III relating to these areas shall not entail harmonisation of Member States' laws or regulations.
6. The scope of and arrangements for exercising the Union's competences shall be determined by the provisions relating to each area in Part III.

EXCLUSIVE COMPETENCES

The first category involves the exclusive competences of the Union, where it is the Union that enjoys the power to legislate or to empower member states to do so. Article 13 sets out the specific areas of exclusive competence as follows:

Article 13

Areas of exclusive competence

1. The Union shall have exclusive competence in the following areas:
(a) customs union;
(b) the establishing of the competition rules necessary for the functioning of the internal market;
(c) monetary policy for the Member States whose currency is the euro;
(d) the conservation of marine biological resources under the common fisheries policy;
(e) common commercial policy.

2. The Union shall also have exclusive competence for the conclusion of an international agreement when its conclusion is provided for in a legislative act of the Union or is necessary to enable the Union to exercise its internal competence, or insofar as its conclusion may affect common rules or alter their scope.

The purpose of exclusive competence is to establish uniformity and to avoid risk of distorting the single market. Yet the choice of exclusive competences was not entirely uncontroversial, and certainly not unimportant as they enjoy the privilege under EU law of not being subject to the application of the principle of subsidiarity.[1] Nor is enhanced co-operation to be permitted in the field of exclusive competence.[2] No previous EU Treaty had spelt out what the exclusive competences were, so the Convention had to codify a large corpus of EU case law and well-established practice. The presumption made is that exclusive competences have a basic value to the development of Europe's economic integration; that they are prerequisites of the Union and lynchpins of the acquis communautaire; and that they cannot feasibly be shared with member states. Yet the fact that these competences are exclusive to the EU means neither that they are inevitably the most important competences currently possessed by the EU nor that member states have no role whatsoever to play. For example, the Union's exclusive competence in competition policy does not eliminate national competition rules but, rather, obliges them to conform to the discipline of the European single market. There have been a number of cases brought before the Court of Justice where the Commission's attribution of exclusivity to the harmonisation of national laws in the field of the internal market has been successfully challenged.[3]

The inclusion of marine conservation in the list of exclusive competences

---

[1]   Article I–11.3.
[2]   Article I–44.1.
[3]   For example, on tobacco advertising.

looks mightily odd, and offends Scottish Nationalists, but the Convention and the IGC were of the view that, for the sake of conserving stocks, the Commission and Council needed to keep full control over the size of the fishing catch.

The question of international agreements is more complicated still. As long ago as 1971 the Court ruled that, as regards common commercial policy, the EU has exclusive competence to enter into external agreements once it has adopted a common internal rule.[4] Problems arose over the interpretation of how wide the jurisdiction of the EU should be in relation to mixed international agreements involving issues that were only partly within its exclusive competence and partly enjoyed concurrently with member states. Controversy persisted because whereas EU trade in goods is subject to QMV in the Council, trade in services is not. The Commission is joined by member states in WTO negotiations in services, transport and intellectual property. The French government was particularly insistent in the Convention and the IGC that this distinction should not be blurred.

Nevertheless, it should not be lost sight of that Article 13.2 would strengthen the exclusive competence of the Union in respect of international agreements that stem from EU legislation, that enable the Union to exercise its internal competence or that affect the scope of EU common rules. This threefold provision is broader than the Treaty's current definition which merely implies a link between internal and external competence.

SHARED COMPETENCES

Article 14 lays down the second and most common category of EU competence. These are competences attributed to the Union but shared with member states, and where both the Union and the states may adopt laws and regulations. The states shall exercise their competences in these areas only where the EU has not exercised its competence, or has decided to stop exercising it. This is the case with all the sectoral common policies of the Union with the exception of competition policy, commercial policy and monetary policy for the euro group – which are exclusive (Article 13) – and policies where the EU merely supports or complements national policy (Article 17). The Constitution intends that in the common policies in the areas of shared competence the Union should concentrate on resolving cross-border problems, on setting minimum standards and on eliminating barriers to trade. However, in accordance with the principles of subsidiarity and proportionality, the Union institutions are

---

[4] Case 22/70, *ERTA* [1971], ECR 263, confirmed by subsequent case law.

impelled to seek, find and formulate in legislative or regulatory terms the added value of taking action at the Union level.

Article 14

Areas of shared competence

1. The Union shall share competence with the Member States where the Constitution confers on it a competence which does not relate to the areas referred to in Articles I–13 and I–17.

2. Shared competence between the Union and the Member States applies in the following principal areas:

(a) internal market;

(b) social policy, for the aspects defined in Part III;

(c) economic, social and territorial cohesion;

(d) agriculture and fisheries, excluding the conservation of marine biological resources;

(e) environment;

(f) consumer protection;

(g) transport;

(h) trans-European networks;

(i) energy;

(j) area of freedom, security and justice;

(k) common safety concerns in public health matters, for the aspects defined in Part III.

3. In the areas of research, technological development and space, the Union shall have competence to carry out activities, in particular to define and implement programmes; however, the exercise of that competence shall not result in Member States being prevented from exercising theirs.

4. In the areas of development co-operation and humanitarian aid, the Union shall have competence to carry out activities and conduct a common policy; however, the exercise of that competence shall not result in Member States being prevented from exercising theirs.

The reference to Part Three of the Constitution with respect to social policy and public health is clumsy but was considered essential in order to delimit strictly the conferral of competence on the Union in those areas. Part Three lays out in much greater detail the objectives of the common policies and the role of the EU institutions in both formulating and implementing them. In all cases, the provisions concerning EU competences should be read with Part

Three in mind, where their scope and the arrangements for exercising them are more fully determined.[5]

In the field of social policy, the reservation amounts to the prohibition of EU harmonisation of national laws with the intention of preserving member state discretion to design and finance their own social security systems.[6] In the field of public health, EU legislation is permissible to protect the trade in drugs, blood and organs, in veterinary and phytosanitary measures, and in order to combat serious cross-border health risks.[7] In either case the adoption of EU law does not prevent a member state from imposing higher standards of social welfare policy as long as national law is compatible with the EU Constitution.

Special provisions are made with respect to two policies: research and development and international development. The preservation of national particularities is considered so important in these fields that the existence of common EU policies must not be allowed to preclude the maintenance of individual member state policies. France and the UK were the member states most anxious to retain such clauses in the Constitution. Giscard lobbied successfully for the inclusion of space policy as an adornment to mundane scientific research and technological development.

Equally defiant of the conventional classification of the Union's concurrent competence were its competences in the fields of economic policy or foreign and security policy. In both cases the British government was in the vanguard of those who sought to limit the conferral of competence on the Union to the maximum possible extent. While rather grudgingly admitting that national policies had to be co-ordinated at EU level, the UK wished to emphasise that the policies would continue to be conducted by national governments. One may question – and many did – whether this was, in fact, an appropriate emphasis to be making when the economic performance of the EU was plainly faltering and the fruits of common foreign and security policy were mainly risible. Earlier drafts had been both more fluent and more decisive in giving the Union powers to co-ordinate national policies: a future revision of the Constitution may wish to revisit them – particularly in view of the low-level performance of the member states' current efforts to coordinate their national economic and foreign policies.

The precise objectives of these coordinated policies are confined to Part Three of the Constitution, and even there one finds very little content. Search Part Three for the economic policy programme of the Lisbon agenda, for example, and one will be disappointed. It may be that a renegotiated Constitution would

---

[5] Article I–12.5.
[6] Article III–210.
[7] Article III–278.

want to make much more visible the actual content of the policies the Union was inviting its citizens to support. Greater visibility within the Constitution of the content of the EU's economic and foreign policies, as opposed to the procedures which run them, would certainly have helped the Yes campaigners in France and Holland. In any case, Articles 15 and 16 of the Convention's Constitution read as follows:

Article 15

> The co-ordination of economic and employment policies
> 1. The Member States shall co-ordinate their economic policies within the Union. To this end, the Council of Ministers shall adopt measures, in particular broad guidelines for these policies.
> Specific provisions shall apply to those Member States whose currency is the euro.
> 2. The Union shall take measures to ensure co-ordination of the employment policies of the Member States, in particular by defining guidelines for these policies.
> 3. The Union may take initiatives to ensure co-ordination of Member States' social policies.

Article 16

> The common foreign and security policy
> 1. The Union's competence in matters of common foreign and security policy shall cover all areas of foreign policy and all questions relating to the Union's security, including the progressive framing of a common defence policy that might lead to a common defence.
> 2. Member States shall actively and unreservedly support the Union's common foreign and security policy in a spirit of loyalty and mutual solidarity and shall comply with the Union's action in this area. They shall refrain from action contrary to the Union's interests or likely to impair its effectiveness.

However one might regret the trodden-over language, a number of things are already crystal clear from these clauses. First, the Union enjoys under the Constitution the competence to co-ordinate national policies, and has instruments to deploy in pursuit of co-ordination. Second, co-ordination in the economic and employment sphere is not confined to members of the euro group. Third, the EU is instructed to devise guidelines for national economic and employment policies. Fourth, the imperative of a common foreign and security policy is without limitation and may well lead to common defence. It might have been helpful if these four points had been drummed home in the French referendum campaign.

COMPLEMENTARY COMPETENCES

After some fairly ill-tempered debate, the Convention agreed to designate seven policy sectors for the Constitution where the Union may support member state action without superseding it. In all such cases, the Union's legally binding acts shall not entail harmonisation of national laws or regulations. Nevertheless, growing concern about the comparative weakness of public administration in several of the accession states led to the important addition of 'administrative co-operation' as an area into which the EU has potential to develop its role. Article 17 reads as follows:

Article 17

> Areas of supporting, co-ordinating or complementary action
> The Union shall have competence to carry out supporting, co-ordinating or complementary action. The areas of such action shall, at European level, be:
> (a) protection and improvement of human health;
> (b) industry;
> (c) culture;
> (d) tourism;
> (e) education, youth, sport and vocational training;
> (f) civil protection;
> (g) administrative co-operation.

Powerful lobbies in the Convention and at the IGC insisted that tourism could not be treated like any other industry, and that sport also deserved its own specific legal base in the Constitution. If the Constitution enters into force before 2012, the EU can help out with the London Olympics. Indeed, Union action in these areas often has a high relevance for local authorities, universities as well as the general public. More emphasis on developing a European cultural policy may even reap dividends in the context of referendum campaigns on EU issues, to which, it seems, several member states are irrevocably committed.

COMPETENCE FLEXIBILITY

The European Union has enjoyed since its foundation a degree of flexibility about competence. As we have seen, the European Commission has from time to time implied competences and rulings of the Court of Justice have inferred competences. There has also been extensive use of Article 308 of the Treaty of Rome which allows the EU institutions (with the Council acting by unanimity) to take appropriate measures to fulfil an objective of the Treaty even where the Treaty itself has not provided a specific legal base. There was considerable debate in the Convention about whether the Constitution's new emphasis on conferral of competences rendered the so-called flexibility clause superfluous. Eurosceptics alleged that the clause is a dangerous weapon in the hands of the overwhelmingly centralising Brussels institutions. But the majority fought successfully to include such a clause, albeit redrafted, in the new Constitution. Accordingly, the clause now reads as follows:

Article 18

Flexibility clause
1. If action by the Union should prove necessary, within the framework of the policies defined in Part III, to attain one of the objectives set out in the Constitution, and the Constitution has not provided the necessary powers, the Council of Ministers, acting unanimously on a proposal from the European Commission and after obtaining the consent of the European Parliament, shall adopt the appropriate measures.
2. Using the procedure for monitoring the subsidiarity principle referred to in Article I–11(3), the European Commission shall draw national Parliaments' attention to proposals based on this Article.
3. Measures based on this Article shall not entail harmonisation of Member States' laws or regulations in cases where the Constitution excludes such harmonisation.

It should be stressed that Article 18 does not allow the EU to interfere in any way it fancies, but only in strictly defined circumstances in pursuit of a constitutional objective. Any decision to deploy the article would have to be by unanimity and subject to the subsidiarity test of national parliaments; and it may not be used to blur the distinction between shared and complementary competences. Its advantage is not that it may be used to avoid the necessity of a major constitutional amendment but in order to provide the possibility to act in circumstances that the authors of the Constitution did not foresee. In the past, the comparable article has been used to smooth the introduction of the euro, to prepare countries to fulfil the conditions for membership, and as a legal basis for contractual ties with third countries. It has allowed the EU to fill in some gaps in the Union's functional powers pending future treaty revisions, particularly during the building of the complex edifice of the single market.

The Constitution's consolidation of current competences and its extension of specific legal bases should make it unlikely that the flexibility clause will need to be much used. In any case, use of the flexibility clause alongside the principle of conferred competences will naturally be subject to judicial review by the Court of Justice. Its very existence might well discourage the Court from being tempted in its case law to infer a creeping transfer of competence by other routes. A notable improvement in the new formulation is that it provides for the actual consent of the European Parliament whereas Article 308 merely allows for its consultation. MEPs have tended previously to oppose extensive use of this article because it provided neither for QMV in Council nor for codecision with Parliament. The Commission can be expected to be less keen on its deployment in the future, given that it requires the unanimous agreement of an improbable twenty-five ministers.

No federal system has a system of delimiting competences that is perfect. Grey areas about who does what tend to persist, and are frequently subject to adjudication by the supreme court. Overall, the Constitution seems to have done a good job in setting out the competences of the Union in a logical fashion. The Convention was certainly seized of the statement in the Laeken Declaration that some citizens wanted the EU to play a greater role in some areas and a reduced role in others. Its consultations with representatives of the political parties and civil society confirmed that dilemma. It is to be hoped that one day, blessed by a constitution similar to this one, the Union will be able to concentrate on its essential tasks, to intensify action where necessary, to lighten its interventions where possible – and in all cases to justify itself to its citizens.

CHAPTER 7

The institutions: who does what?

Any Member of the European Parliament is constantly made very well aware of a widespread public and media ignorance about how the European Union is run. With the exception of some lively moments in the European Parliament hemicycle, the institutions themselves are hardly telegenic. Modern office buildings and flag posts against a background of lowering Brussels skies lack the historical resonance of the recuperated Reichstag building or even the folklore charm of the Palace of Westminster. Endless photo-shoots of groups of mostly men in suits fail to transmit either the substance or the drama of the power politics being played out at meetings of the Commission or European Council. The institutions' moveable feast of Brussels, Luxembourg and Strasbourg seems odd and costly. Simultaneous interpretation, whispered through headphones in a style first used at the Nuremberg trials, gives the whole scene a conspiratorial air. Media coverage of EU affairs is more opinionated than informed, and in any case sparse. For national political parties, as for the press, the EU is second order politics. It is little wonder that few people seem to know who does what at the top level of the Union. Even the Yes campaigners (with a few honourable exceptions) in France and Holland had to struggle to explain accurately the workings of the EU or to debate from a convincingly informed standpoint the strengths and weaknesses of the system.

The Constitution attempts to clarify matters. Lacking the courage to describe the EU institutions as the system of government it indubitably is, the Constitution falls back on 'institutional framework'. It describes for the first time the institutions' purpose. Article 19.1 says that the Union shall have an institutional framework whose aim shall be to 'promote its values, advance its objectives, serve its interests, those of its citizens and those of the Member States', and 'ensure the consistency, effectiveness and continuity of its policies and actions'.

Having named the institutions – European Parliament, European Council, Council of Ministers, European Commission and Court of Justice, in that order

– the Constitution provides that: 'Each institution shall act within the limits of the powers conferred on it in the Constitution, and in conformity with the procedures and conditions set out in it. The institutions shall practise mutual sincere co-operation'.[1] From this we can infer that the institutions are not self-serving, that they are all grounded in the Constitution, that they form something of a team with joint responsibility for the good governance of the Union, while respecting their own and each others' functions. In short-hand, and somewhat euphemistically, this is called 'the institutional balance' – a balance which the Laeken Declaration asked the Convention to keep. (It did not.)

Subsequent clauses in Part One (Articles 20 to 32) go on to describe in succinct form the functions and composition of the different institutions. These neat descriptions are in themselves novel, and all the more welcome for that. The final section of Part Three of the Constitution is entitled *The Functioning of the Union*. This develops the institutional articles in Part One, and comprises a number of important second tier provisions that knit the constitutional fabric together, notably the details of the budgetary and codecision procedures. Together with a number of Protocols and Declarations, Articles 330 to 436 lay down in more detail the rules concerning the composition and functioning of each institution, and the way they interact with each other. A third tier of institutional rules, in which the working methods of each institution are more precisely elaborated, is to be found in their own Rules of Procedure.[2]

EUROPEAN PARLIAMENT

The European Parliament, enjoying a much enhanced standing under the Constitution, is properly described for the first time.[3] Article 20.1 says:

> The European Parliament shall, jointly with the Council, exercise legislative and budgetary functions. It shall exercise functions of political control and consultation as laid down in the Constitution. It shall elect the President of the Commission.

Overall, among the institutions, the Parliament comes out best from the Constitution. Use of the ordinary legislative procedure is more than doubled. Codecision plus QMV expands into some totally new areas such as the citizens'

---

[1] Article I–19.2. One assumes that the Court of Justice is absolved from this last stricture.

[2] The current rules of procedure of the Commission and Parliament can be accessed fairly simply via the Europa web site, www.europa.eu.int. The current rules of procedure of the Council of Ministers are to be found in OJ L 106, 15 April 2004. Pending its grounding in the Constitution, the rules of procedure of the European Council do not, as yet, exist.

[3] One drawback remains that Protocol No. 6 continues to insist that the Parliament meets in both Brussels and Strasbourg.

initiative[4], a European space programme[5] and humanitarian aid[6]; into areas where the Parliament is at present only consulted, notably the Common Agricultural Policy and Common Fisheries Policy[7], border controls, asylum and immigration[8], and staff regulations[9]; and into areas where the Parliament has at present no say at all, such as movement of capital to and from third countries[10], and the common commercial policy[11].

According to the Constitution, the Parliament will eventually consist of 750 MEPs (against 732 at the moment). The smallest states will have six seats and the largest 96. MEPs are elected every five years, the next election being in 2009.[12] In good time before the next election, there would have to be agreement on the redistribution of seats between member states.[13] Malta will have one more seat and Germany three less: all the others are up for grabs.[14] The Parliament will both initiate this reform and give its final consent to it; but the European Council will have to act by unanimity to approve it. The Parliament also has the chance to initiate a new framework law reforming the uniform electoral procedure. This could ensure the creation of regional constituencies in the larger member states or even, as Laeken had mooted, the addition of a transnational list for the election of a certain proportion of MEPs.[15]

Another European law will establish a statute for Members of the European Parliament laying down their terms and conditions of employment. At present MEPs are paid the same as their respective national MPs, leading to a situation in which the ratio of a Hungarian MEP's salary to that of an Italian is 1:14. This issue has been a running sore in the Parliament, and tortuous negotiations between MEPs and their governments have taken years to achieve a consensus on a package that includes a common salary, taxation and pension scheme with a straightforward system for the reimbursement of travel and other expenses. The Members' Statute is another anomalous item whereby the Parliament has the

---

[4] Article I–47.
[5] Article III–254.
[6] Article III–321.
[7] Article III–231.
[8] Articles III–254, 266 and 267.
[9] Article III–427.
[10] Article III–157.
[11] Article III–315.
[12] Article I–20.
[13] Declaration No. 40 allows for the current Parliament (2004–09) to grow to 785 seats should Bulgaria (18 seats) and Romania (35) join the Union – as, indeed, they are expected to do. The size will then shrink to 750 in July 2009.
[14] Article I–20.2 and Article 1 of Protocol No. 34 on the Transitional Provisions relating to the Institutions and Bodies of the Union.
[15] Article III–330.1.

right of initiative and of final approval, after consulting the Commission and after having obtained the consent of the Council. The Council has to act unanimously on the question of MEPs' taxation.[16] At the time of writing, a political agreement has at last been reached: MEPs voted in July 2005 to accept a package which meant for many of them a significant loss of income and a less favourable deal than that enjoyed by their counterparts in national parliaments.[17]

The Constitution provides for a normal European law to regulate political parties at the EU level – the careful use of which could provide a much-needed sinew of democracy to connect the European Parliament better with its electorate.[18] Other articles lay down Parliament's powers to set up committees of inquiry, to receive petitions from the citizen, to appoint the European Ombudsman, and to adopt its own Rules of Procedure by a majority of its component Members. Parliament will normally act under the Constitution by a simple majority of the votes cast except where the Constitution provides otherwise, as at the second reading stage of the ordinary legislative procedure.[19]

While the Commission remains responsible for the formal drafting and introduction of a law, MEPs can exert real political pressure on the Commission to act even when it is unwilling to do so. If the Commission declines to follow Parliament's lead it has to justify its decision before Parliament.[20] Crucially, Parliament gains the right under the Constitution to initiate revision of the Constitution itself.[21] That is a highly significant step forward towards the constitutionalisation of the European Union, ending as it would the member states' monopoly over treaty change.

Parliament retains its right both to approve and to censure the whole Commission. The Convention did not agree with some MEPs that Parliament should also have the right to sack individual Commissioners. However, over the years, MEPs have gradually acquired the informal power to bring individual Commissioners to book. This is reflected in a Framework Agreement between the Parliament and the Commission which provides for the day-to-day workings of the inter-institutional relationship. In the latter half of 2004, President-elect Barroso was unable to proceed to appoint the team of Commissioners served up to him by the European Council because of objections raised by Parliament during its hearings of the individual candidates. As a

---

[16] Article III–330.2.
[17] MEPs' salary is to be set at 38.5 per cent of that of a judge of the European Court of Justice – which means currently €7000 per month.
[18] Article III–331.
[19] Article III–396.7.
[20] Article III–332.
[21] Article IV–443.1.

result of Parliament's unprecedented rebuttal of the prospective college, one nominee was withdrawn by her government, another resigned and a third had his portfolio switched by Barroso. From the ensuing crisis emerged a new Framework Agreement that has greatly increased the Commission's accountability to the Parliament.[22] It was agreed that if Parliament votes by a substantial majority to withdraw confidence in an individual member of the college, the President will either ask that member to resign or the President will come before Parliament to justify his refusal to do so. That concession gives MEPs the potential firing mechanism they have hitherto lacked to go for the 'nuclear option' and censure the whole college.

The European Parliament's initial rejection then later approval of the EU's new executive provoked much media comment. The reportage was such that the discerning public could see MEPs behaving exactly like it expects of parliamentarians. As for the Commission, although its confirmation in office was difficult and protracted, the college emerged strengthened. It is impossible now for critics to accuse the Commission of being unelected bureaucrats. Overall, the crisis over the approval of the Barroso Commission breathed some welcome democratic life into the constitutional process. Perhaps more should have been made of the event in the French and Dutch referendum campaigns: both countries' chosen Commissioners, although approved, featured prominently during the parliamentary hearings and its dénouement.

EUROPEAN COUNCIL

The one body that was not best pleased by the early tribulations of the Barroso Commission was the European Council, whose first selection was rejected by the Parliament. The European Council would be further tamed by the Constitution under which it is turned into a fully-fledged institution of the Union, thereby obliging the heads of government to abide by the inter-institutional rules. The powers of the European Council, composed of the heads of state or government, have grown rather haphazardly over the years. The fact that the Council of Ministers has had to share more and more legislative power with the Parliament has been compensated for by the emergence of the European Council at the top of the hierarchy. Indeed, Jean Monnet only persuaded Valéry Giscard d'Estaing, when President of France in 1974, to accept the introduction of direct elections to the European Parliament on condition that the summit meetings of the European leaders, at that stage

---

[22] European Parliament Resolution on the Framework Agreement, 26 May 2005, A6–0147/2005.

spasmodic, would become formalised as a regular European Council. The arrival on the scene of the European Council bore witness to the growing importance of European integration to national politics. But the European Council has tended to complicate decision making at the Council of Ministers level not only by treading wilfully on prerogatives but also by providing an excuse for ministers not themselves to make progress on a problematical dossier. Whereas the classic institutions of the European Community – Commission, Council and Parliament and Court – have been required to act only within the limits of the powers conferred upon them by the Treaty, no such injunction applied to the European Council.[23] Hence the significance of Article 21.1 of the Constitution, which grounds the European Council within the Constitution and prohibits it from interfering directly in law making, as follows:

> The European Council shall provide the Union with the necessary impetus for its development and shall define the general political directions and priorities thereof. It shall not exercise legislative functions.

The European Council is composed of heads of state or government and the President of the Commission. It meets at least quarterly, and takes its decisions by consensus.[24] Until now the chairmanship of the European Council has rotated between serving presidents or prime ministers every six months. The Constitution makes the job more permanent, for a term of two and a half years, renewable once.[25] Neither the Commission President nor the new-style President of the European Council, who would no longer hold national office, would vote. How the European Council adjusts to its new situation may depend heavily on the qualities of the person selected to be its 'full-time' chairman.[26] To signify the close liaison between Jacques Chirac and Gerhard Schröder, the Constitution allows one head of government to speak and vote on behalf of one other. Abstentions will not prevent the adoption of a decision by unanimity. After the Constitution comes into force, the European Council would have to adopt its first Rules of Procedure by simple majority. One would await to see those with interest.

COUNCIL OF MINISTERS

Article 23.1 on the ordinary Council of Ministers says:

> The Council shall, jointly with the European Parliament, exercise

[23] Article 7 TEC.
[24] Article I–21.
[25] Article I–22.
[26] Article III–341.

legislative and budgetary functions. It shall carry out policy-making and co-ordinating functions as laid down in the Constitution.

The Council of Ministers consists of one representative of each member state government who must be able to commit that government. Apart from some important exceptions laid down in the Constitution, the Council is to decide by QMV.[27] It is to meet in various policy configurations, led by a General Affairs Council (usually made up of foreign ministers). Its work is prepared by a powerful Committee of Permanent Representatives (COREPER). In a very important constitutional innovation, the Council will have to meet in public 'when it deliberates and votes on a draft legislative act'.[28]

We have already noted how controversial the issue of the QMV threshold became at the IGC. The eventual settlement defined the normal majority (when the Council votes on a Commission proposal) as 55 per cent of member states representing at least 65 per cent of the population. In an additional, and complicating, key brought in to satisfy the wounded pride of Poland and Spain, the IGC also decided that the qualified majority had to comprise at least fifteen member states and the blocking minority at least four. (This element becomes redundant once the membership of the EU reaches twenty-eight states.) In abnormal procedures (when the Council is not voting on a legislative proposal of the Commission), the threshold is to be 72 per cent of the member states representing 65 per cent of the population.[29] Under the terms of the Constitution, the new rules on qualified majority voting are only due to come into force, to replace those of Nice, on 1 November 2009.[30]

In another important reform, heralded by a debate at the Seville European Council in June 2002, the Constitution changes the system of presidency of the Council of Ministers. Since the beginning of the European Community, the chair has rotated among member states every six months. With six fairly cohesive founder member states that system achieved some continuity. With twenty-five disparate member states, it is collapsing. The Constitution now ordains, therefore, that the presidency of the different Council formations will be managed by teams of three member states rotating every eighteen months, with each of the three chairing each formation in turn for six months.[31]

The notable exception to this circus is the Foreign Affairs Council which is to be chaired by the new post of Union Minister for Foreign Affairs. This person is to be appointed and sacked by the European Council, acting by QMV, with

27   Article I–23.
28   Article I–24.6. See also Article I–50.
29   Article I–25.
30   Article 2 of Protocol No. 34.
31   Article I–24.7.

the agreement of the President of the Commission. He or she will also be a Vice-President of the Commission, responsible to the Council for the conduct of common foreign, security and defence policy and to the Commission for the conduct of the Union's external relations.[32] The new post – which will probably be styled 'Minister Vice-President' – combines the current roles of the Council's High Representative for foreign and security policy, Javier Solana, and the European Commissioner for external affairs, Benita Ferrero-Waldner. Solana has already been nominated for the new job and so, if confirmed in it by the European Parliament, he would then have to give up the other post that he combines currently with that of High Representative, which is Secretary-General of the Council. If and when the Constitution comes into force, a new, stand-alone Secretary-General will be appointed. (The long-serving French deputy to Solana is Pierre de Boissieu.)

The new Foreign Minister is to take over the chairmanship of the Foreign Affairs Council as soon as he is appointed. As far as the presidency of the other Council formations is concerned, the last two countries to take office under the old regime are Austria in the first half of 2006 and Finland in the second. Thereafter, team presidencies of three member states, balanced by both size and geography, are scheduled to preside for a period of eighteen months. The first cluster, from January 2007 until June 2008, is Germany, Portugal and Slovenia. The second, until December 2009, is France, the Czech Republic and Sweden.

In a parallel provision to that enjoyed by the Parliament, the Council can also invite the Commission to submit a proposal to it, legislative or otherwise, with the similar proviso that the Commission would have to justify a refusal to do so.[33]

Under the terms of the Constitution, the Council of Ministers undergoes important, long-awaited, structural reform. It will then have to adapt its own Rules of Procedure to suit, taking this and other procedural decisions by simple majority.

EUROPEAN COMMISSION

The European Commission retains its prerogatives under the Constitution, but has them spelt out comprehensively for the first time. Article 26.1–2 on the Commission says:

> 1. The Commission shall promote the general interest of the Union and take appropriate initiatives to that end. It shall ensure the application of

[32] Article I–28. When Solana, as expected, becomes the first Foreign Minister, he will join the Commission. His Spanish compatriot Almunia will have to leave the college at that stage.
[33] Article III–345.

the Constitution, and measures adopted by the institutions pursuant to the Constitution. It shall oversee the application of Union law under the control of the Court of Justice of the European Union. It shall execute the budget and manage programmes. It shall exercise co-ordinating, executive and management functions, as laid down in the Constitution. With the exception of the common foreign and security policy, and other cases provided for in the Constitution, it shall ensure the Union's external representation. It shall initiate the Union's annual and multi-annual programming with a view to achieving Inter-institutional agreements.

2. Union legislative acts may be adopted only on the basis of a Commission proposal, except where the Constitution provides otherwise. Other acts shall be adopted on the basis of a Commission proposal where the Constitution so provides.

The right to initiate the Union's multi-annual programme with a view to reaching a formal inter-institutional agreement with the Council and Parliament is an extension of the Commission's powers. It is intended to bring more strategic coherence to the work of the institutions, to improve parliamentary scrutiny and to bind together more effectively the two executive branches of the Union (Commission and Council). President Barroso is already experimenting with the first five-year programme.

The Constitution strengthens the powers of the Commission to enforce compliance with EU law. As soon as the Court of Justice has ruled on non-compliance, the Commission will be able to specify the amount of the fine which will be imposed automatically by the Court in the event of continued non-compliance.[34] Such a streamlined process would have brought France's refusal to import British beef in the wake of the BSE crisis to a speedy climax.

The wide extension under the Constitution of the ordinary legislative procedure coupled with the abolition of the pillars offer large potential for a Commission that has a coherent legislative programme at home and well-focussed strategies abroad. A strong Commission would exploit the democratic opportunities arising from the fact that, under the Constitution, it is to be held more accountable by MEPs than in the past. The good governance of the Union demands a strong executive, and the Constitution provides for that. For the Commission to reach its potential it must aim to consolidate its position in the period immediately after the entry into force of the Constitution during which the new institutional provisions are being put into effect – particularly

[34] Article III–362.

in relation to the external action service, the Foreign Minister and the 'full-time' President of the European Council.

Relevant provisions in Part Three secure the Commission's prerogatives, at least on paper. Its independence is again underlined, as is the need for integrity. Members of the Commission must 'refrain from any action incompatible with their duties. Member States shall respect their independence and shall not seek to influence them in the performance of their tasks'.[35] Commissioners can be sacked by the Court of Justice if guilty of serious misconduct or otherwise unable to fulfil their duties. The President is empowered to allocate and reshuffle portfolios within the Commission. The Commission takes decisions, including the adoption of its Rules of Procedure, by simple majority.

A tricky matter for the IGC to resolve concerned the future size and shape of the Commission. It was agreed that members of the Commission should be chosen for a term of five years from persons of general competence, European commitment and indubitable independence. The college appointed in 2009 is to have, like the present Commission, one member per member state. The college appointed in 2014 will correspond to two-thirds of the membership, unless the European Council, acting unanimously, loses its nerve. In a decision which may come back to haunt us, the Constitution insists on strictly equal rotation between nationalities.[36] The IGC rejected a proposal from the Convention that member states would have to put forward a number of possible candidates for the Commission from which the President-elect would be able to choose. Apart from a larger role for the Parliament in his or her election, the powers of the Commission President remain substantively unchanged. The Council 'by common accord with the President-elect' will nominate the college which will then require a vote of consent by the Parliament.[37] The President will dispose portfolios.

COURT OF JUSTICE

Under the present Treaty, the European Court of Justice is enjoined, cryptically, to 'ensure that in the interpretation and application of this Treaty the law is observed'.[38] The Court's main task is to hear cases brought by the member states and the institutions against one another, and to settle disputes. But its power of judicial review is not unlimited. The present Treaty seeks to protect the second and third pillars (respectively, common foreign and security policy

[35] Article III–347.
[36] Article I–26.6.
[37] Article I–27.
[38] Article 220 TEC.

and police and judicial co-operation in criminal matters) from interference by the Court. It also makes it very difficult for ordinary citizens to get redress from the Court unless they can prove they are directly and individually and adversely affected.[39] Many members of the Convention were anxious to improve citizens' access to justice, especially with regard to fundamental rights. But, as expected, they met concerted opposition from several member states, especially the UK.

The Treaty of Nice had made some useful reforms of the internal structure of the EU Court system. The Constitution built on these by making three changes of terminology. The entire judicial system becomes the 'Court of Justice of the European Union'. The Court of First Instance, created in 1989 to help the Court of Justice, becomes the 'General Court'. Judicial panels become 'specialised courts'. The Court of Justice is to be composed of one judge per member state. The General Court (currently the Court of First Instance) is to have at least one judge per member state. Judges and Advocates-General are to be appointed by the common accord of member states for renewable terms of six years. A panel of seven former members of the Court, one of whom is appointed by the European Parliament, must be consulted over these judicial appointments.[40] Article 357 (second paragraph) says:

> The panel shall comprise seven persons chosen from among former members of the Court of Justice and the General Court, members of national supreme courts and lawyers of recognised competence, one of whom shall be proposed by the European Parliament. The Council shall adopt a European decision establishing the panel's operating rules and a European decision appointing its members. It shall act on the initiative of the President of the Court of Justice.

The Court's procedure on compliance has been streamlined, thereby greatly enhancing the Commission's ability to enforce compliance by member states to their obligations.[41] The Constitution also made some significant changes to the scope of jurisdiction of the Court. The requirement of individual concern will no longer be necessary in order to challenge a 'regulatory act which does not entail implementing measures'.[42] This enhances the right of an individual to approach the Court. The Committee of the Regions gains the right to address the Court in defence of its prerogatives.[43] And as we discuss later,

[39]   Article 230 TEC.
[40]   Article I–29.2.
[41]   Article III–362.
[42]   Article III–365.4.
[43]   Article III–365.3.

national parliaments may approach the Court, via their governments, to protect their prerogatives under the terms of the Subsidiarity Protocol. There is also a useful widening of the scope of the Court's jurisdiction to give preliminary rulings not only on the validity and interpretation of acts of the EU institutions but also of its 'bodies, offices and agencies'.[44]

The abolition of the third pillar means that the scope of the Court's jurisdiction widens to include all actions of the Union concerning the development of the area of freedom, security and justice except that it will not have jurisdiction to review the validity or proportionality of national police and security service operations.[45] But in general the possibility for a member state to choose whether or not to accept the jurisdiction of the Court in the field of police and judicial co-operation in criminal matters has been removed by the Constitution.[46]

As far as common foreign and security policy is concerned, the jurisdiction of the Court would be extended with respect of sanctions. The Court would gain the power to rule on direct or individual challenges against sanctions and other restrictive measures imposed by the Union, although it would not have jurisdiction over the common policy as such.[47] In other words, the Constitution would not allow the European Parliament to sue the British government in the Court of Justice for unlawfully invading Iraq.

In general, the Court has the authority it needs to interpret the Constitution. It can anticipate a rise in the volume of litigation, not least with respect to the Charter, and worries have been expressed about how expeditiously the Court will be able to dispatch justice. However, the Treaty of Nice has helped matters by allowing rulings to be made without first hearing an Opinion from an Advocate General. This, coupled with the wide use of chambers, has made the Court much more efficient. In 2004 the Court dealt with a total of 665 cases, thirty per cent more than in 2003.[48]

Nevertheless, to ensure efficacy, the Court of Justice still needs to firm up the commitment of national courts to co-operate closely with it in seeking to uphold the rule of the EU Constitution. For that reason, Article 29.1 of the Constitution, which sets out the role of the Courts, instructs member states to ensure that national judicial systems become more effectively integrated into the EU judicial system:

[44] Article III–369.
[45] Article III–377.
[46] Article 35.2 TEU.
[47] Article III–376.
[48] Of these, only 12 per cent were heard in full Court, the rest by chambers of five or three judges.

The Court of Justice of the European Union shall include the Court of Justice, the General Court and specialised courts. It shall ensure that in the interpretation and application of the Constitution the law is observed.

Member States shall provide remedies sufficient to ensure effective legal protection in the fields covered by Union law.

Article 29.3 follows on:

The Court of Justice of the European Union shall in accordance with Part III:
(a) rule on actions brought by a Member State, an institution or a natural or legal person;
(b) give preliminary rulings, at the request of courts or tribunals of the Member States, on the interpretation of Union law or the validity of acts adopted by the institutions;
(c) rule in other cases provided for in the Constitution.

OTHER BODIES

The Constitution affords the status of 'institution' to the European Central Bank and the Court of Auditors. The former, whose job it is to issue the euro and, together with national central banks to 'conduct the monetary policy of the Union', remains strongly independent. Members of the executive board of the European Central Bank are appointed by the European Council, acting by QMV and after consulting the Parliament, for a non-renewable term of eight years.[49]

The one significant – and very sensible – change to the constitution of the Central Bank is that, under the terms of the Constitution, the President and other members of the Executive Board will be appointed by the European Council acting by QMV.[50] The current Treaties stipulate 'by common accord' – which proved a very difficult mountain to climb at the time of the appointment of Wim Duisenberg, the first President, in May 1998.

Against expectations, no changes were made by the Convention or the IGC to the composition of the Court of Auditors, which remains at the increasingly inflated size of one member per member state. The British were keen to reduce the size of the Court but failed to garner support for their view. The auditors are appointed by the Council of Ministers, acting by QMV and after consulting

[49] Articles I–30 and III–382.
[50] Article III–382.2.
[51] Article I–31 and III–385.

the European Parliament, for a renewable term of six years.[51]

The terms of office of the Economic and Social Committee and the Committee of the Regions is extended to five years from four. Their opinions are to be forwarded directly to Parliament as well as to the Commission and Council. Neither body, despite their pleadings, made it to the elevated standing of EU institution. The Economic and Social Committee and the Committee of the Regions remain advisory bodies, composed of representatives of economic and civil society and of regional and local authorities, respectively.[52] Both bodies have 350 members and are appointed by the Council, acting unanimously on a Commission proposal.[53]

No change is made in the Constitution to the status or powers of the European Investment Bank.

RESPECTING THE INSTITUTIONAL COMPROMISE

We have noted earlier that if the Constitution fails to enter into force the problems that led the member states to set up the Convention will not have gone away. Nowhere is this more true than in respect of the institutional reforms proffered by the Constitution. There is, first of all, the question of efficiency. The institutions will not work very well, either individually or collectively, under the terms of the Treaty of Nice. They will not work at all if they remain unreformed and the membership of the EU expands to more than twenty-seven. Secondly, there is the question of democracy. Without the Constitution the institutions of the Union will remain much less accountable to the citizen. Thirdly, there is the issue of effectiveness. Without reform of the instruments and procedures, the Union will be hard pushed to improve the quality of its political and legislative outcome. Unless the fruits of the constitutional reforms can be harvested, the Union risks being unloved at home and ignored abroad.

There will be some, faced with the possible demise of the Constitution, who prefer to cherry-pick those institutional reforms presaged in the Constitution that they like best: a smaller Commission, the installation of the Foreign Minister, transparency in the Council, for example. But the fact is that very few individual elements of the reform package can be extricated without provoking controversy. The Constitution strengthens not one but all the institutions. The success of the Convention and the IGC was the accomplishment of a comprehensive, complex and sophisticated package deal.

---

[52] Article I–32.
[53] Articles III–386 and 389.

The Constitution is a delicate compromise, but it hangs together. Unpick only a small number of bricks and the whole edifice will be jeopardised. In any case, almost none of the institutional reforms, however attractive, can be legally introduced without a revision of the Treaty of Nice – so that another IGC followed by the laborious process of ratification will still be necessary.

This is not to conclude that the Constitution, or those who wrote it, achieved perfection. There are things which could yet be improved and which, if handled well, might foster a rising degree of acknowledgment and even popular support. At the end of the book we examine what aspects of institutional reforms might benefit from further thought in the context of a wider renegotiation of the Constitution. Before then, we need to look further into the balance between the institutions, and into how they work in practice.

CHAPTER 8

Shifting the institutional balance

The Constitution clarifies definitively the settlement of powers between the institutions. The European Parliament and Council of Ministers are the two chambers of the legislature. The Commission is the main executive authority, which initiates legislation and seeks to steer the Union according to the common interest of the whole, but the Council of Ministers retains some important executive powers. The European Council of heads of government provides top leadership. The Court takes on more and more the characteristics of a supreme federal court. And, overall, the constitutional innovations perpetrated by the Convention and the IGC record a decisive shift in the balance between the institutions in favour of the European Parliament.

We have become fairly familiar with the fact that, in the European Union, executive power is shared between the Commission and Council, that legislative power is shared among Commission, Council and Parliament, and that significant limitations are placed on the role of the Court of Justice. The Laeken Declaration prompted the Convention to ask itself whether the Council should act in the same manner in both its legislative and its executive capacities. But it also asked if the role of the Council should be strengthened – a question not posed, incidentally, about the Court. The mood of the Convention became fairly clear from early on in its deliberations, and was in favour of a greater separation of powers, particularly with respect to the judiciary. It was argued that the ambiguous nature of the power of the executive within the Union made it doubly important to extend the Court's powers of judicial review. At the same time, there was much weight placed, especially on behalf of national governments, on the need to maintain the famous 'institutional balance' – a concept which was never defined but which was taken to mean the avoidance of a concentration of power in the hands of one institution at the expense of the others. Conservatives in the Convention used the mantra of institutional balance to encourage caution; progressives used it to advance the cause of the 'Community method' – in other words, to protect the classical role of the supranational institutions.

The Convention debate had raged along two planes. The first concerned the traditional battle between federalist and intergovernmentalist forces, characterised by the continuing struggle for power between the Commission and Parliament on the one side and Council on the other. The second concerned the vested interests of the member states determined by their size. One immediate effect of the enlargement of the Union was to pitch larger states against smaller states with an unprecedented degree of vehemence. The launch of a third campaign – that between old and new member states – was threatened, but wiser heads, including that of Giscard, prevailed.

Given the argumentative circumstances at the outset of the Convention and the difficulties it faced, it is remarkable that a settlement was concluded at all and that the Constitution was written and agreed, at least at the level of the EU institutions. Many in the Convention were sorry not to have had another few months of work into the autumn of 2003 in which to tackle more fully the more stubborn institutional questions and to delve more deeply into the policy chapters of Part Three. It is always tempting in such circumstances to delay in the hope of getting a better settlement. But there is also always a danger in lingering on in any negotiation. Deals struck at an earlier stage in the process can begin to unravel. Diplomacy drawn out for its own sake can make things infinitely worse. The Irish presidency was undoubtedly right to push as hard as they did for closure of the IGC on the night of 18 June 2004. One could sense towards the closing stages of the conference that the overriding need was to finish and go home: had the conference gone on it faced the looming risk of a deep institutional crisis with severe political consequences. The public would not have understood, and certainly would not have forgiven, a failure on the part of their leaders to settle their constitutional quarrels. In this sense, the public will prevailed, and the deal was done.

LINGERING DOUBTS

Heartfelt relief at the end of the intergovernmental conference, however, did not mean that all parties went home without some doubts. Everyone knew, for example, that in practice the principle of 'equal rotation' of nationalities in the reduced Commission will be very difficult to achieve without rancour. A Declaration had to be added to the Constitution to warn of the fears of those member states which will be excluded from the future, smaller Commission.[1]

---

[1]   Declaration No. 6.

Numerous references have been inserted about the need to respect the demographic and geographical diversity of the Union.[2] Even the final, tortuous agreement on the QMV thresholds of the Council was qualified by a Declaration – albeit supposedly transitional – which says that if three-quarters of the states or states representing three-quarters of the population object to a decision being taken by QMV, they can force a reconsideration of the issue at stake.[3]

Strong reservations were also expressed in the IGC about the Convention's wish to differentiate more clearly between the Union's executive and legislative powers. Many members of the Convention would have preferred to create a completely separate formation of the Council solely devoted to law making. Alarm from sectoral departments inside national administrations to the potential loss of control over the legislative process caused the proposal for a separate Law Council to be abandoned. In its place, the Convention reached a botched compromise, welding a Legislative Council and the General Affairs Council together. Perhaps fortunately, this clumsy arrangement was defeated early on in the IGC. Only the commitment to more transparency and to the re-organisation of Council agendas into two parts, legislative and executive, was retained.[4]

RUNNING THE COUNCIL

The Constitution creates particular new challenges in respect of the presidencies of the European Council, Council of Ministers and COREPER. The reforms are radical: a non-prime ministerial chair of the European Council for thirty months, team presidencies of the Council of Ministers for eighteen months, and, in the Foreign Minister, an executive chairman for foreign affairs. But could the new system obtain the greater coherence and consistency that the Convention, more ambitious than the IGC, sought? In particular, what sort of creature might the new full-time President of the European Council turn out to be? This question troubled the Convention, not least because the strongest advocate of the idea was the British government.

Unlike their mainland counterparts, British prime ministers are largely untrammelled by domestic constitutional niceties. They have no coalition partner to keep in trim. They are usually in command of a substantial parliamentary majority at Westminster. Like Margaret Thatcher before him, the only significant opposition that Tony Blair cannot avoid is at meetings of

[2] For example, Article I–26.6 and Declaration Nos. 3 and 4.
[3] Declaration No. 5. This constituted a revival of the notorious Ioannina clause, forced on the Council by the British in 1994.
[4] Article I–24.6.

the European Council. Here he is often out-gunned and contradicted. He has a bad memory of his own first term as chair of the European Council in 1998. More recently his experiences of the European Council have been soured by continuing rows, especially with Jacques Chirac, over Iraq, the reform of the financial perspectives and the CAP.

No wonder, then, that Blair's main preoccupation with the Convention concerned the leadership of the European Council. His representative in the Convention, Peter Hain, peddled a 'job description' for a new-style, full-time 'chair' of the European Council. Hain's memo was not a modest pitch. The appointment would be made from the small club of ex-heads of government. Hain's 'chair' would not only run the meetings of the European Council but have sweeping powers to 'deliver' its political strategy, to speak for the Union in world summitry, to intervene in the work of the sectoral Council of Ministers, to represent the Union in front of national parliaments, to choose the High Representative for foreign and security policy, and, threateningly, to supervise the Commission in what Hain called 'functional areas of shared competence'. He, or improbably she, would have their own secretariat. In short, the British were proposing to set up an executive president of the European Council who would lord it over the rival President of the Commission. Hain argued that all nationalities could have their turn at this job, but everyone suspected how effortlessly such a plan would turn out to have established a directory of the bigger member states.

The British plan for a super-president of the European Council might have satisfied Tony Blair's quest for strong leadership, but it raised alarm elsewhere. It was ironic that the British continued to rail against the supposed threat of a centralised European super-state when it would be difficult to invent anything as certain to centralise power in Brussels than the replacement of the present collegiate system of governance of the Union with the presidential model now proposed by London. One was led to wonder whether the British plan had been properly thought through even in its own terms. Was No. 10 Downing Street really content to have its phone calls from the White House on permanent divert to the EU 'chair' in Brussels?

In January 2003, to counter the British initiative, and to mark the fortieth anniversary of the Elysée Treaty (and of De Gaulle's *Non* to UK membership), Gerhard Schröder and Jacques Chirac launched a plan for a fixed president of the European Council elected not from outside but from one of its number. This President of the European Council would cohabit *à la française* with the President of the Commission. Somewhat awkwardly, the double-hatted Secretary or Minister responsible for foreign and security policy would be answerable to both Presidents. The significance of the Franco-German plan was not that it convinced many (it did not) but that it was part of a larger package between Paris and Berlin. Germany agreed to accept a full-time Presidency of the European Council; France agreed to support more codecision for the European Parliament, the election of the Commission President by MEPs and an extension of QMV even in foreign policy and justice and home affairs.

When the Convention debated the matter, it was presented with a fresh proposal from a number of its senior members to integrate all the Union's executive functions under a single President. He or she would chair not only the Commission but also the European Council, giving general political impetus and direction to the affairs of the Union. This would allow the European Council to draw upon all the executive resources of the Union, be they in the Commission or the Council. The new style President would be responsible for delivering the decisions of the European Council as well as for running the Commission. A unified presidency would have the advantage of forcing the separation of the Council's legislative from its executive tasks. The Law Council, chaired by a government minister (who could be elected, just like the President of the European Parliament, by his own peers) would continue to work methodically in codecision with the Parliament. The executive Council would meet in a reduced number of formations to run economic policy, foreign, security and defence policy, and police affairs and criminal justice. The presidents of the executive Councils would be the appropriate Vice-Presidents of the Commission. They would be answerable before the European Parliament for the activities of the Council and would speak for the Union in world affairs.

The Convention as a whole, however, found this idea of an integrated presidency ahead of its time. Only the 'Minister Vice-President' survived to chair the Foreign Affairs Council. The Convention, however, managed to hold open the possibility of an eventual move towards an integrated presidency by declaring merely that the President of the European Council may not hold a national office.[5] This leaves open the option of inviting a future serving President of the Commission to chair the European Council as well.

In order to stabilise the work programme of the institutions and to encourage continuity, the Convention agreed to establish under the authority of the European Council a new multi-annual strategic programme. This would be decided by the heads of government but initiated by the Commission, after consultation with the Parliament. This important proposal, now incorporated in Article 26.1 of the Constitution, would effectively put an end to the current six-monthly programmes of the rotating Council presidencies, which are

[5]   Article I–22.3.

pretentious and distracting. The rolling multi-annual strategy of the European Council should be a useful tool, with immediate advantages for focus, continuity and scrutiny. Within the context of the overall policy strategy, the Commission will continue to produce its annual legislative programme.

On the understanding that there was potential for the Commission to strengthen its strategic role in relation to the European Council, the Convention eventually accepted the proposal for a full-time chair of the European Council, although with clearly circumscribed powers. The Convention fought off the British plan for an executive President of the European Council. It salvaged what it could from the Franco-German initiative, and kept the door open for a future more integrated presidency of Council and Commission. From an amalgam of the three proposals, the final agreement was wrung.

There were good practical reasons for this. Habitually, the president-in-office of the European Council tours the capitals of all member states during his six-monthly term. Enlargement to twenty-five countries and beyond renders even that a major logistical exercise. Domestic engagements suffer, and fleeting glory in the chancelleries of Europe is not always reflected positively in public opinion polls back home.

The decision of the Convention to accept some sort of more permanent presidency of the European Council was immediately shown to be a wise one. The shambles of the Berlusconi presidency from July to December 2003, climaxing in the disastrous IGC summit in Brussels, dispelled any second thoughts. Nothing could be worse than that.

The final version of this controversial provision reads as follows:

Article 22

The European Council President
1. The European Council shall elect its President, by a qualified majority, for a term of two and a half years, renewable once. In the event of an impediment or serious misconduct, the European Council can end his or her term of office in accordance with the same procedure.
2. The President of the European Council:
(a) shall chair it and drive forward its work;
(b) shall ensure the preparation and continuity of the work of the European Council in co-operation with the President of the Commission, and on the basis of the work of the General Affairs Council;
(c) shall endeavour to facilitate cohesion and consensus within the European Council;

(d) shall present a report to the European Parliament after each of the meetings of the European Council.

The President of the European Council shall, at his or her level and in that capacity, ensure the external representation of the Union on issues concerning its common foreign and security policy, without prejudice to the powers of the Union Minister for Foreign Affairs.

3. The President of the European Council shall not hold a national office.

According to the provisions of the Constitution, there will be no government machine to back up the new-style President. Although responsible for running the meetings of the European Council, it will be the General Affairs Council of Ministers, chaired by a team presidency of a different duration, which is responsible for preparing and ensuring the follow-up to the meetings of the European Council.[6]

Whether or not the proposed new style presidency of the European Council will ever be an assured success depends to a large extent on the competence of the first holder of the job. One may hope for a good short-list. It is not unknown for ex-premiers and presidents to become in some serious way discredited or even dishevelled once they leave national office. The first post-holder, who was to have been found and elected during 2006, would be wise not to interfere too obviously with the work of the President of the Commission, the Foreign Minister or the presidency-in-office of the General Affairs Council. Clear lines of demarcation and engagement, especially in international relations, will have to be drawn up. He or she will have their work cut out to establish a good working relationship with the twenty-five heads of government – especially those whose governments were currently serving as members of the team presidency of the Council of Ministers. Relations with the European Parliament could also prove critical, especially when allies are needed at one of the Union's perennial moments of crisis.

Concentration on the relative powers of the individual institutions tends to cloud the fact that the Union works best when a spirit of partnership between them is at its most elevated. The success of the Convention and the IGC in assembling a large consensus around the Constitution generated sufficient good will to raise expectations that any shortcomings in the institutional reform package would not, in the event, matter too much. Continuing failure to finalise the constitutional settlement will not only dash such optimism but heighten tension and aggravate the institutional weaknesses in the current state of affairs.

---

[6] Article I–24.2.

CHAPTER 9

Exercising the powers

Having looked at the powers and composition of the institutions, as well as the shifting balance between them, we turn to examine how these powers are planned to be exercised under the Constitution.

The Convention made enormous strides in rationalising the instruments at the Union's disposal and in simplifying decision-making processes. Its proposals, eventually accepted by the IGC, gave practical expression to the wish of the Laeken Declaration to separate out more clearly the Union's exercise of legislative from executive powers. Transparency of decision making and execution of policy are thereby much improved.

The Constitution settles on six 'legal acts' of the Union, set out in Article 33. This reduces the number of EU instruments from fifteen under the Treaty of Nice. Of the ones suppressed, the most notable are 'conventions' in the field of justice and home affairs and 'common strategies', 'joint actions' and 'common positions' in the field of foreign and security policy. In hierarchical order the new acts instruments are as follows:

- European law – binding in its entirety and directly applicable across the EU;[1]
- European framework law – binding as to the result to be achieved but leaving to the relevant national authorities the choice of form and methods;[2]
- European regulation – an executive act intended to implement certain provisions of the Constitution or a European law or European framework law;
- European decision – an executive act binding only on those to whom it is addressed;
- Recommendation – with no binding force;
- Opinion – equally, with no binding force.

[1] Under the existing Treaty, this is called a regulation, and automatically becomes part of national law.

[2] Under the existing Treaty, this is called a directive, and requires transposition into national law (in the UK, by a Statutory Instrument).

LAW MAKING BY QMV AND CODECISION

Under the Constitution, European laws and framework laws are to be enacted by the 'ordinary legislative procedure'.[3] No law can come into being unless voted for both by the Council of Ministers and by the European Parliament, if necessary after a process of conciliation between the two. Both chambers act at key stages of amendment by QMV.

The normalisation of the use of QMV in the Council plus codecision with the Parliament is a great achievement of the Convention. The gradual spread of the practice has not been uncontroversial. On the contrary, every extension has had to be fought for at successive IGCs. Even the Laeken Declaration did not dare to envisage that QMV plus codecision would become normal practice.

Once upon a time almost all substantive decisions in the Council were taken by unanimity. Only procedural decisions required a simple majority vote. The insistence on unanimity was thought to oblige all member states to respect and implement the decision. But progress on complicated legislative matters was slow or imperceptible, especially after the number of ministers around the Council table grew from six to nine in 1973. It was agreed that if the complicated package of single market measures was ever to be agreed, there had to be greater use of qualified majority voting. The gradual introduction of QMV after the Single European Act came into force proved decisive in enabling the Council to pass legislation. It is not only the incidence of QMV being used, but that the potential deployment of QMV applies pressure on all ministers to seek a compromise. Nobody likes to be out-voted, and revenge is sweet. The Council still prefers to act by consensus. Nevertheless, QMV has been undeniably useful in disentangling issues. With increased use of QMV it was no longer possible for a single member state to block progress on one dossier because it harboured some serious grievance about another. Removal of the power of veto has encouraged ministers and officials to act in a generally more constructive manner. The lack of a veto power enhances trust at the federal level of any system of multi-state governance.

Codecision was first introduced by the Maastricht Treaty into fifteen areas of EU activity. The Treaty of Amsterdam more than doubled that number to thirty eight, and the Treaty of Nice added another five items where codecision had to be used. The Constitution adds another forty-three items, making eighty six in all. This would leave only thirty measures where abnormal procedures are prescribed.

The Treaty of Amsterdam was notable for improving the codecision procedure in two respects. First, it enabled the Parliament and Council to reach agreement at first reading. Second, it set a deadline of six to eight weeks for the convening

[3]   Article I–34.1.

of the conciliation committee if, after two readings, the two legislative chambers cannot agree. Both Amsterdam and Nice reduced the number of exceptions to the general rule that codecision with the Parliament must be accompanied by QMV in the Council. Pending the coming into force of the Constitution, only three such anomalies remain where codecision is coupled with unanimity: social security for migrant workers, freedom to practice for professional workers, and cultural policy.[4] The Constitution excises that anomalous procedure.

Despite the normalisation of QMV plus codecision, however, a new anomaly has been created by the Constitution in three areas – social security for migrant workers, judicial co-operation in criminal law and the definition of crime. In these three fields the UK government has insisted on introducing to the Constitution provision for an 'emergency brake' which will allow it to block the use of the ordinary legislative procedure whenever it wants to do so.[5] We examine the emergency brake in more detail later on.

Nevertheless, the Convention and IGC could not have made so much progress on extending QMV plus codecision (almost) across the board unless recent experience of the procedure had proved fruitful. During the term of the fifth legislature (1999–2004), 403 legislative acts were adopted under the codecision procedure. 124 of those concerned the harmonisation of national laws in order to boost the single market.[6] The next most common areas for use of the codecision procedure after legal harmonisation were environment policy, maritime and air transport, public health, the right of establishment and common statistics policies. Only two directives failed – concerning company takeovers and access to port services – when MEPs rejected at third reading the compromises reached in the conciliation committee. More recently, in July 2005, the Parliament took the unprecedented step of defeating a directive – on the patenting of computer-implemented inventions – at second reading. Roughly speaking, a quarter of the draft acts are agreed at first reading and half at second reading, while the remaining quarter become subject to conciliation. About half of the amendments tabled by Parliament find their way into the final law.

The role of the European Commission is crucial to the success of the ordinary legislative procedure. In the first place, the Commission launches the legislative proposal. It can withdraw it at any stage up to, but not including, conciliation. The Commission also retains the right to re-launch a defeated proposal on its own initiative in the future. During the second reading, where the Commission gives a negative opinion on a proposed amendment from Parliament, Council has to act by unanimity to approve it. Once into the conciliation process the

---

4   Respectively, Articles 42, 47 and 151 TEC.
5   Articles III–136, 270 and 271 respectively.
6   Under the legal base of Article 95 TEC.

Commission's job is not to press its own proposal but to broker agreement between Parliament, acting by an absolute majority of half its membership, and Council, acting by QMV. Following the recent enlargement the official conciliation committee has grown to an improbable size for a negotiating team, with twenty-five members on each side. So the role of the Commission as facilitator in a smaller and informal 'trialogue' promises to be even more important.

In addition to establishing codecision as the norm, the Convention and the IGC managed to somewhat simplify the procedure, and to lay it out better.[7] It is made crystal clear that the Parliament enjoys parity with the Council at each stage of law-making. The article that sets out the ordinary legislative procedure is one of the key provisions of the Constitution. It is as follows:

Article 396

1. Where, pursuant to the Constitution, European laws or framework laws are adopted under the ordinary legislative procedure, the following provisions shall apply.

2. The Commission shall submit a proposal to the European Parliament and the Council.

First reading

3. The European Parliament shall adopt its position at first reading and communicate it to the Council.

4. If the Council approves the European Parliament's position, the act concerned shall be adopted in the wording which corresponds to the position of the European Parliament.

5. If the Council does not approve the European Parliament's position, it shall adopt its position at first reading and communicate it to the European Parliament.

6. The Council shall inform the European Parliament fully of the reasons which led it to adopt its position at first reading. The Commission shall inform the European Parliament fully of its position.

Second reading

7. If, within three months of such communication, the European Parliament:
(a) approves the Council's position at first reading or has not taken a decision, the act concerned shall be deemed to have been adopted in the wording which corresponds to the position of the Council;
(b) rejects, by a majority of its component members, the Council's position at first reading, the proposed act shall be deemed not to have been adopted;

---

[7] Compared, that is, with Article 251 TEC.

(c) proposes, by a majority of its component members, amendments to the Council's position at first reading, the text thus amended shall be forwarded to the Council and to the Commission, which shall deliver an opinion on those amendments.

8. If, within three months of receiving the European Parliament's amendments, the Council, acting by a qualified majority:

(a) approves all those amendments, the act in question shall be deemed to have been adopted;

(b) does not approve all the amendments, the President of the Council, in agreement with the President of the European Parliament, shall within six weeks convene a meeting of the Conciliation Committee.

9. The Council shall act unanimously on the amendments on which the Commission has delivered a negative opinion.

Conciliation

10. The Conciliation Committee, which shall be composed of the members of the Council or their representatives and an equal number of members representing the European Parliament, shall have the task of reaching agreement on a joint text, by a qualified majority of the members of the Council or their representatives and by a majority of the members representing the European Parliament within six weeks of its being convened, on the basis of the positions of the European Parliament and the Council at second reading.

11. The Commission shall take part in the Conciliation Committee's proceedings and shall take all necessary initiatives with a view to reconciling the positions of the European Parliament and the Council.

12. If, within six weeks of its being convened, the Conciliation Committee does not approve the joint text, the proposed act shall be deemed not to have been adopted.

Third reading

13. If, within that period, the Conciliation Committee approves a joint text, the European Parliament, acting by a majority of the votes cast, and the Council, acting by a qualified majority, shall each have a period of six weeks from that approval in which to adopt the act in question in accordance with the joint text. If they fail to do so, the proposed act shall be deemed not to have been adopted.

14. The periods of three months and six weeks referred to in this Article shall be extended by a maximum of one month and two weeks respectively at the initiative of the European Parliament or the Council.[8]

---

[8] A final paragraph details the special procedures when abnormally the legislative initiative is made not by the Commission but by a group of member states, the European Central Bank, the Court of Justice or the European Investment Bank.

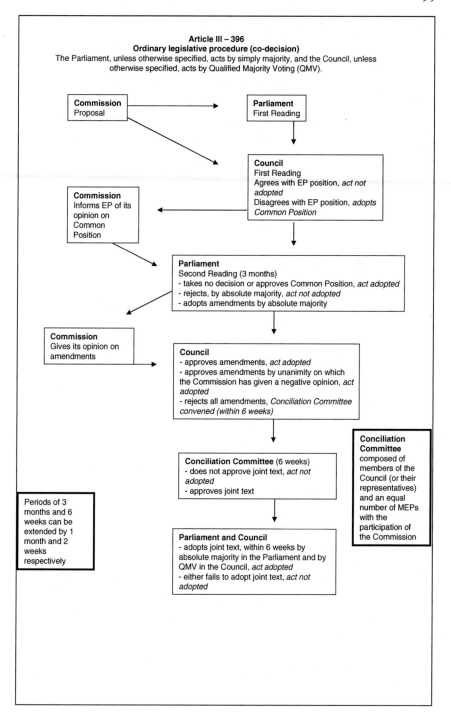

Article III – 396
Ordinary legislative procedure (co-decision)
The Parliament, unless otherwise specified, acts by simply majority, and the Council, unless otherwise specified, acts by Qualified Majority Voting (QMV).

Commission
Proposal

Parliament
First Reading

Council
First Reading
Agrees with EP position, *act not adopted*
Disagrees with EP position, *adopts Common Position*

Commission
Informs EP of its opinion on Common Position

Parliament
Second Reading (3 months)
- takes no decision or approves Common Position, *act adopted*
- rejects, by absolute majority, *act not adopted*
- adopts amendments by absolute majority

Commission
Gives its opinion on amendments

Council
- approves amendments, *act adopted*
- approves amendments by unanimity on which the Commission has given a negative opinion, *act adopted*
- rejects all amendments, *Conciliation Committee convened (within 6 weeks)*

Conciliation Committee (6 weeks)
- does not approve joint text, *act not adopted*
- approves joint text

Conciliation Committee
composed of members of the Council (or their representatives) and an equal number of MEPs with the participation of the Commission

Periods of 3 months and 6 weeks can be extended by 1 month and 2 weeks respectively

Parliament and Council
- adopts joint text, within 6 weeks by absolute majority in the Parliament and by QMV in the Council, *act adopted*
- either fails to adopt joint text, *act not adopted*

STREAMLINING DECISION MAKING

The Constitution makes an important advance in consolidating the ordinary legislative procedure by dropping entirely an existing 'co-operation procedure' in which the Council has the decisive say. The co-operation procedure, once more common, is now little used, applying as it does to only four provisions of the rules for economic and monetary union.[9] But its suppression by the Constitution is nevertheless satisfactory.

Use of another abnormal procedure, where the Council decides after receiving the formal opinion of the Parliament (called the 'consultation' procedure), is reduced in number to twenty. While its powers of codecision widen, Parliament's formal right of assent (renamed 'consent') in specific circumstances is retained – mostly for international and financial agreements.

The increased salience of European laws or framework laws adopted under the provisions of Article 396 would also reduce the need for ad hoc 'inter-institutional agreements' between the Commission, Council and Parliament. For example, whereas the arrangements for 'comitology' – that is, the committee system charged with overseeing the implementation of law within member states – is subject today to an inter-institutional agreement, under the Constitution comitology would be regulated by a law established under the ordinary legislative procedure. However, the Constitution still provides for inter-institutional agreements of a practical nature, which may be binding.[10]

In addition, the European Parliament would still be able to pass formal 'resolutions', the European Council presidency would still produce its 'conclusions' and the Council of Ministers will still make its 'communications', but none of these would have the force of Union legislation.

The Parliament, for its part, has always voted in plenary in public, often with roll call votes so that the individual choices of MEPs are published. But to reflect the more open spirit of the Constitution, Parliament could well consider how it might enlarge the transparency of the legislative procedure, especially in the relevant programme committee where the broad mandate of the Parliament's negotiating team is established. Only the proceedings of the conciliation committee and the associated trialogues need remain closed because they are a negotiation, and conciliation would be unlikely to work efficiently if exposed to the glare of publicity. In any case, the results of the

---

[9] Article 252 TEC. Two of the four moved to codecision (Articles 99.5 and 106.2 TEC) and two to consultation (Articles 102.3 and 103.2).

[10] Article III–397.

conciliation procedure are now posted quickly on the website, and all other phases of the process are public.[11]

Parallel to the work of the Convention in 2003 a new inter-institutional agreement on better law-making was painstakingly negotiated between the three institutions.[12] Its aim is to improve the timetabling and co-ordination of the legislative process as well as to sharpen the monitoring of how EU law takes effect inside member states. All the institutions involved in the ordinary legislative procedure are to be bound to increase the use of regulatory, financial and environmental impact assessments. The Commission, in particular, will have to justify its decision to choose the legislative route (as opposed to the option of an executive legal act). It can expect to have its justification more heavily scrutinised than before by the Council, the European Parliament and even national parliaments. Ex-post review of EU laws and framework laws will be enhanced by the wider scope of the Court's jurisdiction.

EXECUTIVE ACTS

As we have seen, although the Commission is the main executive authority of the Union, it has to share some of its executive powers with the Council of Ministers. In the Convention a tough battle was fought to reduce, if not quite eliminate, the Council's executive powers. Under present arrangements, the job of the Commission is to ensure the application of the Treaty and the implementation of EU policy, to help shape the decisions of the Parliament and Council, to make recommendations and issue opinions, and also to exercise certain powers conferred on it by the Council.[13] The Council enjoys executive authority in the original field of the common market not only to confer powers upon the Commission but also to take executive decisions itself, for example, to fix agricultural prices, and to 'ensure co-ordination of the general economic policies of the Member States'.[14] The Council is given the 'power to take decisions ... [t]o ensure that the objectives set out in this Treaty are attained'.

Great progress was made in the Convention in clarifying who could delegate executive authority to the Commission and under what terms. A greater willingness on behalf of the legislator to delegate technical minutiae to the Commission has been recorded in the Constitution: MEPs of a non-scientific

[11] Rules governing public access to official documents are set out in Regulation (EC) 1049/2001.
[12] OJ C 321, 31 December 2003.
[13] Article 211 TEC.
[14] Article 202 TEC.

inclination will be particularly gratified. 'Delegated European regulations' will have to be authorised in a European law or framework law, requiring the consent of both Council and Parliament. Essential political choices would still have to be made in the legislation itself and not in the executive act. The objectives, content, scope and duration of the delegation would have to be specified in the law. The Commission is committed to continuing the practice initiated in the financial services sector – the so-called Lamfalussy procedure – to consult with experts appointed by the member states before it drafts amendments to its executive acts in response to changed technical or market conditions.[15] Both legislative chambers also have the power to call back the delegation.[16]

COMITOLOGY

More difficulty was experienced by the Convention in reaching agreement on how to implement legally binding acts of the Union – either regulations or decisions – inside the member states. Article 37 concerning 'implementing acts' stipulates that member states are obliged to adopt all measures of national law necessary to ensure implementation.[17] In theory, the Commission is responsible for overseeing the implementation of EU legal acts at the European level. In practice, of course, the Commission needs the participation of the member states both to formulate the necessary implementing measures and to monitor their efficacy. Since 1987, and in response to the growing use of codecision in the area of the single market, the Union has managed the drafting of implementing measures through a complex system of committees, known as 'comitology'. There are three types of committee, all composed of national government officials and all chaired by the Commission. There are almost 250 of these committees, dealing annually with about 1750 acts.

Advisory Committees give the Commission maximum discretion, and have been used for fairly technical questions. Management Committees oblige the Commission to refer to Council any matter where its decision differs from the view of the Committee, expressed by QMV. Council may overturn the Commission's decision, acting by QMV. This procedure is used for the management of common policies and spending programmes. Regulatory Committees oblige the Commission actually to acquire the

[15] Declaration No. 8 to Article I–36.
[16] Article I–36.
[17] This clarifies the position established by Article 10 TEC.

approval of the Committee, acting by QMV, before taking action. If the Committee fails to act, the matter is referred back to Council which can take the necessary decision by QMV. If the Council fails to act, the Commission can finally adopt the implementing measure itself unless the Council does not object by QMV. Since a revision of the system in an inter-institutional agreement of 1999, and in order to assist the scrutiny by the European Parliament of the comitology decisions, all documents are now made public and the Commission delivers an annual comitology report.

Under the Constitution, where uniform implementation is required it would be the Commission which is normally granted the necessary powers to ensure implementation. In some 'duly justified specific cases', however, including agricultural prices and fishing quotas, it would still be the Council which remains responsible.

The Constitution makes one important improvement to the existing comitology procedure.[18] At present the Council decides on the rules governing the Commission's exercise of these executive powers by unanimity, after having received the opinion of the Parliament. Under the Constitution, a European law would be required to 'lay down in advance the rules and general principles concerning mechanisms for control by Member States of the Commission's implementing powers'.[19] This is a big step forward for the Parliament and, by implication, a significant step forward for the Commission. It should lead to a rationalisation of the burdensome comitology system, including the possible abolition of the Regulatory Committee. It will be possible to make specific allowance for 'sunset' clauses that would mandate the legislator to review a law after a certain, specified time. But in the Convention and the IGC, many governments, led by the British, proved terribly jealous of the Commission's executive powers and tried unsuccessfully to resist the Parliament's encroachment upon the Council's hitherto untrammelled powers of discretion in this field.

In another change made by the Constitution, greater emphasis will have to be placed on the principle of proportionality (Article 11) in the drafting of EU legal acts, of either a legislative or an executive nature.[20] Furthermore, there will have to be fully reasoned justifications for the choice of instrument on a case by case basis. And we have already noted the Commission's commitment to verify all its legislative proposals against the provisions of the Charter of Fundamental Rights.

[18] Article 202 TEC.
[19] Article I–37.3.
[20] Article I–38.

In summary, the Constitution made very good progress in simplifying and in making more transparent the exercise of powers at the Union level. Conversely, rejection of the renegotiated Constitution would make things needlessly complicated all over again – to the undoubted detriment to the quality of European public policy.

CHAPTER 10

A more vital democracy

The European Convention was in large part a parliamentary forum. In a striking contrast with previous Intergovernmental Conferences, a positive argument for the development of European parliamentary democracy was able to be delivered directly by those with a vested interest, namely Members of the European Parliament. Never before had the systematic case for a stronger European Parliament been put – and heard – inside official circles with such force and coherence.

It was not only the Euro MPs in the Convention, however, who argued for more power for Parliament. Others, especially national MPs from integrationist minded parties, took the view that left to their own devices the member states and the Council would continue to fail to reverse public disquiet about the EU. Aware of the limitations of national parliaments in influencing, let alone setting, the EU's political agenda, the Convention took bold decisions on extending European Parliamentary powers with relative ease. Long-standing frustrations of the European Parliament over its exclusion from real decision making in the Common Agricultural Policy were met, therefore, not only in the budgetary field but also with respect to structural reforms. After difficult negotiations in the Convention and at the IGC, the essential power over the purse strings, enjoyed by the Parliament for many years, was successfully preserved. The Parliament's power as co-legislator was extended by the Constitution, as was its capacity to influence the choice of the new European Commission. MEPs consolidated their claim to accept or reject all international agreements of the Union in the sphere of exclusive or shared competence. They won a number of other long sought after concessions – such as the right to permit the delegation of executive powers to the Commission (and to withdraw the permission), and the right to give consent to the operation of closer co-operation among a limited number of member states.

Growing self-confidence within and without the Convention allowed MEPs to push for the inclusion of a new chapter in the Constitution entitled *The Democratic Life of the Union*.[1] To fulfil its potential and to confound

[1] Articles I–45 to 52.

euroscepticism, the Constitution had to be able to address and transcend the caricature of the Union as some vast, undemocratic, over-centralising plot. The effort at constitutionalisation would hardly be valid without having shifted that particular misapprehension.

The participation in the Convention of the EU's newcomers accentuated the importance of changing the discourse. The membership negotiations with the ten new countries had been mainly about economic rules, the harmonisation of law and the crossing of various political thresholds, spiced by the promise of money. Until they experienced the Convention, the new member states had no first-hand experience of EU politics in the raw. Some of the Convention members from the accession states gave a less than joyous reception to the revelation that the European Union was a rapidly developing federal system of representative democracy. The more conservative elements, especially from Poland, the Czech Republic and Slovakia, did not at all like what they heard and read in the Convention. The Convention was blamed for upping the threshold of membership, and for shifting the goal posts after the game had started. The UK government found some ready support among the soon-to-be members for its own more eurosceptical positions.

Representative democracy

Valéry Giscard d'Estaing, who was never able to evince enormous enthusiasm for EU enlargement, joined with MEPs in wishing to accentuate the democratic nature of the political system. He quickly accepted the need for special constitutional provisions on the democratic life of the Union. Accordingly, the Constitution spells out three democratic principles which should inform the system of government of the EU. Article 45 says that the EU shall observe the republican principle of democratic equality between its citizens. Each citizen will 'receive equal attention' from the institutions.

There follows a neat, and entirely novel, encapsulation of the long-standing federalist contention that citizens are represented directly in the European Parliament while the states are represented directly in the Council, which also enjoys democratic legitimacy, as follows:

Article 46

The principle of representative democracy
1. The functioning of the Union shall be founded on representative democracy.
2. Citizens are directly represented at Union level in the European Parliament.

Member states are represented in the European Council by their Heads of State or Government and in the Council by their governments, themselves democratically accountable either to their national Parliaments, or to their citizens.

3. Every citizen shall have the right to participate in the democratic life of the Union. Decisions shall be taken as openly and as closely as possible to the citizen.

4. Political parties at European level contribute to forming European political awareness and to expressing the will of citizens of the Union.

Who in good faith, having read that, could accuse the European Union of being unrepresentative? However, while the Constitution helps consolidate the theory of parliamentary democracy at the European level, it is up to its practitioners to breathe democratic life into the system of government. And one of the weakest links in the democratic chain is that of the European political parties.

The party groups in the European Parliament work quite well. They ensure that Parliament's political and legislative decisions are genuinely transnational, and they make the workings of the Parliament surprisingly smooth. Likewise, the Convention itself contributed to the development of political party consciousness at the EU level. Had it not been for the party caucuses within the Convention the constitutional outcome would have been different, and of a lesser calibre. But the weakness of this EU level party activity is that its roots are shallow. The existing transnational party formations are fairly feeble federations of national political parties. European parliamentary democracy lacks, for the moment, one of the essential sinews of democracy, that is, popular party forces that can articulate fluently the anxieties and aspirations of the citizen and direct them to the top level of government. The future of political parties is one of the most interesting conundrums posited by the Constitution. Would the constitutionalisation of the EU presage the development of proper European political parties? A Statute of European Political Parties was enacted in 2002, at the height of the Convention, laying out the legal framework and financial conditions for this much-needed development to take place. The new law on political parties foreseen by the Constitution could build on this foundation and promote the direct party membership of individual citizens with a view to those parties taking over responsibility for fielding candidates at future European Parliamentary elections and contributing to other EU-wide citizens' initiatives and referendum campaigns.[2]

---

[2] Article III–331.

Participatory democracy

Article 47, on the principle of participatory democracy, introduces another novelty. It grants the right to one million citizens coming from a 'significant' number of member states to make an 'appropriate' proposal for a new legal act to the Commission. A law is to be promulgated to specify how precisely this citizens' initiative will work. Drawn from both Swiss and American experience, the introduction of this form of direct democracy has much potential to engage the citizens in law making at the federal level. In a Union of 455 million people a petition of one million is far from being an unreasonable hurdle. Already organisations of civil society count their fee-paying membership in millions, and many of these nationally based bodies are collaborating closely with similar, like-minded organisations in other member states. Even the transnational federations of political parties, as well as the trade unions, can command impressive membership figures, at least in theory. A legislative petition would be one way of mobilising membership and of dispelling apathy. A resourceful Commission and/or Parliament, possibly stymied by the Council, might well succeed in stimulating public interest in a favoured legislative proposal by themselves promoting a petition.

One should not be surprised, therefore, if the adoption of the Constitution were soon to prompt a spate of attempted citizens' initiatives. It is likely that the introduction of this provision will trigger moves to increase further the elements of participatory democracy within the European Union. As we know all too well, referendums are increasingly fashionable among national leaders nervous of European Union politics, not only as a means of neutralising parliamentary debate about the ratification of Constitution itself, but also of requiring popular consent to future enlargement of the Union. The rush to plebiscite is proving infectious. The lack of a provision in the Constitution for the holding of EU-wide referendums was a constant source of regret to some keen *conventionnels*, particularly from Italy.

Might one also expect an early citizens' petition to widen the constitutional privileges of God or to assert a point of view on a lively social issue, such as hunting, shooting, euthanasia, same sex partnerships, stem cell research, contraception or abortion? The Commission will need to exercise political skill at a high level in order to cater for the receipt of constitutional initiatives expressing such diverse populist sentiment. The new delimitation of competences as set out in the Constitution should help it to cope.

Open government

It may not be enough for the Commission merely to react to the rise of the citizens' initiative. A prudent Commission might try to manage its public relations with organisations of civil society in such a way as to train their activities along constructive lines. Article 47 provides for 'open, transparent and regular dialogue' with civil society, 'broad consultations' by the Commission with concerned parties, and 'autonomous social dialogue' with employers and workers organisations. Existing treaty commitments to taking decisions as openly and as closely to the citizens as possible are repeated.

In Article 50, transparency, much lauded by the Scandinavians, achieves yet greater prominence. As we have already noted, the Convention pushed to get open law making in the Council of Ministers. This pressure was at first resisted by those governments who hankered after the old-style diplomatic role of the Council and feared a lurch towards rendering the Council too evidently the second chamber of a bicameral federal legislature.

It was accepted that EU law making needs less public moments when the deals between member states and political parties are thrashed out. In this the EU is not abnormal. The conciliation process between Council and Parliament at the second stage of the codecision procedure does not lend itself to the public gaze. What has been reprehensible in the past, however, is the propensity of ministers and officials to brief against each other, largely to the disbenefit of the Brussels press corps. The distinctiveness of national positions is exaggerated, with a resulting loss of focus on the common interest. The public reflection of what goes on in Council is cast in the language of defeats and victories, battlefield cries which defy the true nature of the Council meetings themselves.

The Council is actually a better instrument for decision making than it allows itself to appear to be. Its reputation will be much enhanced as soon as the interested press and public are permitted to follow the reasonableness of the arguments on matters often of considerable complexity. Experience of the very public Convention suggests that ministers begin to settle on reaching a conclusion once they know they are under scrutiny. It is surely possible to retain privacy but suppress secrecy. Above all, it matters for democratic reasons that the public know how their government representative argues and votes towards the closure of the law making process. Ministers are no different from MEPs in this respect. The Constitution has accepted this. Its stipulation that what goes for the Parliament in the way of openness must also go for the Council is a big breakthrough for European parliamentary democracy.

Associated with the debate about opening up the proceedings of the Council was the question of access to official documents. There has been a running squabble between the European Parliament on the one hand and the Commission and Council on the other about how liberal to be with putting working papers, at various stages of completion, into the public domain. An ethical cultural divide between northern and southern Europe about the correct level of responsibility of Commissioners, both individually and collectively, was not dealt with capably by either the Santer or the Prodi Commissions. A number of 'whistle-blowers' have emerged, with more or less personal credibility, to remind Parliament and press that all was not well within the services of the Commission. The Council has had to confront the problem that what would be a closed document in one member state would be open in another.

The Convention tussled with the issue of access to documents. Quite properly, it decided to provide for a new law which should lay down the principles and limits which, on the grounds of public or private interest, should govern the right of access.[3] (At present, the Council's policy on access to documents is decided only according to its own rules of procedure.) Moreover the Constitution widens the scope of the future legislation from that of the existing treaties and case law – which specifies just the Commission, Council and Parliament – to all the EU institutions, bodies, offices and agencies, and 'whatever the medium'. Member states should not be immunised from more open practices at the EU level of government; nor should the agencies of the Union dealing with material sensitive to the citizen such as Europol be wholly exempt from the norms of good governance.

Article 51 picks up the provision in the Charter of Fundamental Rights concerning the protection of personal data, and also provides for an EU law or framework law to lay down the rules governing the behaviour of the EU institutions and member states when acting for the EU institutions on data protection. An independent authority will be established to monitor the application of these rules. In the case of access to documents, as in the case of the citizens' initiative, Parliament will be fully involved in the design of the implementing legislation.

It is proper that the Ombudsman makes his first constitutional appearance in this chapter on democratic life.[4] The first holder of the post, from 1995, was the enigmatic Finn, Jacob Söderman. He was succeeded in mid-2003 by Nikos Diamandouros. Both men played an influential part in raising awareness within the institutions of the importance of good administration. The existence of the Ombudsman provided part of the answer to the complaint that the Constitution provides few quick, cost-effective or non-judicial remedies for the citizen whose interests have been abused by the EU institutions and their agencies (including national, regional and local government when executing EU law and policy). Some members of the Convention would have preferred to have given greater emphasis to the importance of the Ombudsman. But at least he is there, entrenched, and now cannot be marginalised, even by the

[3] Article III–399.
[4] Articles I–49 and III–335.

European Parliament which elects him. His existence is of special significance for the new member states where standards of probity and efficiency in public administration have yet to excel.

PRIESTS, MULLAHS AND MASONS

An oddity, inserted by the Convention only towards the end of its proceedings, is a clause that elevates the status of 'churches and non-confessional organisations'.[5] The provision attempts to allay the fears of the Christian churches about the lack of a specific reference to Christendom in the Preamble to the Constitution. Clergy, led by the Vatican but supported by the Greek Orthodox, Lutheran and Calvinist churches, presented a rare display of ecumenical unity in their lobbying of the Convention. The more conservative ecclesiastical elements feared that the insistence in the Charter of Fundamental Rights on freedom of religion and worship would jeopardise the established churches, not least with respect of Islam. Few Church representatives appeared to understand the difficulty faced by the Convention in bridging the vast cultural divide between France's aggressive laicism, forged at the Revolution, and the pious elements to be found in several national constitutions, such as those of Greece, Ireland and Poland, where the church enjoys a very privileged status. The solution found by the Convention, under Giscard's stern supervision, was, in the end, quite proper. It applied the useful Catholic principle of subsidiarity. The Constitution 'respects and does not prejudice' the national status of churches and faith communities. However, 'recognising their identity and their specific contribution, the Union shall maintain an open, transparent and regular dialogue' with these churches. In other words, churches shall be regarded as worthy members of European civil society, but their privileged dialogue with the institutions will have to be open and transparent.

How representatives of the EU's twenty million Muslims will wish to exploit the provisions of Article 52 is unclear. It is greatly to be hoped that European Islam engages fully in the processes of citizenship and constitutional democracy. Certainly it is in the interests of Turkish and Balkan aspirations to EU membership that Muslims participate strongly in the inter-faith dialogue envisaged under the provisions of the Constitution.

To placate the humanists and freemasons another, fairly bizarre, sub-clause was added to provide that the Union 'equally respects' (but not so equally that it 'does not prejudice') the status of 'philosophical and non-confessional organisations'.

[5] Article I–52.

CHAPTER 11

The role of national parliaments

Article 46.2 reminds us that national governments are democratically accountable to their national parliaments. The Convention learned to accept that the 'democratic deficit' much bandied about by critics of the European Union was not solely the fault of the EU institutions but also of national institutions which fail, for one reason or another, to connect the citizen with the new, federal dimension of politics. The decline of national politics has been starkly demonstrated by the success of the No votes in France and the Netherlands. In both countries, all the official mainstream political parties of left and right, and their two national parliaments, were in favour of Yes. Whereas the first victim of the Noes is the European Constitution, longer-term damage may have been inflicted on the standing and vitality of national parliamentary democracy in those two countries (and in the case of France, on the credibility of the Fifth Republic's presidential system).

The Convention was in any case wise to pay heed to the plight of national parliaments in the European dimension, and right to try to enhance parliamentary democracy not only at the European level but also at that of the member state. Two Protocols to the Constitution, hard-fought in the Convention, seek to refurbish the EU's relationship with national parliaments.[1] In essence, these Protocols deal with the matter of the EU's compliance with the principle of subsidiarity in the new constitutional order. The Constitution invites member state parliaments to assess the scale and effects of any draft EU legislation in areas of shared or complementary competence in order to reassure themselves that the EU is the better level at which to legislate. The Protocols require the Commission to communicate directly with national parliaments rather than indirectly, as it does now, through governments. Parliaments are to have six weeks in which to raise a reasoned objection to a draft law on the grounds of a breach of the principle of subsidiarity. The Council will not begin

---

[1] Protocol No. 1 on the role of national Parliaments in the European Union and Protocol No. 2 on the application of the principles of subsidiarity and proportionality.

its deliberation on the legislation until the six week period has expired. If one third of national parliaments objects the Commission will 'maintain, amend or withdraw' the draft, and give reasons for its decision.[2]

The implication of subsidiarity may be that decisions should be taken 'as close to the citizens as possible', but the constitutional test is whether there is added value in trying to achieve the intended objectives at Union level. The objectives themselves are not to be put to the test. National parliamentary scrutiny should bear upon both the scope and force of the intended law as made explicit in its drafting, as well as on any likely but unintended consequences. As EU law has primacy over national law, it is important to verify whether the proposed legislative intervention at the EU level will be improbably disruptive at the national level, creating disconcerting legal uncertainty and giving rise to significant potential for judicial conflict.

NEED FOR CO-ORDINATION

Six weeks is a short time for national parliaments to undertake the intensive research that is needed to furnish them with the arguments required to formulate a convincing, critical, reasoned opinion on a new legislative proposal, especially as the drafting of their opinion will have to be assisted in most cases by consultations outside parliament.

The Constitution gives two votes to each member state parliament in order to meet the constitutional requirements of parliaments in federal states where, for example, the Bundestag and Bundesrat have distinct roles to play. The Convention's assumption was, however, that in states with bicameral parliaments in all but exceptional circumstances the two votes would be exercised as one.

Within the same six weeks as they need to achieve internal cohesion, national parliaments would also have to seek and find consensus with other national parliaments if the quorum of one third is ever to be reached. The Convention intended that the reasoned opinions should be either identical or at least similar in order to trigger the constitutional early warning mechanism. It was fully aware that in circumstances where one parliament, say the Italian, were to complain that the scale and effects of a draft law did not go far enough, yet where another parliament, say the British, were to grumble that the same law went too far, the Commission would be perfectly free to ignore them both. Random or contradictory opinions or those that are not reasoned on the grounds of subsidiarity are a waste of everyone's resources.

---

[2] Protocol No. 2, Article 7.

Each national parliament has to decide for itself how much time and effort it wishes to expend in co-ordinating its views with others. Less proactive parliaments should be aware that if no other parliament takes the initiative, the job will be done on their behalf by the German Bundesrat. It is up to national parliaments to make better use of the machinery they already have for inter-parliamentary co-operation. Irregular conferences between the relevant committees of national parliaments on problematical dossiers, such as reform of the CAP, might be of benefit.

The Constitution does not, indeed cannot, oblige national parliaments to react formally to each piece of draft legislation. In the governance system of the European Union, failure to act is the default option. It will not be dishonourable to choose not to intervene. In fact, one suspects that the issuing of formal reasoned opinions from all twenty-five national parliaments will become a rare exception rather than the general rule. The early warning mechanism will work none the worse for being deployed irregularly and with discretion.

National parliaments in general should avoid becoming preoccupied with the operation of the early warning mechanism to the exclusion of the more political scrutiny of EU affairs. For example, the multi-annual work programme, the legislative programme, the budgetary settlements, the annual report on comitology, Green and White Papers, and developments in the field of foreign, security and defence policy are all central features of the contemporary European Union, equally deserving of scrutiny by national parliaments.

Whereas the Constitution permits the intervention of national parliaments on the grounds discussed, it lays down specific obligations on the European Commission to consider the regional and local dimension, to assess the financial, regulatory and environmental impact of its proposals, and, not least, to explain and justify itself more fully and systematically than it does at present. The Commission's success in carrying out these obligations is a very much more important factor in ensuring compliance with the principle of subsidiarity than is the role of national parliaments. National parliaments would do well to pay particular attention to the Commission's annual report on the application of subsidiarity. They might usefully invite their national Commissioner to discuss it.

LIMITATIONS OF NATIONAL PARLIAMENTS

It is worthwhile recalling, therefore, how thoroughly the role of national parliaments was dealt with by the Convention. There were lively debates on the matter at all levels: in the party groups, in two working parties, in the Praesidium and in the plenary. Eventually a large and strong consensus was formed around the proposals that were finally adopted too by the IGC.

The Constitution succeeds in balancing an enhanced role for national parliaments with respect for the role of the EU legislator. Each EU institution must respect the principle of subsidiarity. That means that it is not just the Commission's job to articulate the common interest of every member state but also that of the European Parliament, which represents the citizen directly, and of the Council of Ministers, which represents national governments directly and, therefore (one must assume), national parliaments indirectly. Parliament and Council together are responsible for deciding whether a draft law from the Commission is good, bad or indifferent. All three institutions consult widely about draft legislation, and these consultative procedures would be strengthened by the Constitution. The new transparency of the legislative work of the Council will be a huge help to effective parliamentary scrutiny of the performance of national ministers and officials.

The role of national parliaments is both a real one and is genuinely respected. But it is different from that of the EU legislator itself, to whom the duty of law making falls. One is aware that there are still some in the UK and Danish parliaments, and maybe elsewhere, who believe that the Constitution's early warning mechanism is in some way deficient or insufficient. That was the view taken by Gisela Stuart and David Heathcote-Amory, the two representatives of the House of Commons in the Convention, as well as by Denis MacShane, then British Minister for Europe. In their favourite parlance of football, they would exchange the 'yellow card' for the 'red card'. The fact is, however, that to give national parliaments the right of veto over EU legislation would create de facto a third legislative chamber. There is no parliament in the democratic world that has three chambers. One can hardly imagine that its creation in the EU would contribute to the Constitution's goals of simplicity or efficiency. Nor would it be understood by the discerning citizen. The 'red card' proposal would sharply undermine the legitimacy of both the European Parliament and the Council of Ministers. While no UK government has been particularly keen to grow the powers of the European Parliament, one cannot imagine it was ever part of a British government scheme to weaken its very own institution of the Council. (Indeed, rather the opposite.)

Moreover, it is not as if the EU has not had experience of a parliamentary chamber made up of national MPs. The European Parliament used to be made up of delegations of national parliamentarians. In 1979 that system was abolished because it did not work, because MPs had domestic rather than EU mandates, because they could give neither the time nor focus to EU affairs, because they were all elected at different times and for different periods, and, ultimately, because the growing importance of the European dimension to law and politics demanded a more focussed and professional approach. Given the much greater complexity and sophistication required of EU law makers today than thirty years ago, it defies belief to think that a reincarnation of the old system could work. National MPs, peers and senators have a job to do in the EU, but it is not the job of the MEP, who enjoys a direct popular mandate as EU legislator. It would be reactionary nonsense to pretend that the collective will of the EU's twenty-five national parliaments was in some sense a more pure expression of democracy than that of the European Parliament and Council of Ministers acting jointly.

The national parliaments of the European Union have a variety of constitutional functions and representative capacities. What they all have in common, however, is the duty to sustain the government of the day. How often could one expect a parliamentary revolt against the government on the grounds of a European policy – especially when the revolt has to be concocted in a reasonable way within six weeks? Given the strong ties of representation and accountability that bind national parliaments with the Council, the likelihood is that the early warning mechanism will seldom if ever be used without the complicity or connivance of governments. Indeed, the British government intends, within the six week period, to issue the Westminster parliament with official advice about whether or not each piece of draft EU law accords with the principle of subsidiarity. It seems that national parliaments are not always the independent creatures they imagine themselves to be. This raises obvious questions about the efficacy of national parliaments as tools of national government policy.

Perhaps the real significance of the early warning mechanism is not that it is practicable, but that it lends itself to the development of good governance in the EU. The importance of the mechanism lies not in the frequency or regularity of its use but in the stimulus it should give to improved and informed parliamentary scrutiny of EU affairs in general. The true objective, after all, is to improve the quality of public policy stemming from Brussels and Strasbourg. National parliaments can make a genuine contribution to achieving this goal not particularly by verifying the application of subsidiarity at the early legislative phase (the operation of the early warning mechanism), but more so by helping the EU institutions monitor the effect of EU law once in place, by reflecting more regularly and politically upon the European integration process, and by working as a conduit between the federal institutions on the one hand and domestic media and public opinion on the other.

The Constitution prompts us to remember that, in the first instance, governments in the Council are democratically accountable to national parliaments. It gives national parliaments greater potential to get generally more engaged with the European dimension to politics. National parliaments have now no excuse not to comply – whether or not the Constitution enters into force.

CHAPTER 12

Paying for the Union

The present financial system of the Union is often accused of being unfair, convoluted, untransparent and disproportionate. The amount of money at the disposal of the EU represents only 2.5 per cent of all public spending, and is therefore much too small to permit the EU a serious role in macroeconomic stabilisation policy. Nevertheless, the Convention did not seek to stretch the Laeken mandate in so far as money questions were concerned. It was accepted that the EU budget would be maintained at much its present size in spite of the fact that that would perpetuate the curious constitutional imbalance between the Union's small financial clout on the one hand and its large political and legislative powers on the other. The Convention allowed the constitutional moment to pass without forcing an injection of fiscal federalism into the veins of the Union. It accepted the Commission's contention that EU finance is not so much about redistributing resources between member states but more about maximising the impact of EU common policies so that the added value of every euro spent at European level is enhanced.

THE CURRENT FINANCIAL SYSTEM

The Union's present revenue system of 'own resources' has existed almost unchanged since 1988. It has four elements: agricultural levies, customs duties, a proportion of national VAT receipts (capped), and a payment related to the gross national income (GNI) of each member state. Only the first two, which are rapidly diminishing, stem from the EEC's classical competences of the CAP and customs union and are authentically 'own' resources. The last two are really intergovernmental transfers.

There was certainly discussion in the Convention about the need at some early future date to consider creating a new, fifth own resource for the Union. The Convention flirted with some possibilities for adding to the existing revenue streams which could complement the EU's newer political objectives. These included the assignation of seignorage from the European Central Bank, an extended VAT resource or taxation hypothecated for the EU on energy production and/or consumption.

A notional ceiling has been set on overall EU revenue of 1.24 per cent of EU GNI. As a mark of the relative paucity of the Union's own resources, this sum has to be compared with national state expenditure, which averages out at 47 per cent across the EU as a whole. The Swedish state tops the list by raising and spending almost 60 per cent of its country's wealth. No EU government spends less than a third of its GNI. The wide variation in the size of the national public purse is reflected in the tax burden on individuals. In 2003 Sweden recorded the highest tax to GDP ratio at 51 per cent; Latvia, at 29 per cent, the lowest. In terms of direct taxation as the share of the total tax take, Danes score 60 per cent, Poles 20 per cent.

In practice, EU spending in recent years has been much less than its theoretical maximum income of 1.24 per cent GNI. Since 1988 an inter-institutional agreement has set a medium-term 'financial perspective' that determines overall planned expenditure and assigns sums to various broad categories. The present agreement, reached at the Berlin European Council in 1999, runs out in 2006. In October 2002, however, because of the imminent enlargement, CAP spending was fixed for the period 2007–13. The prospect of long, tough negotiations over the new medium-term agreement formed a backdrop to the work of the Convention and the IGC.

The EU budget is not allowed to go into deficit. Just over 40 per cent of the EU budget is nowadays spent on direct support for the agricultural sector mainly by subsidising farmers' incomes and by countryside management schemes. The rest is spent through structural and cohesion funds, particularly in order to stimulate economic activity in the poorer regions as well as infrastructural development, on R&D and on administration. EU spending in 2004 was €111 billion, which is about 1.14 per cent of GNI. On 15 December 2003 the prime ministers of Austria, France, Germany, the Netherlands, Sweden and the UK wrote to President Prodi asserting that commitments in the EU budget for the enlarged Union should be restricted to a mere one per cent of GNI. Such a policy implies a cut of €11 billion from the 2005 budget. It will be interesting to see where precisely these national leaders are willing to accept cuts. The British government has already indicated that it is prepared to sacrifice almost all its current receipts from EU structural funds. France has yet to reveal where it is preparing to make any cuts whatsoever.

Curiously enough, these same states (with the exception of Germany) lent their support to a British proposal in the Convention which was intended to reduce the budgetary powers of the Commission and Parliament but which in practice could well have led to an increase in the overall size of the EU budget.

The British proposal was first put forward in February 2003 by Peter Hain but was later adopted by the Council of Finance Ministers (Ecofin) and dispatched by the Council president Guido Tremonti as a gratuitous contribution to the IGC.

The so-called 'Ecofin proposal' was rather crude. It suggested a single reading of the draft budget and that any cut in the budget had to be agreed by both the Council and the Parliament. In case of failure to agree, the lower sum proposed by either party would carry the day (unless the previous year's budget was higher). This would have meant that any member state wishing to oppose a cut would simply have to try to scupper the whole budgetary process, and would no doubt have to be bought off with costly concessions. Both institutions would be tempted to propose a zero increase in a sector preferred by the other, making the prospect of conciliation slender indeed. Fortunately, the IGC rejected Tremonti's proposal just as the Convention had earlier rejected Hain's. What did the Convention propose?

OWN RESOURCES

After a difficult negotiation in two working groups, the Convention agreed a complex package of measures. To the budgetary and financial principles it added 'sound financial management'.[1] On own resources, the Convention stuck to the current system whereby the revenue ceiling and the categories of revenue source are decided by an abnormal 'European law of the Council'. This involves unanimity between the member states. The European Parliament is merely consulted. The agreement then has to be ratified in all member states according to their own constitutional requirements (usually, by a vote of the national parliament).

To move some way towards a lightening of the procedure, the Convention proposed that whereas the own resources ceiling should remain rigid, the modalities of the own resources decision would be subject to another atypical law of the Council, this time decided by QMV after having obtained the consent of the Parliament. By 'modalities', the Convention meant primarily the revision of one of the existing revenue streams or the creation of a new one. The Convention left unresolved an ambiguity about whether payment derogations and abatements would fall in this category of matters to be decided by QMV, not least because it was thought to be inconceivable that any root and branch reform of the own resources system could be imposed on unwilling member states. The UK, however, forever fearful for the future of its budget rebate won by Margaret Thatcher in 1984, contested even that modest element

---

[1]   Article I-53.6.

of QMV when it came to the IGC. The compromise reached at the IGC was to ensure that all the essential political choices concerning the own resources system, including the implementing measures, should be made by unanimity and 'ratified' by national parliaments. Article 54.4 was modified by the IGC to link any revision of own resources to the implementing measures foreseen in this paragraph, thereby preventing the adoption within the implementing measures of decisions likely to affect the UK rebate.

FINANCIAL PERSPECTIVES

It was widely agreed within the Convention that the process of setting the financial perspectives, now subject to a voluntary inter-institutional agreement, should be integrated formally into the Constitution and that the agreed financial plan should become obligatory upon the budgetary authority (Council and Parliament). The MEPs in the Convention suggested that the financial perspectives should become broader in terms of categories of expenditure and more flexible, so as not to pre-empt the scope of the annual budgetary decision making. The new approach should allow for more regular review of decisions on finance to match the rolling programme of medium-term strategy that is to take place under the auspices of the European Council. The Convention proposed that the new-style financial perspectives should therefore be re-named the 'multi-annual financial framework', and that this should be agreed by QMV in the Council and with the consent of the European Parliament – although QMV would not apply until the second round of negotiations following the entry into force of the Constitution (possibly as late as 2017). The Convention suggested that the new financial framework should be shortened from seven years to five and that the categories of expenditure should be both broad and few.

Here, however, the Convention stumbled across hard politics. France and Ireland were determined to protect the bulk of CAP spending from any subversive attack by the British, Dutch and Scandinavians. The Dutch, for their part, linked their grudge against the UK rebate to the financial perspectives: if the British insisted on a veto over EU revenue, the Dutch would insist on a veto on EU spending. At the IGC, the Netherlands challenged the proposed shift to QMV even though the Convention proposed to postpone it until the next but one round of negotiations. The final Constitution, therefore, retains unanimity for the financial perspectives, but permits the European Council, acting unanimously, to switch to QMV at a future date once the Dutch have been satisfied that they have a fair deal.[2] The present Dutch government

---

[2] Articles I–55 and III–402.

professes its willingness to move to QMV when the time is ripe.[3] This is a prominent example of the use of the device of the *passerelle*, or bridging clause, which introduces an element of flexibility into the Constitution.

THE CONVENTION'S BUDGET PROPOSALS

The present budgetary procedure dates from 1975. It is complicated and tortuous, with two different procedures for the 'compulsory' and 'non-compulsory' sectors. The European Parliament is prevented from exercising its full budgetary authority over the compulsory segment, which includes the Common Agricultural Policy. Overall, however, Parliament has the power to reject the budget at its third reading by a two-thirds majority. The Council uses QMV to amend Parliament's first reading. To confirm its adherence to its original modifications, Parliament needs a three-fifths majority at its second reading. If no budget can be agreed at all, the previous annual budget is voted through on a monthly basis. It was hoped that the Convention could streamline this budgetary process by introducing more elements from the tried and tested codecision procedure used for ordinary legislation.

As far as the Union's annual budget is concerned, important changes are made in the Constitution.[4] The arcane distinction between compulsory and non-compulsory expenditure is abolished, which fulfils a key ambition for the European Parliament. The Convention agreed with its MEPs, and proposed that Parliament should have uniform powers over the whole annual budget, including the anomalous stand-alone European Development Fund and not excluding the CAP.

The Convention proposed that, once the Commission had launched its draft budget, Council should act in the first instance by QMV. In order to prevent the budget's adoption at first reading, Parliament would have to amend it by an absolute majority of its Members. Council would accept Parliamentary amendments, and therefore adopt the budget, at its second reading by QMV. If Council were minded to reject the amendments, a conciliation committee would be convened. In the committee the Parliamentary delegation would act by simple majority and the Council delegation by QMV. The results of the conciliation would be adopted by QMV in Council unless vetoed by a three-fifths majority of Parliament. If no conciliation were to prove possible, or if Council were to reject the compromise, Parliament could re-impose its first amendments by a three-fifths majority. Where Parliament failed to confirm its amendments, the Council version would apply.

[3] Declaration No. 42 by the Kingdom of the Netherlands to Article I–55.
[4] Article I–56.

The IGC's budget settlement

The consensus that formed around the Convention's proposal was less assured than it looked. Misgivings were expressed in the Council about the rather complex package delivered up by the Convention. Some were nervous at the likelihood of a breakdown at the conciliation stage and, therefore, of having to have recourse to the messy system of provisional monthly twelfths. Certain member states were clearly unhappy about the abolition of compulsory expenditure. Moreover, it was obvious that it would be very tempting for the Parliament to engineer a breakdown of the conciliation process in the expectation that the three-fifths majority of votes cast could be reached at third reading. Under pressure from some finance ministers, the Italian presidency tabled a proposal at the IGC that effectively deprived the Parliament of its last word.

This initiative caused a furore in the Parliament, where some Members rather cheekily demanded their own 'red line': not only the codecisional procedure for the budget but also the famous last word that was a key feature of the old system with respect to non-compulsory expenditure. The European Parliament invited the national parliaments to send their delegates to the Convention back to Brussels for a joint meeting which took place on 5 December 2003. The Italians made one final move in the days before the summit level IGC on 12–13 December.[5] The presidency proposed giving the final last word to the Council, who would be able to veto the whole package by QMV. Whether or not this would have commanded consent of the leaders will never be known, as, along with the other substantive compromises put forward by the Italians, it was never discussed at summit level. Following the breakdown of the IGC at the Brussels summit, the Irish presidency took up the reins. After a period of careful consultation, the Irish re-introduced a proposal that had been discussed at the instigation of the French over a year beforehand, but rejected. In June 2004, it was now accepted in full by the IGC.

The first phase of the process sticks to that of the Convention proposal. In other words, the Council will act in the first instance by QMV and the Parliament can make amendments by an absolute majority or the budget shall stand adopted. Council will accept Parliament's amendments by QMV or reject them and convene a conciliation committee. Here the Irish proposal changed from that of the Convention. The conciliation committee's position will stand if either Council or Parliament fails to act. If Parliament accepts the compromise position (by simple majority) but Council rejects it (by QMV), the compromise still stands unless Parliament musters a three-fifths majority

---

[5] CIG 60/03 ADD I, 9 December 2003.

to re-impose its first reading amendments. In a rather surreal final scenario, provision is also made for the compromise to be rejected outright by Parliament (acting by absolute majority) or by Council (by QMV) if Parliament fails to act. No matter how the draft budget is defeated, however, the Commission will have to submit a new proposal. The final article laying down the process for the annual EU budgetary law is as follows:

Article 404

European laws shall establish the Union's annual budget in accordance with the following provisions:

1. Each institution shall, before 1 July, draw up estimates of its expenditure for the following financial year. The Commission shall consolidate these estimates in a draft budget which may contain different estimates.

The draft budget shall contain an estimate of revenue and an estimate of expenditure.

2. The Commission shall submit a proposal containing the draft budget to the European Parliament and to the Council not later than 1 September of the year preceding that in which the budget is to be implemented.

The Commission may amend the draft budget during the procedure until such time as the Conciliation Committee, referred to in paragraph 5, is convened.

3. The Council shall adopt its position on the draft budget and forward it to the European Parliament not later than 1 October of the year preceding that in which the budget is to be implemented. The Council shall inform the European Parliament in full of the reasons which led it to adopt its position.

4. If, within forty-two days of such communication, the European Parliament:

(a) approves the position of the Council, the European law establishing the budget shall be adopted;

(b) has not taken a decision, the European law establishing the budget shall be deemed to have been adopted;

(c) adopts amendments by a majority of its component members, the amended draft shall be forwarded to the Council and to the Commission. The President of the European Parliament, in agreement with the President of the Council, shall immediately convene a meeting of the Conciliation Committee. However, if within ten days of the draft being forwarded the Council informs the European Parliament that it has approved all its amendments, the Conciliation Committee shall not meet.

5. The Conciliation Committee, which shall be composed of the members of the Council or their representatives and an equal number of members representing the European Parliament, shall have the task of reaching agreement on a joint text, by a qualified majority of the members of the Council or their representatives and by a majority of the representatives of the European Parliament within twenty-one days of its being convened, on the basis of the positions of the European Parliament and the Council.

The Commission shall take part in the Conciliation Committee's proceedings and shall take all the necessary initiatives with a view to reconciling the positions of the European Parliament and the Council.

6. If, within the twenty-one days referred to in paragraph 5, the Conciliation Committee agrees on a joint text, the European Parliament and the Council shall each have a period of fourteen days from the date of that agreement in which to approve the joint text.

7. If, within the period of fourteen days referred to in paragraph 6:

(a) the European Parliament and the Council both approve the joint text or fail to take a decision, or if one of these institutions approves the joint text while the other one fails to take a decision, the European law establishing the budget shall be deemed to be definitively adopted in accordance with the joint text, or

(b) the European Parliament, acting by a majority of its component members, and the Council both reject the joint text, or if one of these institutions rejects the joint text while the other one fails to take a decision, a new draft budget shall be submitted by the Commission, or

(c) the European Parliament, acting by a majority of its component members, rejects the joint text while the Council approves it, a new draft budget shall be submitted by the Commission, or

(d) the European Parliament approves the joint text whilst the Council rejects it, the European Parliament may, within fourteen days from the date of the rejection by the Council and acting by a majority of its component members and three-fifths of the votes cast, decide to confirm all or some of the amendments referred to in paragraph 4(c). Where a European Parliament amendment is not confirmed, the position agreed in the Conciliation committee on the budget heading which is the subject of the amendment shall be retained. The European law establishing the budget shall be deemed to be definitively adopted on this basis.

8. If, within the twenty-one days referred to in paragraph 5, the Conciliation Committee does not agree on a joint text, a new draft budget shall be submitted by the Commission.

9. When the procedure provided for in this Article has been completed, the President of the European Parliament shall declare that the European law establishing the budget has been definitively adopted.

10. Each institution shall exercise the powers conferred upon it under this Article in compliance with the Constitution and the acts adopted thereunder, with particular regard to the Union's own resources and the balance between revenue and expenditure.

THE POWER OF THE PURSE

So – for readers who are managing to hold on – how are we to assess this complicated tripartite package deal covering the revenue system, medium-term financial planning and the annual budget? First, the EU's income will be strictly controlled by member state governments, whose legitimacy will be enhanced by having to seek and win the consent of their respective national parliaments to any change; the European Parliament, in a secondary role, will only be consulted over revenue. Second, the multi-annual financial perspectives will be reformed and made compulsory, and will gradually be liberated, all being well, from the rigidity of unanimity; Parliament will use its power of consent to induce some (presumably significant) element of codecision. Third, the Union's annual budget will be determined by QMV and genuine codecision between Council and Parliament.

What took the Convention and the IGC by surprise was the jealous reaction of the finance ministers who appeared not only unwilling to accept the Convention's first proposals but also were clearly unhappy about the existing financial system and budgetary procedure. The status quo, in other words, was unstable. Some ministers of finance seemed determined to row back the budgetary powers of the Commission and European Parliament. Such a challenge to its powers of the purse provoked MEPs into a vehement and successful defence of Parliamentary prerogatives.

The final settlement engineered under the Irish presidency managed to reduce the opportunities for the whole financial and budgetary process to break down. Member states retain their privileges. The standing of the Parliament has been preserved. The role of the Commission has been slightly enhanced. The Constitution ensures that there is more likely to be a new annual budget every year that commands the consent of all three institutions, Council, Parliament and Commission. Furthermore, the Commission is set to re-gain

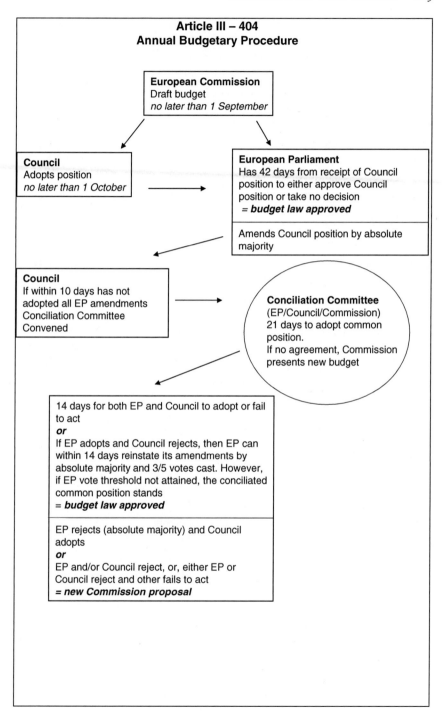

Article III – 404
Annual Budgetary Procedure

European Commission
Draft budget
no later than 1 September

Council
Adopts position
no later than 1 October

European Parliament
Has 42 days from receipt of Council
position to either approve Council
position or take no decision
= budget law approved

Amends Council position by absolute
majority

Council
If within 10 days has not
adopted all EP amendments
Conciliation Committee
Convened

Conciliation Committee
(EP/Council/Commission)
21 days to adopt common
position.
If no agreement, Commission
presents new budget

14 days for both EP and Council to adopt or fail
to act
or
If EP adopts and Council rejects, then EP can
within 14 days reinstate its amendments by
absolute majority and 3/5 votes cast. However,
if EP vote threshold not attained, the conciliated
common position stands
= budget law approved

EP rejects (absolute majority) and Council
adopts
or
EP and/or Council reject, or, either EP or
Council reject and other fails to act
= new Commission proposal

the right of initiative in the unlikely event of a stand-off between Council and Parliament. In practice, the final combative phases of the procedure are unlikely to be needed. The combination of the Convention and the IGC – without much help from Ecofin – has simplified and shortened the budgetary procedure as well as ensured genuine codecision between Council and Parliament.

Whether or not the member states were wise to stick to the rigid procedure for the settlement of the Union's supply of revenue, only time will tell. The new multi–annual financial framework has to be in place during 2006 in good time for the making of the 2007 budget. It will have to provide adequate financial means to allow the Union to address its future challenges both equitably and effectively. EU spending must provide good added value as well as accord with the constitutional principles of subsidiarity, proportionality and solidarity. Improved budgetary discipline is also necessary, especially inside the member states where the bulk of EU money is actually spent. A new law will lay down the control and audit obligations of member states which should provide the Commission with greater powers to enforce compliance.[6] In general the three institutions will have to pay greater heed to the advice of the Court of Auditors and to be more accountable to each other if the EU budget is to be properly managed at the EU level, faithfully implemented at the national level, and correctly discharged. Even though the EU budget will remain very small in real terms, the citizen needs and deserves more reassurances that what money is raised for and spent by the Union is good value.

MONEY TROUBLES

While the Constitution's proposals for the reform of the financial system are good if modest, their reception has been complicated by the deepening row over the new financial perspectives for the years 2007 onwards. The European Parliament has been quite helpful in proposing an overall spending level of 1.07 per cent GNI, mid-way between the Commission's initial proposal of 1.15 per cent and that of the net contributory states, for the period 2007–2011. Unfortunately, the European Council meeting of 16–17 June 2005 not only failed to take up such constructive proposals as existed but succeeded only in making the situation much worse. Tony Blair's refusal to negotiate seriously about reducing the UK rebate unless Jacques Chirac agreed to renege on the European Council's 2002 agreement on the financing of the CAP – an agreement in which, it must be recalled, Blair was complicit – was hardly conducive to achieving a satisfactory outcome. Nobody, and certainly not the

---

[6] Article III–407.

French, can object to the UK government's desire to spend proportionately more on European R&D and to better reflect in EU spending priorities the policy objectives of the Lisbon agenda designed to boost Europe's economic performance. The British case is not helped, however, by its resort to simplistic arguments against the Common Agricultural Policy.

First, the CAP is in the middle of a long process of radical reform that has already stemmed the production of excessive surpluses in most products. That process continues with the Commission's bold proposals to reform the sugar regime. Second, the CAP is not simply an agricultural policy but also a social policy for the rural communities: obliterate direct support for farmers and much of Europe's countryside will have to be abandoned. Third, the current reforms of the CAP include the promotion of useful schemes that improve the rural environment and help the conservation of precious resources, including flora, fauna and, not least, water. Fourth, the EU has already agreed in principle to scrap export subsidies for food. The next target is a large and steady reduction of EU farm tariffs within the context of the WTO's Doha Round. Fifth, if the EU is serious in wishing to reduce CAP spending as a proportion of its budget there are a number of things it should do. Increasing expenditure elsewhere is always an option. Capping subsidies to the larger farms is another – a recommendation of the Commission hitherto rejected by both France and the UK. A more drastic solution would be to accept a much larger measure of co-financing between the EU and national budgets, a reform that would have the effect of cutting France's receipts from the EU disproportionately to those of the UK. The Commission, which is reluctant to adopt this approach, would have to be instructed to come forward with a package of measures designed to prevent the partial re-nationalisation of the CAP from descending into a break-up of the European common market for food. In order to carry out the promised restructuring of farming in Central Europe, co-financing should be restricted for a decade to the fifteen older member states.

The presumption in London is that the UK will have to wield its veto to prevent the British rebate from being snatched away.[7] What the British tend to forget, however, is that a veto for the UK means a veto for everyone else too. No other member state supports the retention in its present form of the British abatement which was designed at an earlier phase of the Union's history to cope with rather different circumstances than those which pertain today. It seems perverse, to put it mildly, that countries much poorer than Britain in terms of GDP per capita should be obliged to pay into the coffers of HM Treasury. Other richer countries, notably the Netherlands, feel at least as

---

[7] After receipt of its abatement and taking all EU spending inside the UK into account, the cost of EU membership for Britain was, in 2003, a mere €46 per person.

aggrieved as the British about being big subscribers to the Union budget. The Dutch, with support from the Commission, favour a generalised corrective mechanism as a solution to their present inequitable situation.

The Constitution does not propose a softening of the present unanimity requirement for deciding the revenues of the Union. Nonetheless, it is clear that unanimity about the future financing of the Union is improbably difficult to achieve in a Union of twenty-five member states where the disparity between rich and poor is wider than ever. There seems no prospect whatsoever of reaching agreement if the debate is fixated on the UK abatement versus French receipts from the CAP. So all the institutions should agree to schedule in the near future a much more radical review of the own resources system than took place in the Convention or is possible today. Some greater element of fiscal federalism is certain to emerge as part of the eventual package.[8] The new settlement will have to be driven by the force of logic: gross contributions should relate to the ability to pay and net contributions should accord more faithfully than they do now to the commonly agreed political priorities of the Union as a whole. Arguments based on the Thatcherite premise of 'getting our money back' would be out of place in a Union that had self-confidently resolved its constitutional disputes and had set its political priorities for the years ahead with courage and conviction.

These financial issues are far from irrelevant in the context of a possible renegotiation of the Constitution, not least because they coincide. The inequitable size of the Dutch net contribution to the EU budget was a live issue during the referendum campaign in the Netherlands, and informed the rather grudging (and much less than convincing) endorsement of the Constitution even by some members of the government. The Dutch would seem to need a fair settlement of the financial question before they could be asked to vote again – whether the Constitution is renegotiated or not. If renegotiations are to take place, however, it will be helpful to write into the appropriate policy chapters, now found in Part Three, details of the reformed rural policies of the Union as well as those relating to economic competitiveness (the Lisbon agenda). It would be sensible also to re-open the debate about constitutional hostages to fortune. Should the Union really continue to cripple itself by an exaggerated insistence on the need for rigid unanimity for all financial decisions? In the short term, however, the priority must be to settle the transitional multi-annual financial framework for 2007 onwards.

---

[8] For a good discussion of these issues, see Iain Begg, *Funding the European Union*, Federal Trust, London, March 2005.

CHAPTER 13

Re-ordering the world

The member states of the European Union began as early as the 1970s to develop a European identity in world affairs through intergovernmental procedures dubbed 'political co-operation'. The Treaty of Maastricht established common foreign and security policy as a second pillar of the Union, even providing for 'the eventual framing of a common defence policy' which could 'in time lead to a common defence'. Shamed by European inaction throughout the early years of the Balkan crisis, a tentative outline agreement had been reached in Berlin in June 1996 about future co-operation between the EU, WEU and Nato.[1] By 1997, in the Amsterdam Treaty, EU leaders were ready to establish the post of High Representative for common foreign and security policy, who would double up as the Secretary-General of the Council. Amsterdam also provided for the EU to attempt certain peace-keeping and humanitarian missions by enshrining the so-called Petersberg Tasks.[2] The Treaty of Nice added to the function of the High Representative the permanent structures of an EU Political and Security Committee, a Military Committee and an EU Military Staff.

Lagging behind both the rhetoric and the improving institutional provisions, however, is military capability. All Europe's national armed forces suffer from out-of-date equipment, costly duplication, poor co-ordination and low standards of inter-operability. Most European armies are made up of poorly trained and weakly motivated conscripts. Even the two countries with the most professional military could not easily fight on the same side: British planes, for example, cannot land on French aircraft carriers. In December 1998, at a summit meeting at St Malo, Tony Blair and Jacques Chirac agreed to take a number of bilateral steps towards greater military co-operation. St Malo was taken, quite rightly, as a signal that British policy under the 'New Labour' government would be more pro-European than its Tory predecessors. But the

---

[1] The members of WEU were Belgium, France, Germany, Greece, Italy, Luxembourg, The Netherlands, Portugal, Spain and the UK. Mr Solana was its last secretary general.

[2] The WEU defence ministers met in the Petersberg Hotel overlooking the Rhine in June 1992.

St Malo agreement did not bury entirely the long-standing quarrel between London and Paris about how the EU should connect up with Nato.

Ambiguity about what Nato was actually for after the collapse of the Soviet Union had led the organisation, at American insistence, into enlargement. This expansionism on the part of Nato, however, risked antagonising Russia without securing the US objective of strengthening the European pillar of the Atlantic Alliance. Spurred on by St Malo, the European Council at Helsinki in December 1999 not only agreed to make Turkey a candidate for EU membership but also declared a much-trumpeted 'headline goal' to establish by 2003 the capacity to deploy within sixty days and sustain for one year between 50,000 and 60,000 troops. This proved too ambitious. Serious divergences continued among the Nato allies, amplified by Vladimir Putin. At Nice in December 2000 Blair and Chirac presented contradictory pictures to the media of what they thought they had agreed.

We have noted earlier how the attack on the World Trade Centre of 11 September 2001 was a catalyst to European integration. George W. Bush spoke, apparently with conviction, about the need for America's allies to come to the defence of Western liberty and democracy. This was taken by the EU to be a welcome change of tack from his previous policy, which had been to withdraw from American multilateral commitments. A fortnight after 9/11 Blair told the Labour Party conference: 'The kaleidoscope has been shaken. The pieces are in flux. Soon they will settle again. Before they do, let us re-order this world around us'.

For the European Union, the invitation to 're-order the world' meant a radical revision of its common foreign and security policy. In particular, it became impossible to justify the continued existence of the three pillars of the Maastricht Treaty that had separated out both foreign and security policy and internal security policy from the mainstream thrust of integration in the social and economic fields. On 9/11 the icon of globalised capitalism had been attacked by foreigners on domestic flights, rather undermining the architectural conceit of the EU's three pillars. Many of the perpetrators of 9/11 had been recruited and trained inside the European Union; many of those who died were European citizens. Was Europe next?

The Laeken European Council in December 2001 had no difficulty in agreeing to enrich the mandate of the Convention by inviting it to consider the Union's security predicament. The desire to rectify Europe's sad divisions and perpetual weakness in the field of foreign and security policy became a major driving force behind the work of the Convention. A working group, chaired by Commissioner Barnier, began to piece together a coherent response to the security crisis. Aided and encouraged by High Representative Solana, the group addressed the issues that had divided the European partners for so long, including EU relations with Nato, and whether or not a core group of integration-minded and militarily capable member states should be permitted to go forward further and faster than others.

At one stage it looked as though the very public and intense quarrel between France and Britain on the latter's decision to invade Iraq would sink the Convention altogether. Guy Verhofstadt, the main author of the Laeken Declaration, reacted by inviting the leaders of Germany, France and Luxembourg to join him in a summit meeting at the Palais d'Egmont in Brussels on 29 April 2003. Despite huge British hostility, the four leaders agreed to work towards the formation of a military core group, and to invite others to join them. This startling event proved to be the stimulus the Convention needed to make bold constitutional proposals for permanent 'structured co-operation' in the field of defence.[3]

Equally helpful to the Convention was the fact that, after more than six years of negotiation, the EU-Nato package – known as 'Berlin Plus' – came into force on 17 March 2003. Berlin Plus managed to square the interests of the EU's Nato members with (i) the non-European members of Nato, (ii) the non-EU European members of Nato, and (iii) the non-Nato EU members.[4] Under its terms, EU led crisis management operations will have assured access to Nato's planning capabilities and access to Nato's military assets on a case by case basis. The EU and Nato agreed on mutual arrangements for consultation in a crisis, involving in the first instance the EU's High Representative Javier Solana and Nato's Secretary-General Jaap de Hoop Scheffer, both Brussels based. In almost all circumstances, the Deputy Supreme Allied Commander Europe (a European) will become the EU Operation Commander. His headquarters will remain at SHAPE in Mons in Belgium.[5] To date, there have been three EU military operations – all fairly successful: in Macedonia (Concordia), in the Democratic Republic of Congo (Artemis), and now in Bosnia-Herzegovina (Althea).

'MUTUAL POLITICAL SOLIDARITY'

Article 40 of the Constitution says that the Union 'shall conduct a common foreign and security policy, based on the development of mutual political

---

[3] The ramifications of Verhofstadt's initiative rumbled on. In June 2004 Blair vetoed the appointment of the Belgian prime minister as the new President of the Commission, preferring the Portuguese prime minister who had supported the invasion of Iraq.

[4] Respectively, (i) Canada and the USA, (ii) Bulgaria, Iceland, Norway, Romania and Turkey, and (iii) Austria, Finland, Ireland and Sweden.

[5] One should never underestimate the importance of location in European politics. The siting of the EU's military wing became very controversial when the Belgians proposed Tervuren, a suburb of Brussels, for a standalone HQ.

solidarity among member states, the identification of questions of general interest and the achievement of an ever-increasing degree of convergence of Member States' actions'.

The European Council is to be responsible for determining the strategy and objectives of common foreign and security policy. The Council of Ministers would work within the strategic guidelines established by the heads of government. Both bodies can take decisions. The common policy can be put into effect by the Foreign Minister and the member states themselves, 'using national and Union resources'.[6] Although legislation is naturally excluded, the European Parliament will be 'regularly consulted on the main aspects and basic choices' of the common policy.[7] The Council will act on the basis of a proposal from the Foreign Minister (with or without the Commission's formal support), or from a member state.

The mutual obligation to consult is strict – and stricter than the UK wanted. Member states shall 'consult one another ... on any foreign and security policy issue which is of general interest in order to determine a common approach. Before undertaking any action on the international scene or any commitment which could affect the Union's interests, each Member State shall consult the others ...'.[8]

The British made a terrible fuss about retaining unanimity for all EU decisions in the field of foreign and security policy, and appeared to have convinced many at Westminster that the Convention was a foreign plot to send British soldiers into battle by QMV. Under the terms of the Constitution, unanimity will indeed be the norm, but there are significant exceptions as set out in Article 300 in Part Three. There is a facility for qualified abstention, which means that the member state or states concerned, while accepting that the majority view commits the Union, will not need to apply the decision. However, one third of member states representing one third of the population forms a blocking minority. The same Article, moreover, also provides for real QMV whenever the Council adopts decisions giving effect to the strategic decisions of the heads of government. So the potential scope for using QMV in foreign and security policy seems, in fact, rather wide and not, as continually claimed by British ministers, nugatory. In addition, there is also the insertion of a *passerelle* clause in Article 40.7 which would allow the European Council, acting unanimously, to extend QMV to all decisions in common foreign and security policy – without the by-your-leave of national parliaments.

Faced with a strong majority of opinion in the Convention and a significant

[6] Article I–40.4.
[7] Article I–40.8.
[8] Article I–40.5.

majority of opinion in the IGC that supported these arrangements, the UK was forced to insist on the inclusion of an emergency brake clause. This states that any one member of the Council may block the use of QMV for 'vital and stated reasons of national policy' – in which case the Council may decide by QMV to refer the matter to the European Council for a decision by unanimity.[9] One can imagine how popular the UK will be if it tries to press this brake. One may equally imagine how frustrated the UK will be if its own goals for common foreign and security policy are frustrated by any other member state bringing the European security limousine to a juddering halt.

The final version of the key foreign policy article is as follows:

Article 40

Specific provisions relating to the common foreign and security policy
1. The European Union shall conduct a common foreign and security policy, based on the development of mutual political solidarity among Member States, the identification of questions of general interest and the achievement of an ever-increasing degree of convergence of Member States' actions.
2. The European Council shall identify the Union's strategic interests and determine the objectives of its common foreign and security policy. The Council shall frame this policy within the framework of the strategic guidelines established by the European Council and in accordance with Part III.
3. The European Council and the Council shall adopt the necessary European decisions.
4. The common foreign and security policy shall be put into effect by the Union Minister for Foreign Affairs and by the Member States, using national and Union resources.
5. Member States shall consult one another within the European Council and the Council on any foreign and security policy issue which is of general interest in order to determine a common approach. Before undertaking any action on the international scene or any commitment which could affect the Union's interests, each Member State shall consult the others within the European Council or the Council. Member States shall ensure, through the convergence of their actions, that the Union is able to assert its interests and values on the international scene. Member States shall show mutual solidarity.

[9]   Article III–300.2.

6. European decisions relating to the common foreign and security policy shall be adopted by the European Council and the Council unanimously, except in the cases referred to in Part III. The European Council and the Council shall act on an initiative from a Member State, on a proposal from the Union Minister for Foreign Affairs or on a proposal from that Minister with the Commission's support. European laws and framework laws shall be excluded.

7. The European Council may, unanimously, adopt a European decision authorising the Council to act by a qualified majority in cases other than those referred to in Part III.

8. The European Parliament shall be regularly consulted on the main aspects and basic choices of the common foreign and security policy. It shall be kept informed of how it evolves.

'OPERATIONAL CAPACITY'

The Constitution reflects important progress in the field of security and defence policy. Article 41 defines the purpose of the common policy as providing the Union 'with an operational capacity drawing on civil and military assets' which the Union may use 'on missions outside the Union for peace-keeping, conflict prevention and strengthening international security in accordance with the principles of the United Nations Charter'. There will not be an EU standing army. Instead, the EU draws on the armed forces of the member states. The Constitution continues:

> The common security and defence policy shall include the progressive framing of a common Union defence policy. This will lead to a common defence, when the European Council, acting unanimously, so decides. It shall in that case recommend to the Member States the adoption of such a decision in accordance with their respective constitutional requirements.

EU security and defence policy 'shall not prejudice' the policies of those member states which 'see their common defence realised in Nato', and shall be compatible with Nato's own policy.[10] In any case, all member states 'undertake progressively to improve their military capabilities'.

A new European Defence Agency is established to develop the Union's capabilities with respect to arms procurement. Member states may choose whether or not to take part in the activities of the Defence Agency. Its tasks are to 'contribute to identifying and, where appropriate, implementing any measure

---

[10] Article I–41.2.

needed to strengthen the industrial and technological base of the defence sector, to participate in defining European capabilities and armaments policy, and to assist the Council in evaluating the improvement of military capabilities'.[11]

The Constitution makes two commitments to collective solidarity. The first concerns a member state which is the victim of armed aggression, in which case the other member states will 'have towards it an obligation of aid and assistance by all the means in their power'.[12] The UK, for reasons of its own, refused to extend this commitment as far as Nato's Article 5 which regards an attack on one member as an attack on all. Nevertheless, it would be implausible for one EU state sharing the same Constitution with another to refuse to help defend it. One can only speculate on the circumstances in which the UK would stand aside from a European Union war. The second commitment concerns a member state which is the object of a terrorist attack or a victim of a natural or man-made disaster, in which case the Union shall mobilise all the instruments at its disposal, including military resources.[13] The UK seemed happy with that one.

The Convention revised and up-graded the Petersberg Tasks which had been devised as guidelines for the EU's emerging security and defence stance in 1992. The new tasks of the Union in the security field are 'joint disarmament operations, humanitarian and rescue tasks, military advice and assistance tasks, conflict prevention and peace-keeping tasks, tasks of combat forces in crisis management, including peace-making and post-conflict stabilisation'. All these tasks 'may contribute to the fight against terrorism, including by supporting third countries in combating terrorism in their territories'.[14]

The Constitution sensibly provides for a certain group of member states to embark upon a particular military mission on behalf of the Union as a whole, where the Council sets the objective, scope and conditions.[15] The Council may entrust the implementation of a task to member states which are 'willing and have the necessary capability for such a task'.[16]

MILITARY CORE GROUP

More controversially, and in a radical departure from the Treaty of Nice, the IGC accepted the Convention's proposal for the formation of a permanent core group, and even improved on its initial formulation, as follows:

[11] Articles I–41.3 and III–311.
[12] Article I–41.7.
[13] Article I–43 and Article III–329.
[14] Article III–309.1.
[15] Articles I–41.4.
[16] Article III–310.1.

> Those Member States whose military capabilities fulfil higher criteria
> and which have made more binding commitments to one another in this
> area with a view to the most demanding missions shall establish
> permanent structured co-operation within the Union framework.[17]

The lifting of the prohibition on enhanced co-operation in security and defence policy is one of the most important reforms envisaged by the Constitution. The core group, selected only from the politically willing and military capable member states, will be established by a decision of the Council acting by QMV. Unlike the euro group, there is no requirement for all member states to join in. The qualifications for participation and obligations of membership are tough. Only members of the core group will admit new members or suspend members, acting by QMV. Other decisions of the core group are to be taken by unanimity. Members of the group are bound in practice to maintain a high level of defence expenditure. They are committed to harmonising the identification of military needs by pooling and specialising their defence means and capabilities. They are obliged to 'take concrete measures to enhance the availability, interoperability, flexibility and deployability of their forces, in particular by identifying common objectives regarding the commitment of forces, including possibly reviewing their national decision-making procedures'.[18] Participating states will have to make good perceived shortfalls in meeting agreed troop, equipment and logistics commitments. They are to commit themselves to acting together in the work of the European Defence Agency and, by 2007, to establishing battle groups capable of fighting. They will harmonise their procurement policies, co-ordinate their training, standardise their equipment and identify common objectives. Any member state which 'no longer fulfils the criteria or is no longer able to meet the commitments' will be in danger of being ousted from the core group.[19]

This provision for structured cooperation in defence has huge potential. It has the facility to overcome the internal incoherence and weakness of Europe's military capacity that has persisted since the failure of the European Defence Community in 1954.

EUROPEAN SECURITY STRATEGY

To put its emerging military effort into a clearer political context, the European Union has now agreed a European Security Strategy. Formulated by Javier Solana and formally adopted by the European Council in December 2003, *A Secure*

[17] Article I–41.6.
[18] Article 2 of Protocol No. 23 on Permanent Structured Cooperation.
[19] Article III–312.4.

Europe in a Better World does not mince its words on Europe's military weakness. Its objectives are to tackle the threats to Europe's security, to extend the scope of security around Europe's borders and to strengthen the international order. The document asserts that the main security threats of weapons of mass destruction and terrorism can only be met by 'effective multilateralism'. The EU, it says, will uphold the UN. It remains committed to the use of force only as a last resort. In contrast to current American policy of making pre-emptive strikes against potential foes, the EU speaks of 'preventive engagement'. One is led to hope nevertheless that what flows from the European Security Strategy in terms of practical results will meet US concerns. Despite the continuing crisis in Iraq, and the fall-out in terms of EU cohesion, the first job of the newly enlarged and constitutionalised European Union must be to repair its transatlantic relations. Solana's security strategy contributes to that process.

Another piece of the emerging jigsaw of the EU's security and defence policy is the European Defence Agency, which the Council has already decided to establish under existing legal bases.[20] It is anticipated that the Defence Agency will gradually take over the work of the existing intergovernmental bodies in the armaments field.[21] It will also work closely with the European Commission in its own efforts not only to boost R&D in science and technology relevant to Europe's security but also to open up the arms market to more competition. The Constitution still allows member states to protect their arms industries from normal single market disciplines for reasons of national security.[22] In addition to the European Defence Agency, which is now up and running, EU defence ministers have been commendable in wasting no time. Small battlefield forces of no more than 1500 EU soldiers, to be deployed within a fortnight over distances of up to 5000 kilometres, are at last being trained and organised. An EU gendarmerie is being proposed to undertake the less military and more civilian type of operation.

One concrete conclusion of the rise of EU security and defence policy is the effective absorption into the EU of the Western European Union.[23] Because its achievements have been modest throughout its fifty year history, the passing of WEU will not be much lamented. But the parliamentary assembly of WEU collected together the defence specialists from national parliaments. The European Parliament, if it were wise, would try to recruit the same MPs to co-operate with it on the scrutiny of the emerging common policy. New

---

[20] Council Joint Action 2004/551/CFSP of 12 July 2004.
[21] The West European Armaments Group (WEAG) and the Organisation Conjointe de Coopération en matière d'Armement (OCCAR).
[22] Article III–436.
[23] Protocol No. 24 on Article I–41.2.

methods of co-operation are needed between MEPs and national MPs in the defence field. National parliaments exercise budgetary powers over defence expenditure and retain an abiding interest in national security. The role of the European Parliament is to foster, influence and monitor the common elements of European security and defence policy. Only a combination of effort between national and European parliamentarians will make an effective difference to the evolution of European security. Big choices, such as whether the EU should get involved militarily in Afghanistan or Iraq, should not be made without the consent of Europe's parliaments – with or without the EU Constitution in place.

Not least among the security preoccupations of the European Parliament is arms control. MEPs are of the view that the current EU Code of Conduct on arms exports is insufficiently rigorous in controlling unethical commercial practices or in combating illegal arms trafficking. Parliament is demanding binding EU rules on arms brokering, as well as a drive by the EU to achieve an international arms trade treaty. Best practice in the field of arms procurement engendered by the European Defence Agency could spill over into European arms exportation. An arms control policy grounded within the evolving European Security Strategy, coupled with the revised institutions and procedures promised by the Constitution, would indeed give Europe the chance to do great good in the world.

The potential loss of the Constitution is particularly regrettable in the field of security and defence policy, and particularly in so far as the United Kingdom is concerned. The British government can contribute positively to the rapid development of the common European security and defence policy, and at last seems willing to do so. It would indeed be bizarre for the British not to participate significantly in the one area of European integration where they have a commanding lead over other member states. It is no longer convincing to argue that Nato is enough. Nato has not contributed much to the integration of European armed forces or to getting good value for money. With the exception of its belated assault on Serbia, Nato has not earned itself an assured reputation in world affairs since the loss of its raison d'être at the end of the Cold War. Nato has been unable to devise a strategy for the 21st Century that unites its European and US wings. Greater EU autonomy in military matters will provide for the USA a more responsible and respectable partner. The Constitution provides the ways and means to achieve this without threatening to turn the EU into a military superstate. For the UK, the special relationship with the USA is over. It is prudent now for the British to take out insurance cover against the contingency that one of Tony Blair's successors either chooses not to seek, or does not acquire, a good relationship with one of the illustrious successors of George W. Bush.

CHAPTER 14

Freedom, security and justice

Minded of the deteriorating security situation, the Convention was almost united in wanting to bring cooperation in the field of interior affairs within the mainstream of Union activities. However, as some governments could not bring themselves entirely to follow the logic of the Convention's purpose in abandoning the third pillar, Article 42 of the Constitution was devised to make continued special provisions in this field. It establishes that the Union 'shall constitute an area of freedom, security and justice:

(a) by adopting European laws and framework laws intended, where necessary, to approximate laws and regulations of the Member States in the areas referred to in Part III;
(b) by promoting mutual confidence between the competent authorities of the Member States, in particular on the basis of mutual recognition of judicial and extrajudicial decisions;
(c) by operational co-operation between the competent authorities of the Member States, including the police, customs and other services specialising in the prevention and detection of criminal offences'.

The European Council laid down political guidelines for development of this policy at Tampere in October 1999. The Commission of Romano Prodi (1999–2004) made considerable progress in shaping an ambitious legislative programme involving measures to strengthen the external borders of the Union, to develop common asylum and immigration policies, and to approximate the definition of crimes and penalties. The Commission and Parliament would like to go further in the direction of combating discrimination on the grounds of racism and xenophobia. There does not seem to have been any reluctance on the side of the police and customs to collaborate with each other – rather the contrary. In the judicial area, however, more systematic coordination is required: hence the emphasis in the Constitution on mutual recognition in the field of criminal justice. National parliaments are given the option of participating in the evaluation of the principle of mutual recognition.[1]

AMBITIOUS OBJECTIVES AND ABNORMAL PROCEDURES

As a further legacy of the Maastricht pillar arrangement, various abnormal procedures are installed in Part Three as a result of a rearguard action fought by some national ministers of the interior, notably the British Home Secretary. Representatives of national parliaments appeared in general to support the cautious approach adopted by governments. Given the complexity and sensitivity of EU involvement in justice and home affairs, it is a remarkable achievement of the Convention that it managed to broaden the scope and objectives of these common policies while at the same time assuaging most if not all of the initial hostility voiced in national capitals.

Article 257 sets out the overall compass of the area of freedom, security and justice:

1. The Union shall constitute an area of freedom, security and justice with respect for fundamental rights and the different legal systems and traditions of the Member States.

2. It shall ensure the absence of internal border controls for persons and shall frame a common policy on asylum, immigration and external border control, based on solidarity between Member States, which is fair towards third-country nationals. For the purpose of this Chapter, stateless persons shall be treated as third-country nationals.

3. The Union shall endeavour to ensure a high level of security through measures to prevent and combat crime, racism and xenophobia, and through measures for co-ordination and co-operation between police and judicial authorities and other competent authorities, as well as through the mutual recognition of judgments in criminal matters and, if necessary, through the approximation of criminal laws.

4. The Union shall facilitate access to justice, in particular through the principle of mutual recognition of judicial and extrajudicial decisions in civil matters.

Member states retain the right to initiate legislation, alongside the Commission, with respect to judicial co-operation in criminal matters, police co-operation and administrative co-operation.[2] The Convention insisted, however, that one quarter of member states would be required to launch a draft

---

[1]   Article III–260.
[2]   Article III–264.

law, which is a significant improvement on the Treaty of Amsterdam arrangements under which any member state could (and did) sally forth on its own.

BORDER CONTROLS

The Constitution provides for EU laws or framework laws concerning visas, border checks, conditions under which third-country nationals may travel within the EU, and the 'gradual establishment of an integrated management system for external borders'.[3] It creates a general legal base for a comprehensive system for asylum and refugees with uniform standards and common procedures. Such a system would respect the Geneva Conventions on the status of refugees, but may offer higher protection. EU legislation may establish a uniform status for asylum seekers and those who seek subsidiary protection, a common system for dealing with a temporary massive influx of refugees, common procedures for granting and withdrawing asylum status, criteria and mechanisms for determining which member state is responsible for each asylum case, common reception standards, and the conduct of co-operation with third countries. In emergencies the Council adopts regulations or decisions on a proposal from the Commission, after consulting the Parliament.[4]

With respect to immigration, and the 'efficient management of migration flows', EU legislation would under the Constitution define the conditions of entry and residence, and the rights of third-country legal residents. EU laws would tackle problems caused by illegal immigration, including repatriation, and combat trafficking, especially of women and children. The EU could adopt incentive measures for the integration of legal immigrants.[5] EU common policy would not affect the right of member states to determine the volume of immigrants they wish to accept, although the policy would be governed by the 'principle of solidarity and the fair sharing of responsibility' between the member states.[6] This last provision is unprecedented, and its implications need to be thoroughly explained to and understood by national ministers, parliaments and media. Asylum and immigration policy can no longer be conceived and implemented on a purely national basis; the EU Constitution provides a strict framework within which a common policy should be developed; that common policy will be firm but fair; a clear distinction is made by the Constitution between asylum on the one hand and immigration on the

3   Article III–265.
4   Article III–266.
5   Article III–267.
6   Article III–268.

other, as well as between legal and illegal immigrants; and decisions on numbers of immigrants will remain a matter of national discretion. It is a pity that the strength of the Constitution's drafting in this sensitive area did not come across with sufficient force in the French and Dutch referendum campaigns where fear of asylum seekers and immigrants played a prominent part. Surely it cannot be beyond the wit of national politicians to argue that pressure from inflows of refugees as well as the growing demand within the EU for immigrant labour pose a common problem demanding shared European solutions – solutions which the Constitution provides.

The Treaty of Amsterdam ordained that after a transitional period of five years QMV could be used in the Council to legislate on policies concerning border controls, visas, third country residence, asylum seekers, refugees and immigration.[7] On 1 January 2005, indeed, QMV was eventually introduced for all these questions except that of legal immigration. This means that, to a large extent, the extension of the ordinary legislative procedure laid down in the Constitution will already be in operation in advance of the entry into force of a renegotiated Constitution. Encouragingly, associated restrictions on the scope of the Court of Justice in this area have also been lifted to coincide with the change in law making procedures.

CIVIL LAW

The Constitution places new importance on integration in the field of civil law as a necessary flanking feature of the single market and as a bulwark of the Union's area of freedom, security and justice. It sets out the circumstances in which the Union will 'develop judicial co-operation in civil matters having cross-border implications, based on the principle of mutual recognition of judgments and decisions in extrajudicial cases. Such co-operation may include the adoption of measures for the approximation of the laws and regulations of the Member States'.[8] EU legislation in this field may provide for mutual recognition and enforcement, exchange of documentation, compatibility of jurisdictions, co-operation in taking evidence, access to justice, elimination of obstacles to civil proceedings, alternative methods of dispute settlement, and training of the judiciary. Although the ordinary legislative procedure is to be used for judicial co-operation in civil matters, special Council measures, with ministers acting unanimously and Parliament only consulted, is to be retained for family law questions.

[7] Article 67.2 TEC.
[8] Article III–269.

CRIMINAL LAW

Equally sensitive is the potential accorded the European Union under the Constitution to make incursions into judicial co-operation in criminal matters. EU measures which may seem perfectly acceptable to deal with cross-border crime can easily impinge upon national courts in their treatment of purely domestic crime over questions such as the admissibility of evidence, the scope of criminal liability, the rights of victims or the choice of jurisdiction. EU legislation is foreseen in relation to rules for mutual recognition of judgments, avoidance and settlement of conflicts between jurisdictions, training of the judiciary, and systems of co-operation. Minimum rules may be established.

In this field of criminal law, the UK insisted on the inclusion of a provision that allows any one member state to object to the use of the ordinary legislative procedure on the grounds that 'fundamental aspects of its criminal justice system' would be affected by the draft law.[9] In that case, the matter must be referred to the European Council, which has four months in which it must either terminate the suspension or request a new draft law. If no action is taken or a new draft law is held up for twelve months, and at least one third of member states wish to adopt the law, they shall be permitted to do so. So there is not only an emergency brake to stop progress by the whole Union but an emergency throttle to accelerate the formation of a core group of integrationist member states so that they might proceed without hindrance. We return to the Constitution's rules on 'enhanced co-operation' in the next chapter.

The Constitution also authorises EU law making to establish minimum rules to combat serious crime with cross-border implications in the following areas: terrorism, trafficking in human beings and sexual exploitation of women and children, illicit drug trafficking, illicit arms trafficking, money laundering, corruption, counterfeiting of means of payment, computer crime and organised crime. Those areas may be extended unilaterally by the Council, acting unanimously after consulting the Parliament. In this field too, the same emergency brake and throttle procedure is prescribed.[10]

Eurojust, established by a Council decision in 2002, is the network of national prosecution authorities. The powers of Eurojust are widened under the Constitution to include investigating and not just prosecuting authorities, and also to oblige member states to launch a prosecution. EU laws are to determine the structure, operation, scope and tasks of Eurojust. They will also make arrangements for European and national parliamentary scrutiny of

[9] Article III–270.3.
[10] Article III–271.

Eurojust.[11] National parliaments can certainly assist the European Parliament in the latter process. The powers of Eurojust may be extended by a unilateral decision of the European Council, acting unanimously, after obtaining the consent of Parliament and after consulting the Commission. Furthermore, the Council, acting unanimously with the consent of Parliament, could establish the office of European Public Prosecutor.[12] Given the reserve expressed about this proposal, however, one should not expect to witness such a development before Eurojust has had much more experience of working alongside a network of national authorities. The Convention, at least, was unconvinced of the need to establish at this stage a wholly new institution.

The Constitution also allows the EU to legislate to develop co-operation between national police forces, including the exchange and storage of data, staff training, research into crime, and the detection of organised crime. The Council alone may legislate, acting unanimously after consulting the Parliament, in the matter of police operations and the involvement of Eurojust and Europol in the internal affairs of member states.[13] Europol is the European Police Office established by a convention in 1995. It collects, analyses and exchanges information among national police authorities. The Constitution gives it a similar legal base to that of Eurojust.[14] As from 2004, Europol and Eurojust exchange information on personal data with each other. Both are destined to develop into more recognisable federal agencies with more powers, a higher profile and a consequent need for greater parliamentary accountability.

JUDICIAL REVIEW

The Constitution envisages important limitations on the powers of the Court of Justice in this field. The Court shall have no jurisdiction to 'review the validity or proportionality of operations carried out by the police or other law-enforcement services of a Member State or the exercise of the responsibilities incumbent upon Member States with regard to the maintenance of law and order and the safeguarding of internal security'.[15] That seems a pity, if inevitable. However, previous limitations on the role of the Court of Justice in the third pillar were much stricter. Under the current treaties, member states have been given the choice of opting into the Court's jurisdiction – an

[11] Article III–273.
[12] Article III–274.
[13] Articles III–275 and III–277.
[14] Article III–276.
[15] Article III–377.

invitation which, needless to say, the UK declined.[16] If and when the Constitution is in force, national courts will be able to make references to the EU Court on all justice and home affairs matters, including asylum and immigration, except for police and security service operations – and except for British and Irish courts in those specific areas where their governments have an opt out.[17]

These procedural devices are evidence of a certain hesitation among member states about deploying the European Union institutions to tackle the international dimension of security. But hesitations or not, cyber-terrorism and international organised crime continue to grow apace. As far as the Convention was concerned, at least, responding to global insecurity through regional integration on the basis of the EU made eminent sense. In the light of the al'Qaeda bombings in Madrid in 2004 and London in 2005 one might expect that any renegotiation of the Constitution would want to take another look at the nervous circumscriptions placed on the jurisdiction of the Court of Justice in the field of security.

[16] Article 35.2 TEU.
[17] Article 2 of Protocol No. 19 on the position of the UK and Ireland on border controls, asylum and immigration, judicial cooperation in civil matters and on police cooperation.

CHAPTER 15

Core groups and semi detached

Enhanced co-operation among a group of member states should be distinguished from a multi-speed Europe in which member states arrive at a common destination in their own time. It is natural that different member states converge at different speeds on objectives that are established by the Union as a whole. The gradual and steady expansion of the membership of the Union is one example of that, as are the variable transition periods that mark the accession treaties. The same approach has been adopted for the euro: in theory, at least, every member state is supposed to adopt the single currency as and when it meets the convergence criteria.

By 'enhanced co-operation', however, the Union means something rather different and a lot more flexible. The Constitution permits a core group of member states to reinforce their integration in a specified policy sector. Although these states have to respect the general provision that their action is designed to protect the interests of the Union and to further the integration process as a whole, it is clear that their choice of policy objectives might be very different to those states which either choose to stay outside the core group or, for one reason or another, are obliged to remain outside. Once established, the inner circle could adopt policies that are divergent from those still pursued by the outer circle. Although it is to be hoped that any core group would succeed over time in recruiting more members, such inclusiveness cannot be guaranteed. In theory, a core group works as a motor of integration, showing the way forward to all by example. In practice, however, once out in front the self-selected core group could swiftly become a co-opting and self-serving club of the élite, creating perforce not a Europe of multi-speeds but of multi-tiers. In other words, a core group formed under the Constitution's provisions of enhanced co-operation may not be a temporary, but a permanent phenomenon. Enhanced co-operation is not for the weak willed. And it certainly has important implications for the way the Union is governed.

The IGC leading up to the Treaty of Amsterdam had drafted a number of provisions designed to authorise reinforced co-operation among a core group of states as a last resort. This innovation had been triggered by increasing alarm at the wayward behaviour of Denmark, the UK and Sweden, and had a particular following in Germany and France. In the event, these provisions have never been utilised, partly because of the high thresholds that have to be crossed in order to do so, but also because of the undeniable headache that their deployment would cause the EU institutions. Moreover, the defeat of the Tories in Britain in 1997 had held out the possibility that the UK would abandon its traditional hostility to much of mainland, mainstream integration.

THE CONVENTION'S APPROACH

At any rate, despite the fact that they had never been deployed, the very existence in the Treaty of the provisions on enhanced co-operation meant that the issue would not go away from the Convention. Only a small minority, arguing that the Union's constitutionalisation required greater conformity, wished to do away with these provisions altogether. The majority feared that to suppress enhanced co-operation within the Constitution would provoke a rise in unregulated coalitions of like-minded states being formed outside the Constitution, on the fringes of the Union. Giscard d'Estaing was keen to point out that the enlargement of the Union from fifteen to twenty-five member states bolstered the case for keeping the provisions for enhanced co-operation in the Constitution. Even the British government accepted the concept of enhanced co-operation for economic issues as long as there was no disruption to the single market, although it opposed the formation of core groups in foreign and security policy. In the end, the Convention chose not only to retain enhanced co-operation, but also to widen its scope and reform its provisions so as to ease its use.

Article 44 of the Constitution says that: 'Enhanced co-operation shall aim to further the objectives of the Union, protect its interests and reinforce its integration process'. Enhanced cooperation is prohibited in the areas of exclusive competence. The threshold for the creation of a core group was lowered from eight out of fifteen member states to one-third of the total membership (that is, in EU–25, nine). The Council decision to authorise enhanced co-operation 'shall be adopted by the Council as a last resort, when it has established that the objectives of such co-operation cannot be attained within a reasonable period by the Union as a whole, and provided that at least one third of the member states participate in it'. Enhanced co-operation must not undermine the single market by creating barriers to trade or distorting competition; nor must it undermine the economic, social and territorial cohesion of the Union.[1] The core croup must respect the competences, rights and obligations of non-participating states, but, conversely, the outsiders shall not impede the implementation of enhanced co-operation.[2]

The rules covering the authorisation of enhanced co-operation were relaxed somewhat by the Treaty of Nice and further by the Constitution.[3] Member states wishing to form a core group will need to address the request to the Commission 'specifying the scope and objectives of the enhanced co-operation proposed'.[4] The Council will act to establish enhanced co-operation by QMV on a favourable proposal of the Commission after having first obtained the consent of the European Parliament. All possibility of a single national veto has been removed by the Constitution. The granting of a comprehensive right of consent to Parliament, which in the previous Treaties was very restricted, is a big breakthrough for MEPs.

By contrast, enhanced co-operation in the field of common foreign and security policy will be authorised by the Council acting unanimously on receipt of the advice of the Foreign Minister and Commission. Parliament will be merely informed.

In all cases apart from military matters (which we examined in chapter 13), the Commission and the participating member states must promote the participation of as many member states as possible.[5] Late or additional applications to join the core group will be authorised by the Commission within four months.[6] If the Commission rejects the application it must explain why and propose measures to allow the applicant member state to catch up. If a second application is rejected, the failed candidate may appeal to the Council, in which the participating states only will decide the matter by QMV. In short, the conditions of entry for late arrivals are tough. In foreign and security policy, new admissions will be decided by the Council, acting unanimously among the participating states alone.

In theory, all member states may take part in Council deliberations on matters subject to enhanced co-operation, even if it is the participating states alone that will take the decisions. Yet whereas the member states adhering to the core group are free to run their own affairs in the Council, the Constitution is silent on the matter of the participation in decisions in the context of enhanced co-operation of MEPs, judges and Commissioners coming from non-

---

[1]   Article III–416.
[2]   Article III–417.
[3]   Article 11.2 TEC.
[4]   Article III–419.
[5]   Article III–418.
[6]   Article III–420.

participating states. The presumption must be that the functioning of these other institutions will not be too badly affected. Members of the Parliament, Court of Justice and the Commission are said to represent the common interests of the Union as a whole and all its citizens, and not just their own constituency, jurisdiction or nationality. Nevertheless, it would be naïve to imagine that utilisation of enhanced co-operation would not put the Parliament, Court and Commission under some considerable strain. If enhanced co-operation becomes fashionable, a future version of the Constitution may have to re-visit the plight of the institutions.

ENHANCED USE OF THE PASSERELLE

A big debate took place within the Convention about how much laxity to grant a core group with respect to revising decision-making procedures, notably by switching from unanimity to QMV. Much against the instinct of the UK government, it was finally agreed to adopt a permissive approach and allow members of the core group to use the full panoply of instruments available to the whole Union, including the *passerelle* clause. Under the Constitution, therefore, member states participating in enhanced co-operation will be able to decide, albeit by unanimity but without the interference of non-participating states, to change the decision-making procedure on any provision of the Constitution from unanimity to QMV and to switch from a Council law under an abnormal procedure to the ordinary legislative procedure.[7] This means that the core group, once established, can drop all the atypical acts, emergency brakes and references to the European Council, and henceforward may proceed to pass laws in the normal way by QMV plus codecision with the Parliament on a proposal from the Commission. The potential consequences of this are large and make the British especially nervous. A bizarre Declaration has been attached to the Constitution which says that member states 'may indicate, when they make a request to establish enhanced co-operation, if they intend already at that stage to make use' of the *passerelle*.[8] (The very same member states may, of course, also not indicate.) As enhanced co-operation is only likely to be needed in precisely those areas where the existence of such abnormalities causes intolerable frustration, the scene is set for the rapid emergence of core groups in social security matters, fiscal policy and in justice and home affairs. In other words, the UK government's campaign to defend its 'red lines' has served to neatly define for the integrationist minded member states where enhanced co-operation could first be tried.

[7] Article III–422.
[8] Declaration No. 27 on Article III–419.

It is evident that under the terms of the Constitution the UK would have no way of stopping the development of an inner core of nine or more member states – presumably members already both of the euro group and the Schengen area – from fulfilling more ambitious plans for political union. If core group politics were to become the predominant practice in the next number of years, however, the risk to the integrity of the Constitution would not be negligible. To make enhanced co-operation work well will require skill, patience and mutual understanding on behalf of the whole Union and all its institutions. It may be anticipated that the Court of Justice will be asked to rule on conflicts arising out of enhanced co-operation in defence of the legitimate interests of non-participant member states. Enhanced co-operation will not be allowed to distort trade or undermine the acquis. It cannot touch the Union's exclusive competences. Non-discrimination on the grounds of nationality will remain the lynchpin of EU law, and non-participant states may have good reason to be especially grateful for the primacy of EU law in years to come.

SCHENGEN

What consequences, if any, does the Constitution hold for the Union's existing forms of differentiated integration? The Schengen Agreement is the most striking example of enhanced co-operation in practice. It was achieved by a roundabout route. In 1985 five member states signed a convention outside the EU Treaty framework at the Luxembourg village of Schengen.[9] The purpose of this agreement was the gradual abolition of passport checks and customs controls at their own respective borders. Revised in 1990, the Schengen Agreement was then absorbed into the Treaty of Amsterdam by Protocol. It was henceforward an integral part of the acquis communautaire and, as such, had to be taken on board by the Constitution too.[10] All ten accession states were obliged to sign the Schengen accord, although its practical application is subject to transitional arrangements. Two non-EU countries, Norway and Iceland, are part of the Schengen area on account of their membership of the older Nordic passport union.

Denmark is a Schengen signatory but ever since it had to renegotiate its terms of acceptance of the Treaty of Maastricht it has had a formalised semi-detached relationship with Schengen.[11] Where unanimity is required in the Council for decisions in the area of freedom, security and justice, unanimity is defined as unanimity minus Denmark, and the QMV thresholds are adjusted

[9] Benelux, France and Germany.
[10] Protocol No. 17 on the Schengen *Acquis*.
[11] Protocol No. 20 on the position of Denmark.

accordingly. Denmark plays almost no part at all in this major Union policy area, with the exception of visa policy. The same, rather astonishing abnegation applies for Denmark, a Nato member, in relation to defence policy. Denmark may suppress this Protocol in whole or in part at any time. (Successful ratification by Denmark of the Constitution might well have triggered a fresh campaign for another referendum whose purpose would have been to jettison the Danish opt-outs on Schengen, defence and the single currency.)

The UK and Ireland are not signatories of Schengen, presumably because of their island mentality. That is why everyone has to queue at British and Irish ports and why European airports have had to build extra terminals. But both countries may elect to opt in to all or some of its provisions on an ad hoc basis, and both have used this facility to some extent. Britain and Ireland have joined the Schengen information exchange system and have adopted much of the Schengen regime on asylum – although not on immigration. The Council acts on requests for opt-ins by unanimity. To protect British singularity against the Constitution's commitment to creating 'an area without internal frontiers', the UK has established another Protocol to verify that it may continue to exercise stringent border controls.[12] (Ireland is not necessarily a willing party to this Protocol but is, as it were, trapped into conformity with it by virtue of its historic Common Travel Area agreement with the UK.)

To complicate matters further, the UK and Ireland have opted out of a large number of key articles involving policies on border checks, asylum and immigration and judicial co-operation in civil matters, and to the evaluation of the effectiveness of these policies.[13] Nor do they recognise the right of the Union to regulate administrative co-operation between themselves and other member states, or to legislate for the gathering of information by police.[14] They will also resist any Court of Justice ruling interpreting these articles. Voting thresholds in the Council are adjusted for these items accordingly. The UK and Ireland have three months after the launching of any measure under these provisions to decide whether or not they wish to join in, but they are unable to form part of any blocking minority. Only Ireland has the right to withdraw from the terms of this Protocol. No wonder the Foreign Office is stuffed with lawyers.

Schengen is the classic example of integration being propelled by a small

---

[12] Protocol No. 18 on the application of Article III–130 to the UK and Ireland.

[13] Protocol No. 19 on the position of the UK and Ireland on policies in respect of border controls, asylum and immigration, judicial cooperation in civil matters and on police cooperation. The relevant articles are found in Sections 2 and 3 of Chapter IV, Title III, Part III.

[14] Articles III–263 and 275.2(a), respectively.

group of states, gradually winning new recruits to the project which is eventually assimilated into the Union's acquis and, ultimately, the Constitution. However, the process is never simple and hardly transparent. Regardless of the merits of the case, the citizen is deprived of the assurance of legal certainty that he and she deserve. The incorporation into the Constitution of the Charter of Fundamental Rights would at least help in this respect. The Charter is intended to be comprehensively binding across the EU: a tentative British exploration of the possibility of gaining opt-outs from the Charter was given short shrift in the Convention.

CONCENTRIC CIRCLES

Just as the Constitution opens up the prospect of more variable geometry within the Union, it follows the same logic for dealing with the Union's immediate neighbours. The Constitution proposes, in effect, to establish a third tier of neighbourly states that would enjoy a privileged partnership with the Union stopping short of membership. There was much debate about suitable candidates for this neighbourhood policy. Giscard clearly meant to include Turkey; most recognised the Ukraine and the Western Balkans in this category; some, mischievously, saw a future for the United Kingdom. The relevant article is not illuminating on detail. It reads:

Article 57

> The Union and its neighbours
> 1. The Union shall develop a special relationship with neighbouring countries, aiming to establish an area of prosperity and good neighbourliness, founded on the values of the Union and characterised by close and peaceful relations based on co-operation.
> 2. For the purposes of paragraph 1, the Union may conclude specific agreements with the countries concerned. These agreements may contain reciprocal rights and obligations as well as the possibility of undertaking activities jointly. Their implementation shall be the subject of periodic consultation.

What is clear, at least, from this formulation – which appears in no former EU Treaty – is that what the Union is offering to its near abroad is co-operation and not integration. The Union has considerable experience of co-operation agreements with countries in its immediate environs. The Barcelona Process, established in 1995, embraces almost all the Mediterranean countries in a dialogue with the EU. Partnership and Co-operation Agreements have been signed with several of the former countries of the USSR, including Moldova and the Ukraine. Democratic progress in the Ukraine is leading to an upgrading of EU relations with that country, and 'reciprocal rights and obligations' would enable the EU to have more leverage than it has had to date on a number of pressing environmental issues, notably Chernobyl.

CHAPTER 16

How to join and leave the Union

The last three articles of Part One of the Constitution concern the terms of Union membership. The condition of eligibility is that first set out in Article 2: the EU is open to all European states that respect its values and 'are committed to promoting them together'.[1] The procedures for accession are not changed substantively from that of the existing Treaty on European Union, save that the Council now has to inform national parliaments as well as the European Parliament that an application has been made. The Council decides to accept or reject membership by unanimity after having received the opinion of the Commission and having obtained the consent of the European Parliament, acting by a majority of its component Members. The accession agreement is made between all the member states and the candidate country and then ratified by all member states according to their constitutional requirements. In Austria and France, at least as far as Turkey is concerned, those requirements will include a referendum.[2]

In December 2004 the European Council decided to open accession negotiations with Turkey. It also established a new framework for all future accession negotiations, including those with Croatia, drawing on the experience of the recent enlargement. The process has become tougher. Permanent safeguard clauses as well as long transition periods and derogations will be considered, not least for the application in practice of the principle of free movement of persons. In a carefully argued passage, the European Council declares:

'The shared objective of the negotiations is accession. The negotiations are an open-ended process, the outcome of which cannot be guaranteed beforehand. While taking account of all Copenhagen criteria, if the candidate state is not in a position to assume in full all the obligations of membership it must be ensured that the candidate state concerned is fully anchored in the European structures through the strongest possible bond.'[3]

[1] Article I–58.1.
[2] France also held a referendum on the accession of the UK, Ireland and Denmark in 1972.
[3] European Council Presidency Conclusions, Brussels, 16–17 December 2004, para. 23.

The heads of government also added the possibility of suspending the accession negotiations on the initiative of the Commission or of one third of member states in the case of a serious and persistent breach of the principles on which the Union is founded (Article 2). The Council will decide by QMV after having given a hearing to the candidate state.

The criteria for suspending accession negotiations are drawn directly from Article 59 of the Constitution. This provides for the suspension of membership on the basis of 'reasoned initiatives' from one third of member states, the Parliament or the Commission. The Council will determine if there is a 'clear risk' of a serious breach of the values laid down in Article 2, acting by a specially high qualified majority of four-fifths of its members, after obtaining the consent of Parliament. The matter then passes to the level of heads of government, where the European Council, having obtained the consent of MEPs, may determine, by unanimity (minus the alleged offender), the existence of a 'serious and persistent breach' of Article 2. The Council, acting again by a super qualified majority, could then suspend certain membership rights, including voting rights, although the offending state would not be released of its obligations under the EU Constitution. Similar procedures are in place to vary or revoke the measures. Parliament acts throughout this procedure by a majority of two-thirds, representing a majority of its component members.

In drawing up its mandate for the opening of membership negotiations with Turkey, the Commission fleshed out the stricter conditions that will apply in this, and doubtless in subsequent cases. It is a pity that more was not made of the fact that the Union has raised the threshold for future accessions in the course of the French, and, especially, Dutch referendum campaigns, where fear of future enlargement, as well as resentment at the recent enlargement, fuelled anti-EU sentiment. A revised Constitution could well install a more explicit rendering both of the original Copenhagen criteria but also of the more recent, tough modifications as a useful contribution to the perfectly legitimate debate about Europe's frontiers.

SECESSION CLAUSE

Article 60, the final clause in Part One, allows a member state to withdraw voluntarily from the Union. This proposal provoked a long discussion in the Convention. In practice, of course, any member could leave the existing Union under the terms of the Vienna Convention on the Law of Treaties simply by revoking its accession agreement. But the Treaty on European Union carries no provision for an orderly secession negotiation. Leaving the present Union would be an ad hoc exercise and almost certain to leave the departing country's relationship with its erstwhile partners in a sorry state.[4] Under the provisions of the Constitution, the seceding country could negotiate 'the framework for its future relationship with the Union' – presumably under the good neighbourly terms of Article 57. In the event that no negotiation were to take place, the Constitution would cease to apply to the disaffected state two years after it had notified the Council of its withdrawal (unless that period was extended by mutual agreement).

The politics of this innovation are interesting. Those in the Convention who were most reluctant to accept the introduction of a secession clause subscribed neither to the eurosceptic nor to the federalist view of the Union. The majority, with Giscard somewhere in its midst, was content to have the importance of the changes brought about by the constitutional process recognised. That was a wise decision. As integration deepens, it is surely right to allow reluctant member states a second thought as to whether they are in for the long haul.

Although it is not true, as some allege, that the UK joined under false pretences in 1973, it is the case that the federal character of the Union has deepened markedly since those days. Membership of the Union should not become an intolerable political burden on the British, or on anyone else. And, in any case, the option of leaving should help to concentrate the mind about staying.

---

[4] It is true that the overseas territory of Greenland left the Union, but its parent member state, Denmark, more or less remained behind.

CHAPTER 17

The Union's common policies

Part Three of the Constitution, entitled *The Policies and Functioning of the Union*, comprises as many as 321 clauses (Articles 115 to 436). Unfortunately, as we have noted already, the Convention had neither the remit nor the time to undertake a substantive overhaul of the common policies of the Union, so most of the policy content of these chapters is taken over directly from the existing Treaty establishing the European Communities (that is the Treaty of Rome, as amended by the Single Act and the Treaties of Maastricht, Amsterdam and Nice). The Convention established working groups to look at only five policy areas – foreign policy, defence, justice and home affairs, social policy and economic governance. Only the first three made significant progress. Nevertheless, Part Three represents an editorial improvement to the existing treaties, including the scrapping of redundant articles, which makes the whole more readable. Many technical amendments were made, especially in relation to the setting up of the euro, and there were important structural changes to ensure harmony and consistency with Parts One and Two of the Constitution as well as to reflect the abolition of the three pillars of Maastricht. Part Three provides the legal bases for the common policies, and it is here that the significant extension of QMV in the Council and codecision with the Parliament is most obviously on display.

HORIZONTAL CONSOLIDATION

Part Three begins with a reiteration of the principles, enunciated in Part One, which are to inform the Union's definition and implementation of common polices. Eight new clauses with horizontal application were inserted by the Convention or the IGC. The first establishes consistency between the common policies of the Union, its overall objectives and the principle of conferral of powers.[1] In the second, the Convention installed the promotion of equality

---

[1] Article III–115.

between men and women: the IGC, fashionably, reversed the order.[2] Article 117 speaks of the need for the common policies to take into account the 'promotion of a high level of employment, the guarantee of adequate social protection, the fight against social exclusion, and a high level of education, training and protection of human health'. Article 118 lays down that, in defining the implementing the common policies, 'the Union shall aim to combat discrimination based on sex, racial or ethnic origin, religion or belief, disability, age or sexual orientation'. 'Environmental protection requirements must be integrated into the definition and implementation of the policies and activities' of Part Three, particularly with a view to promoting sustainable development.[3] Consumer protection shall also be taken into account.[4] A late addition was the need to pay full regard to animal welfare, although only while respecting the 'religious rites, cultural traditions and regional heritage' of the member states, including presumably bull fighting and gastronomic eccentricities.[5]

More controversial was the insertion of an article on 'services of general economic interest', or public utilities such as postal and health services, and the gas, water and electricity supply industries.[6] A rearguard action was fought by those, mainly public sector trade unions, who were frustrated in their efforts to get such a clause into Part One of the Constitution. EU policies to boost competition within the single market, to facilitate cross-border trade and to limit state aids to industry, have ended the protection once accorded to nationalised monopolies. Provision is made for European legislation that will establish principles of universal access to general services and set conditions for their survival in the newly liberalised market place.

In view of the allegations made by certain elements of the French left that the Constitution somehow epitomises the onward march of raw 'Anglo-Saxon liberalism', it seems a pity that the existence of these eight new horizontal articles at the beginning of Part Three has not been more widely disseminated.

ECONOMIC GOVERNANCE

Behind the debate over these horizontal provisions, and in particular the argument over how to protect services of general interest, lay a deeper partisan contest about the reform of the Union's system of economic governance.

[2] Article III–116.
[3] Article III–119.
[4] Article III–120.
[5] Article III–121.
[6] Article III–122.

European economic and monetary union has been founded on the assumption that the single monetary policy is to be complemented by decentralised but co-ordinated national economic policies. Strict convergence conditions are set for joining the single currency in the first place, but the imperative to sustain the monetary union thereafter relies largely on the presumption of financial and budgetary self-discipline and collective political will. The common interest rate is set at the federal level by the autonomous European Central Bank, whose mission is price stability. National budgetary policy for euro group members has to conform to fairly strict guidelines, spelled out in the Stability and Growth Pact. But member states which adopt the euro continue with their own domestic tax and spend policies. In a crisis, there is no EU bail out of national defaulters. There is no provision for the centralisation of taxation beyond the fairly minimal programme to harmonise indirect taxes sufficiently (mainly VAT) to ensure the smooth operation of the single market.

By the time of the Convention there were many, especially but not only to be found on the left, who were keen to review the Maastricht provisions. The Stability and Growth Pact was suffering a gradual loss of authority as a policy tool for the underpinning of economic and monetary union. When Romano Prodi, in an unguarded moment, was driven to call the Pact 'stupid' he was only giving voice to a widespread scepticism that, as an instrument, it was insufficiently robust to guarantee fiscal discipline within the euro group. Germany's experience of reunification had been far more costly to the national treasury than foreseen. The prolonged economic downturn in the late 1990s had not encouraged member states to make much progress on the structural reform of their own economies, notably to liberalise their labour markets or to defuse the 'pensions time bomb' caused by Europe's ageing demography.

Growing concern about the EU's laggard economic performance drove successive meetings of the European Council to establish a set of objectives – notionally to be achieved by 2010 – with the overall aim of boosting competitivity, productivity and employment. This came to be known as the 'Lisbon agenda', named after the European Council under the Portuguese presidency in March 2000. Its mission was to turn Europe into 'the most competitive and dynamic knowledge-based economy in the world capable of sustainable economic growth with more and better jobs and greater social cohesion'. It adopted an essentially liberal approach in which the 'open method of co-ordination', involving bench-marking, peer review, codes of conduct and the sharing of best practice between governments took precedence over economic regulation driven by the Commission.

Dissatisfaction at the ineffective implementation of the Lisbon agenda caused the Convention to establish a working party to review the Union's terms of economic governance. On the surface, this working group, chaired by German social democrat MEP Klaus Hänsch, was seen to be one of the least successful features of the Convention experience. Split as the Convention naturally was on traditional policy lines, the main conclusion reached both in the group and later in the plenary was two-fold: first, that it was too early for a radical revision of the Maastricht rules on monetary union, and, second, that the open method of co-ordination should not be elevated into a policy instrument of general application. The Convention's main objective was to ensure that the Constitution could facilitate the smooth evolution of the economic rule book as and when circumstances demanded it. Those euro group insiders who would have preferred to see established a stronger political discipline in the Council, backed up by centralised, common fiscal policies, were opposed not only by the economic liberals of the euro group but also by the UK government which was reluctant to see the threshold for entry to the single currency pushed upwards by the Constitution.

The Commission, for its part, wanted to strengthen the grip of the Broad Economic Policy Guidelines on the macroeconomic policies of the member states. Under the Constitution, the Commission wins the right to address its opinions about a deteriorating fiscal situation directly to the member state concerned.[7] It can also make a proposal – in place of a recommendation – to the Council, which must act on it 'without undue delay', about whether or not an excessive deficit exists.[8] However, the Commission was frustrated in seeking to extend its powers further to make formal proposals with respect to the action to be taken in circumstances where an excessive deficit is deemed to exist. 'Proposals' would have triggered unanimity (minus the offending state) if the Council had wished to revise the Commission's proposed course of action. This key change, although supported by the Convention, was not accepted by the IGC. France and Germany, stung by criticism from Brussels for their lax budgetary policies, were unwilling to support the enhanced role for the Commission implicit in the Convention's draft.

The Convention was more successful in suggesting changes to the rules in relation to the autonomy of the euro group. This is reinforced, for example, by the provision that a Council decision to allow a new member state to join the euro group must be preceded by a positive recommendation from a qualified majority of current euro group members.[9] This effectively gives the euro group member states complete powers of co-option. The Constitution lengthens the

---

[7] Articles III–179.4 on surveillance of broad economic policy guidelines and III–184.5 on excessive deficits.

[8] Article III–184.6.

[9] Article III–198.2.

list of provisions that do not apply to member states outside the euro group ('Member States with a derogation').[10] Euro group members may have a unified policy and will represent themselves as one within the international monetary system.[11] They have decided to develop, significantly, 'ever-closer coordination of economic policies within the euro area', and, to that purpose, have formalised their 'informal' ministerial meetings.[12]

The latter change raises the important question of who precisely is the spokesman for the euro group on the international stage. There are three contenders for that role: the President of the European Central Bank, the Commissioner responsible for economic and monetary affairs, and the president of the Euro Group Council, Jean-Claude Juncker, who as Luxembourg's finance minister (as well as prime minister) has been elected for two and a half years to chair it and has been named, somewhat glibly, 'Mr Euro'. But this is a delicate matter, and requires each to respect scrupulously the constitutional role of the others. Anything less could damage international market confidence in the euro.

The IGC had to deal sensitively with the Stability and Growth Pact, which continued to lose credibility as a result of its infringement by some member states, notably France and Germany. The IGC did not accept an Italian presidency proposal to enable either the Commission or a member state to bring an action before the Court of Justice in case of a breach of the excessive deficit procedure.[13] However, at Dutch insistence, the IGC adopted a hotly contested – but nevertheless non-binding – Declaration reaffirming its commitment to the Stability and Growth Pact.[14] In this document, the IGC declared that member states 'should use periods of economic recovery actively to consolidate public finances and improve their budgetary positions. ... The Member States will take all necessary measures to raise the growth potential of their economies. Improved economic policy co-ordination could support this objective'.

Shortly after the conclusion of the IGC, in July 2004, the Court of Justice clarified, at the request of the Commission, the respective roles of the Commission and Ecofin in the operation of the Pact. In September the Commission proposed that the Pact should be interpreted more flexibly and that the sanctions possible under the original version should be quietly dropped. It suggested that more attention should be paid to debt sustainability

[10] Article III–197.2 (i) and (j), and Article III–197.4 (a) and (b).
[11] Article III–196.
[12] Protocol No. 12 on the Euro Group.
[13] Article III–184.12.
[14] Declaration No. 17 on Article III–184.

in the surveillance of budgetary positions, as well as to the particular domestic circumstances of each member state, in particular following periods of weak economic growth. It is hoped that earlier warnings of impending excessive deficits and greater peer pressure will help to grow a stronger culture of mutual solidarity between finance ministers. The debate continues.

CITIZENSHIP REVISITED

Part Three lays down precise decision-making procedures with respect to non-discrimination and citizenship.[15] Because citizenship treads on issues traditionally associated with national sovereignty, many of these procedures are abnormal. Although the ordinary legislative procedure will be used to lay down rules to prohibit discrimination on the grounds of nationality, for EU laws banning discrimination based on sex, race, religion, disability, age or sexual orientation, the Council will act unanimously after obtaining the consent of the Parliament. MEPs in the Convention pushed hard until the last minute to get a derogation from that heavy procedure as far as programmes to promote anti-discrimination are concerned. In the end it was agreed that the ordinary legislative procedure may be deployed to 'establish basic principles for Union incentive measures and define such measures, to support action taken by Member States in order to contribute to the achievement of the objectives referred to in paragraph 1, excluding any harmonisation of their laws and regulations'. That modest compromise was only reached by sacrificing some of the Constitution's lucidity.[16] But it does concede to Parliament an element of real codecision in a sphere of legislative activity in which it is highly motivated. MEPs will have to become agile at exploiting their powers of consent, which are sprinkled throughout the Constitution, in order to maximise Parliament's role. The same abnormal legislative procedure is provided where the EU may wish in future to add to the list of citizenship rights laid down in Article 10, but national parliaments are asked to confirm the law.

As far as citizenship is concerned, the checks and balances in the Constitution are poised with care. Arrangements to extend the franchise for municipal and European Parliamentary elections are made by a law of the Council, where the Council acts unanimously after consulting the Parliament. The same procedure applies to extending diplomatic and consular protection. However, a degree of flexibility is permitted if action should prove necessary to help citizens exercise their right to move and reside freely throughout the Union and the Constitution

---

[15]   Articles III–123 to 129.
[16]   Article III–124.2. The ingenious wording was crafted by Giuliano Amato and John Kerr.

has not provided the necessary powers. The ordinary legislative procedure is to be the way of plugging these gaps – without the Council unanimity required by the general 'flexibility clause' (Article 18) unless the measures directly affect passports, identity cards or social security identification.

THE INTERNAL MARKET

There are fewer abnormalities in the large chapter of Part Three that deals with the organisation and management of the single market, including the free movement of persons and services, freedom of establishment, freedom to provide services, the free movement of goods, the customs union, prohibition of quantitative restrictions to trade, free movement of capital and payments, competition policy, state aids policy, taxation policy and approximation of laws.[17] The Council retains its executive power, on a proposal of the Commission, to adopt regulations and decisions 'determining the guidelines and conditions necessary to ensure balanced progress in all the sectors concerned'.[18] On the same basis the Council fixes tariffs and duties, and may take emergency action to safeguard against instability caused by unusual flows of capital or to freeze the assets of terrorists. The Council adopts regulations, on a proposal of the Commission and after consulting the Parliament, on companies' abuse of dominant positions in the internal market, cartel operations and other anti-competitive behaviour, including state aids to industry. The Commission at least retains all its executive powers to uphold the competition and state aids policies. Notwithstanding the exclusive competence of the Union in this area, the Constitution and contemporaneous changes to EU competition policy law and practice make the division of responsibilities clearer between the Commission and national competition policy authorities.

As far as changes in legislative procedures are concerned, QMV replaces unanimity in the Council for laws concerning freedom of movement for self-employed people.[19] The Constitution also provides for legislation to strengthen co-operation between national custom authorities.[20] The ordinary legislative procedure is introduced for free movement of capital including foreign direct investment, financial services and capital markets regulation.[21] Any step backwards from liberalisation of third country capital movements must be

[17] Articles III–130 to 176.
[18] Article III–130.3.
[19] Article III–141.
[20] Article III–152.
[21] Article III–157.

taken by a Council law, with Council acting unanimously after consulting Parliament.

Two issues provoked major quarrels in the Convention and at the IGC, with the UK as main protagonist. One concerned social security for migrant workers, including self-employed and workers' families, where the Convention had first proposed QMV plus codecision (the ordinary legislative procedure). Despite its proclaimed attachment to the completion of the single market and its apparent recognition of the need for a more mobile European workforce, the British government set its heart against any relaxation of the current regime in which the Council decides by unanimity. The British complaint about the potential cost of liberalising social security had been well rehearsed at the time of the Amsterdam and Nice Treaties. The UK again exercised its veto against an extension of QMV, and in order to placate it an emergency brake clause was inserted, as follows:

> Where a member of the Council considers that a draft European law or framework law referred to in paragraph 1 would affect fundamental aspects of its social security system, including its scope, cost or financial structure, or would affect the financial balance of that system, it may request that the matter be referred to the European Council. In that case, the procedure referred to in Article III–396 shall be suspended. After discussion, the European Council shall, within four months of this suspension, either:
> (a) refer the draft back to the Council, which shall terminate the suspension of the procedure referred to in Article III–396, or
> (b) request the Commission to submit a new proposal; in that case, the act originally proposed shall be deemed not to have been adopted.[22]

The best that can be said for this arrangement is that any use of the emergency brake mechanism would receive maximum publicity.

The other fierce controversy, which surfaced early on in the life of the Convention, concerned the harmonisation of taxes. The Union has already found it necessary to move towards the approximation of rates and structures of certain indirect taxes, notably VAT and excise duties on alcohol, tobacco and petrol. Although the principle of competition between tax regimes is generally adhered to, the EU has sought to improve the smooth operation of the single market by reducing very wide disparities in tax rates and structures between member states. The Convention, a large majority of whose members strongly supported QMV for these aspects of fiscal policy, added the qualification that tax harmonisation should be necessary 'to avoid distortion of competition'. As

[22] Article III–136.3.

a derogation from the general rule for tax of unanimity in the Council, it proposed that the Council could nevertheless decide unanimously to use the ordinary legislative procedure for harmonising both indirect and company taxation relating to 'administrative co-operation or to combating tax fraud and tax evasion'.[23] Even this switch to QMV by unanimity proved too much for British Treasury lawyers. At the IGC, the Irish presidency was more sympathetic to the British point of view than its Italian predecessors had been, and the UK was conceded another of its 'red lines'.[24] On his return from the IGC in June 2004, prime minister Blair told an anxious House of Commons that 'this treaty ... keeps unanimity for the most important decisions ... in particular for tax, social security, foreign policy, defence and decisions on the financing of the Union affecting the British budget contribution'.[25] It remains to be seen whether the British victory proves to be the unalloyed success the prime minister claims it to be. Not only was British boasting bound to upset the centre left in mainland Europe, but unanimous agreement on tax policy between twenty-five governments will be very difficult indeed to achieve, especially when the divergence between the high tax and low tax countries is, after enlargement, wider than ever. And, as we have noted before, the British 'red lines' have established some eminently suitable areas for enhanced co-operation among a more homogeneous group of member states.

Harmonisation of direct taxation is even more closely restricted. A European framework law is to establish measures for the approximation of laws with the Council acting unanimously after consulting the Parliament.[26] A new clause has been introduced to provide legislation for the uniform authorisation and protection of intellectual property rights. Decisions on the use of languages for the filing of patents, however, will only be made under a unanimous Council law, with the Parliament merely consulted.[27] Why member states take refuge in unanimity whenever they confront a seemingly intractable problem is something of a mystery. Experience over the patents dossier, critical to boosting Europe's competitiveness, suggests that no QMV means no progress.

THE SHARED COMPETENCE SECTORAL POLICIES

Following the chapter on economic and monetary policy, the Constitution turns to deal individually with the sectoral common policies.[28] The ordinary

---

[23] Convention Draft Constitution Articles III–62.2 and 63.
[24] Article III–171.
[25] HC Debates, 9 June 2004, col. 602.
[26] Article III–173.
[27] Article III–176.
[28] Articles III–177 to 202 cover economic and monetary policy.

legislative procedure is to be used for EU laws establishing incentive measures designed to encourage co-operation between member states in the field of employment policy.[29] In the sensitive field of social policy, the ordinary legislative procedure is to set 'minimum requirements for gradual implementation' relating to improvement of the working environment to protect workers' health and safety; working conditions; the information and consultation of workers; the integration of persons excluded from the labour market; equality between women and men with regard to labour market opportunities and treatment at work; the combating of social exclusion; and the modernisation of social protection systems.[30]

By contrast, the Council acts unanimously after only consulting the Parliament in relation to social security and social protection of workers; protection of workers where their employment contract is terminated; representation and collective defence of the interests of workers and employers, including codetermination; and conditions of employment for third-country nationals legally residing in Union territory. However, with the exception of laws concerning social security and the social protection of workers – the UK 'red line' – Council may decide, acting unanimously on a Commission proposal and after consulting Parliament, to switch the remaining three items to the ordinary legislative procedure. This element of flexibility had been wrung out of the British during the negotiations on the Treaty of Nice. Unlike the general *passerelle* clause (Article 444), this sector-specific *passerelle* is not subject to the consent of national parliaments – a self-denying ordnance which, given the enlarged size of the Union, is commendable. As in the existing Treaty, EU legislation will apply not at all to pay, the right of association, the right to strike or the right to impose lock-outs. And as before, there is provision for binding agreements at the EU level between management and labour which could foreshorten the legislative processes.[31] The Constitution establishes a simple and normal legislative basis for the operation of the European Social Fund.[32]

Provisions on economic, social and territorial cohesion lay down the legislative basis for the European Regional Development Fund and the Cohesion Fund. The former provides targeted development assistance to all the poorer regions of the Union. The latter is designed to contribute to environmental projects and trans-European infrastructure networks in the poorer member states. The extension of the ordinary legislative procedure to

[29] Article III–207.
[30] Article III–210.
[31] Article III–212.
[32] Article III–219.

the setting of the tasks, priority objectives and organisation of what are known as the Structural Funds (Social Fund, Regional Development Fund, Agricultural Guidance and Guarantee Fund) as well as the Cohesion Fund is a big breakthrough, long sought, for the European Parliament. (The Treaty of Nice provides for unanimity in Council and the assent of Parliament.) However, MEPs' rapture will have to be somewhat delayed: at the insistence mainly of the Spanish, the IGC postponed the actual operation of the new procedure until the second revision of the Structural Funds after the coming into force of the Constitution.[33] This will exacerbate the battle for funding between richer and poorer member states. One hopes Spain will not be disappointed as a result of all those national vetoes.

A comparable victory for Parliament transpired in relation to the common agricultural policy and common fisheries policy, where, although QMV has long been used in Council, Parliament has had hitherto only a consultative role.[34] The Constitution gives MEPs equal power with ministers to shape the future direction and pace of CAP reform. This reform should invoke a change in the character of the Parliament's Agriculture Committee. Coupled with the abolition of the distinction between compulsory and non-compulsory expenditure within the EU's annual budget, the Constitution rectifies what has been an unfortunate gap in the powers of Parliament to control what is, after all, the Union's most substantial and venerable common policy. There is no change to the Council's executive power to set, on a proposal of the Commission, the fixing of farm prices, levies, aid and quotas. Efforts in the Convention to change this and to modernise the stated objectives of the CAP and CFP were frustrated. The upgrading of animal welfare in the horizontal clauses at the start of Part Three could have an impact on policy content, however.

EU policy on the environment is aimed at preserving, protecting and improving the quality of the environment, protecting human health, prudent and rational utilisation of natural resources, and promoting measures at international level to deal with regional or worldwide environmental problems. The ordinary legislative procedure pertains for environment policy with the exception of the following anomalous items, where Council unanimity plus codecision continues to apply: 'provisions primarily of a fiscal nature; measures affecting town and country planning, quantitative management of water resources or affecting, directly or indirectly, the availability of those resources, and land use, with the exception of waste management; as well as measures

[33] Article III–223.2.
[34] Article III–231.2.

significantly affecting a Member State's choice between different energy sources and the general structure of its energy supply'.[35] Again, however, the Constitution includes a sector-specific *passerelle* clause to allow the Council of Ministers, acting unanimously on a proposal of the Commission and after consulting the Parliament, to switch these items too to the ordinary legislative procedure, without a referral back to national parliaments.

No change is made to the Convention's provisions on consumer protection, which themselves closely followed the existing Treaty.[36] The ordinary legislative procedure also applies throughout to the common transport policy and to trans-European networks. Parliament is to be consulted by Council in making regulations to outlaw discriminatory charging policies by carriers.[37]

The status of EU common policy for research and technological development gets a boost in the Constitution. 'The Union shall aim to strengthen its scientific and technological bases by achieving a European research area in which researchers, scientific knowledge and technology circulate freely, and encourage it to become more competitive, including in its industry, while promoting all the research activities deemed necessary by virtue of other Chapters of the Constitution.'[38] The ordinary legislative procedure is extended under the Constitution to the design of the multi-annual research and development framework programmes, the creation of the European research area, and the laying down of rules for the participation of researchers and the dissemination of results. EU legislation is also foreseen for supplementary programmes involving a certain number of member states only. Parliament will be consulted in the making of Council regulations and decisions concerning the administration of the research programmes and in the making of Council laws establishing the specific programmes. There was a tussle in the Convention to secure these parliamentary rights. In a substantive change to the common policy, space research, commended by Giscard d'Estaing, wins a clause of its own.[39]

The last common policy in the field of shared competences concerns energy, where the common policy is intended to '(a) ensure the functioning of the energy market; (b) ensure security of energy supply in the Union, and (c) promote energy efficiency and energy saving and the development of new and renewable forms of energy'.[40] The UK government made a great fuss about

[35] Article III–234.2.
[36] Article III–235.
[37] Article III–240.3.
[38] Article III–248.1.
[39] Article III–254.
[40] Article III–256.

maintaining sovereignty over its energy resources under the North Sea, and tried to insist on unanimity for Council decisions relating to exploitation of national energy resources. But the final version of the Constitution retains unanimity only for measures of a fiscal nature – that is, ecological taxation and excise duties on petroleum, diesel and aviation kerosene. Nevertheless, EU laws and framework laws are not to affect a member state's right to 'determine the conditions for exploiting its energy resources, its choices between different energy sources and the general structure of its energy supply'. The outcome is a decent compromise between the nationalistic imperative of the House of Commons in respect of the North Sea and the desire of the whole EU, not apparently excluding the UK government, to liberalise the energy supply markets of Europe.

EURATOM

The European Atomic Energy Community Treaty (1957) is the only one of the EU's historic treaties that has not been swept up inside the new Constitution. Its function has been to regulate at the supranational level the use of nuclear fuel for civilian purposes. Given the essentially controversial nature of nuclear power but also because of lack of time, the Convention was unable to reach consensus on whether to repeal, assimilate or amend the Euratom Treaty. In the end the original Treaty was brought into line with the structure and terminology of the Constitution but left as a free-standing statute with full legal effect. A Protocol binds the Euratom Treaty to the Constitution.[41] It is left to a future version of the Constitution to complete the process, repeal the Euratom Treaty and add an appropriate chapter on nuclear energy in the category of shared competence. Austria, Germany and Ireland have already declared their preference for an early IGC to substantially amend the Euratom Treaty.[42]

THE COMPLEMENTARY POLICIES

The seven policy areas where the Union may take co-ordinating, complementary or supporting action, set out in Article 17, are also accorded more detailed treatment in Part Three. EU legislation in this category excludes any harmonisation of national laws. The 'open method of co-ordination' is much in evidence.

[41] Protocol No. 36 on Euratom.
[42] Declaration No. 44 by Germany, Ireland and Austria.

The most controversial of the policies is public health because of the decision of the Convention to widen EU competence in relation to communicable diseases and bio-terrorism with serious cross border effects. There is also current controversy concerning the appropriate legal base for EU legislation on banning of advertising on tobacco, the extent to which public health concerns should impinge on fiscal policy for tobacco and alcohol, EU restrictions on the sale of health food supplements, and, finally, the implications for national public health services of the EU's attempt to liberalise the markets in services. The Constitution provides that action by the Union shall complement national policies in three specific areas: the fight against major health scourges, by promoting research into their causes, their transmission and their prevention, as well as health information and education; monitoring, early warning of and combating serious cross-border threats to health; and reduction of drug-related health damage, including information and prevention. EU legislation, on the other hand, shall be permissible in order to meet 'common safety concerns' by setting high standards for the trade in medicine, human organs and blood, for measures in the veterinary and phytosanitary fields, and measures concerning monitoring, early warning of and combating serious cross-border threats to health. Laws will also be used to establish incentive measures to combat major cross border health scourges, including protection against tobacco and alcohol abuse.[43]

In addition to legislation, emphasis is put on the need for member states to improve co-ordination between their health services by establishing guidelines and indicators, the exchange of best practice and periodic monitoring and evaluation. Contrary to scare stories in the Westminster parliament and British media, the Constitution does not deprive the UK government or the British Medical Association of their responsibilities in running the National Health Service.

Similar provision for the 'open method of co-ordination' is applied to the other policy sectors in this category, including industry, where the Union's policy objectives are to raise competitiveness by speeding up structural reform and to better exploit the potential of research and innovation.[44] The ordinary legislative procedure replaces unanimity in the Council for laws in respect of cultural policy, where the main goal of EU action is to improve knowledge of European history, to conserve Europe's cultural heritage and to foster artistic and literary creation.[45] The objectives of the new EU policy on tourism are to encourage 'a favourable environment' for the sector and to exchange good

---

[43] Article III–278.
[44] Article III–279.
[45] Article III–280.5.

practice between member states.[46] In the field of education, youth, sport and vocational training policy, the main change to the present Treaty is to encourage youthful participation in the democratic life of the Union.[47] The priorities remain the development of the European dimension in education, particularly through language teaching, and the encouragement of teacher and student mobility. Sport gets a higher profile in the Constitution. In the field of vocational training, the priority is to facilitate the adaptation of the workforce to industrial change.

A new article provides for civil protection in the wake of natural or man-made disasters within the Union as well as 'promoting consistency' in international civil protection.[48] The clause provides the legal base necessary for the operations of the civilian arm of the European security and defence.

Finally, provision is made for administrative co-operation to ensure the more effective implementation of EU law. The Union may support the exchange and training of national civil servants. Out of respect for British sensibilities, the article adds that 'no Member State shall be obliged to avail itself of such support'.[49]

---

[46] Article III–281.
[47] Article III–282.1(e).
[48] Article III–284.
[49] Article III–285.

CHAPTER 18

The Union's external action

We have examined in chapter 13 the main features of the Union's common foreign, security and defence policy, as well as the main institutional innovation, namely the creation of the EU Foreign Minister. Here we look at other aspects of the Union's international relations, including its commercial policy, as well as elaborating on the institutional procedures. In Part Three, Article 292 sets the scene comprehensively, as follows:

> 1. The Union's action on the international scene shall be guided by the principles which have inspired its own creation, development and enlargement, and which it seeks to advance in the wider world: democracy, the rule of law, the universality and indivisibility of human rights and fundamental freedoms, respect for human dignity, the principles of equality and solidarity, and respect for the principles of the United Nations Charter and international law.
> The Union shall seek to develop relations and build partnerships with third countries, and international, regional or global organisations which share the principles referred to in the first subparagraph. It shall promote multilateral solutions to common problems, in particular in the framework of the United Nations.
> 2. The Union shall define and pursue common policies and actions, and shall work for a high degree of co-operation in all fields of international relations, in order to:
> (a) safeguard its values, fundamental interests, security, independence and integrity;
> (b) consolidate and support democracy, the rule of law, human rights and the principles of international law;
> (c) preserve peace, prevent conflicts and strengthen international security, in accordance with the purposes and principles of the United Nations Charter, with the principles of the Helsinki Final Act and with the aims of the Charter of Paris, including those relating to external borders;

(d) foster the sustainable economic, social and environmental development of developing countries, with the primary aim of eradicating poverty;

(e) encourage the integration of all countries into the world economy, including through the progressive abolition of restrictions on international trade;

(f) help develop international measures to preserve and improve the quality of the environment and the sustainable management of global natural resources, in order to ensure sustainable development;

(g) assist populations, countries and regions confronting natural or man-made disasters;

(h) promote an international system based on stronger multilateral co-operation and good global governance.

3. The Union shall respect the principles and pursue the objectives set out in paragraphs 1 and 2 in the development and implementation of the different areas of the Union's external action covered by this Title and the external aspects of its other policies.

The Union shall ensure consistency between the different areas of its external action and between these and its other policies. The Council and the Commission, assisted by the Union Minister for Foreign Affairs, shall ensure that consistency and shall co-operate to that effect.

The projection of Europe's values on the world stage, which is prescribed here by the Constitution, is an unprecedented scale of ambition for the Union. The emphasis on multilateral solutions to global problems, including climate change, and its commitment to the United Nations, was a self-conscious attempt by the Convention to distinguish the EU's international stance from that of the USA at a time of excruciating tension in transatlantic relations.

POWERS OF THE FOREIGN MINISTER

The exact role of the European Council, and of the Union Minister for Foreign Affairs, is spelt out. The European Council will 'identify the strategic interests and objectives' of the Union, and decide, by unanimity, on the duration of any policy and about the means to be made available by the Union and the member states.[1] The Minister will submit proposals to the European Council. Emphasis is put on the need to ensure consistency between the work of Council and Commission. The Minister, with his mandate from the Council in terms of foreign and security policy, and his mandate from the Commission in terms of

[1] Article III–293.

other external action, will be bound to make, where possible and appropriate, joint proposals. The Constitution empowers him to ensure that the constitutional principles of loyalty and mutual solidarity are complied with. He will chair the Foreign Affairs Council and 'conduct political dialogue with third parties on the Union's behalf and shall express the Union's position in international organisations and at international conferences'.[2] The Minister or his representative will also chair the Political and Security Committee, with its important crisis management functions, set up within the Council.[3] The Foreign Minister and the EU's special representatives appointed to conduct certain missions on behalf of the Union will appear regularly before Parliament.[4]

It will be for the Council to take European decisions to implement common foreign and security policies. Member states will keep the Council informed about how they are contributing to the implementation of common policy, and they will consult their partners about new national initiatives. 'Member States shall ensure that their national policies conform to the positions of the Union.'[5] Council decisions will be taken unanimously, but, as we have already noted, unanimity is softened by the possibility of a reasoned abstention.[6] However, if one-third of member states representing one third of the population declare their abstention, the otherwise 'unanimous' decision will be blocked. Therefore, what might start out as a constructive abstention by one or two member states becomes a destructive abstention once joined by nine.

More usefully, there are four instances where real QMV is permitted in the field of common foreign and security policy, as follows:

- when the Council adopts decisions on the basis of a strategic decision of the European Council;
- when the Council adopts a decision proposed by the Foreign Minister under a mandate from the European Council either at his instigation or theirs;
- when implementing a decision defining a Union action or position;
- when appointing a special representative.[7]

As the Foreign Minister is empowered to make proposals to the European Council, the flexibility of the decision-making arrangements is really rather large, and the potential scope of QMV broad – in spite of the fact that decisions in the military or defence field are excluded. To prevent too wide a use of QMV, the British insisted on the insertion of the back-stop provision whereby any

[2] Article III–296.
[3] Article III–307.
[4] Article III–304.
[5] Article III–298.
[6] Article III–300.1.
[7] Article III–300.2.

one member state will be able to refer the whole issue to the European Council for a unanimous decision. Article 300 also includes the *passerelle* clause, prefigured in Article 40.7, which enables the European Council to widen further the scope of QMV.

The horizontal co-ordination of activities within the Council is to be underpinned by co-operation among the diplomatic missions of the member states and of the Union in third countries and within international organisations. The Union is to have 'all appropriate forms of co-operation' with the United Nations, the Council of Europe, the OSCE and OECD.[8] The Foreign Minister will be in charge of these relations, and will supervise the work of the Union's delegations in third countries, which will act in close co-operation with member states' own missions. As far as the UN Security Council is concerned, the Constitution stipulates:

> Member States which are also members of the United Nations Security Council shall concert and keep the other Member States and the Union Minister for Foreign Affairs fully informed. Member States which are members of the Security Council will, in the execution of their functions, defend the positions and the interests of the Union, without prejudice to their responsibilities under the United Nations Charter. When the Union has defined a position on a subject which is on the United Nations Security Council agenda, those Member States which sit on the Security Council shall request that the Union Minister for Foreign Affairs be asked to present the Union's position.[9]

The UK government, along with its French counterpart a Permanent Member of the Security Council, found this last a difficult constraint to swallow. It was also wary of the proposal to establish a European external action service to assist the Minister to fulfil his mandate, as follows:

> This service shall work in co-operation with the diplomatic services of the Member States and shall comprise officials from relevant departments of the General Secretariat of the Council and of the Commission as well as staff seconded from national diplomatic services of the Member States. The organisation and functioning of the European External Action Service shall be established by a European decision of the Council. The Council shall act on a proposal from the Union Minister for Foreign Affairs after consulting the European Parliament and after obtaining the consent of the Commission.[10]

[8] Article III–327.
[9] Article III–305.2.
[10] Article III–296.3.

The creation of this joint civil service, drawing expertise and resources both from the member states and the Commission, is of great significance. The European external action service – in all but name, the EU foreign ministry – is expected to pool intelligence, develop joint analysis and planning capabilities, and speak and act for the Union with a single voice. The inventive discovery of the single voice, in turn, should oblige the EU at a political level to make up its mind about what it wishes to say. The functional effect of the external action service working on the ground in third countries should quickly percolate back up to Brussels and force the Council and Commission together to articulate a consistent and coherent common policy. If the external action service becomes a proven success, the quality and force of European foreign and security policy will have crossed a new threshold of functional integration. For third countries and for international organisations of which the EU becomes a member, the conduct of relations with the EU will become much simpler and more straightforward. In accordance with a decision of the IGC, and in recognition of the complexity of the work involved in establishing the new joint administration, preparatory work to set up the external action service began immediately after the signing of the Constitution in the autumn of 2004.[11] The Commission is understandably anxious to protect its prerogatives in the field of external relations of the Union. The European Parliament is likewise jealous of its constitutional authority over spending from the EU budget on overseas policies and on the administrative costs of common foreign and security policy. The foreign ministries, especially of the larger member states, are not expected to surrender their traditional status or functions to the new administration without the most careful reflection. (The British foreign secretary appears to hate even the terminology, let alone the concept.) However, by the time the new Foreign Minister gets in to work – before the French and Dutch Noes, one had hoped on schedule on Wednesday 1 November 2006 – the Union should have set up the joint external action service in a way that protects the prerogatives of the Commission and Parliament, engages national diplomacies and provides the Minister with the resources, intelligence and instruments he will need to function well.

The financing of the security and defence policy is fairly, and indeed unnecessarily complicated. The administrative expenditure of the institutions, mainly the costs of running the Foreign Minister, the Political and Security Committee and the external action service, are charged to the EU budget. Operational expenditure for the tasks named in Article 309 is seen as a call on the EU budget with the exception of military matters, in which case the

---

[11]   Declaration No. 24 on Article III–296.

Council is to allocate costs on a case by case basis according to a member state's GNI. Member states who abstain from a decision will not be liable to pay for its consequences. The Council will establish procedures, after consulting the Parliament, for appropriations to be made rapidly from the EU budget. National contributions will finance a start-up fund, to be established by the Council acting by QMV, to pay for the early phase of activities not charged to the EU budget.[12]

INTERNATIONAL POLICIES

The basis of the Union's common commercial policy is its customs union, established by the Treaty of Rome. The Constitution adds the liberalisation of foreign direct investment to the goals of the Union, thus: 'The Union shall contribute, in the common interest, to the harmonious development of world trade, the progressive abolition of restrictions on international trade and on foreign direct investment, and the lowering of customs and other barriers'.[13] The Constitution also adds trade in services, intellectual property rights, and foreign direct investment to the exclusive competence of the commercial policy. The ordinary legislative procedure defines the framework of the common commercial policy.

For international trade agreements, the Council authorises the Commission to open negotiations on the basis of the Commission's recommendations. The Commission is assisted by a special committee made up of national representatives appointed by the Council. The Commission reports to the committee and to Parliament. Council acts by QMV to open and close the negotiations – except in the field of trade in services, intellectual property and foreign direct investment where it acts unanimously if the Union's internal rules require it to do so. At the insistence mainly of France (worried about French), the IGC agreed that Council will also act by unanimity in relation to trade in cultural and audio-visual services where the agreements 'risk prejudicing the Union's cultural and linguistic diversity', and in the case of trade in social, education and health services where the agreements 'risk seriously disturbing the national organisation of such services and prejudicing the responsibility of Member States to deliver them'.[14] The Constitution was not, then, as alleged by the French left or boasted by Jack Straw as *britannique* as it seemed.

The practice for trade negotiations under the Constitution is more or less

12 Article III–313.
13 Article III–314.
14 Article III–315.

the same for other international treaties, which is laid out in Article 325. For foreign and security policy negotiations, the Foreign Minister can submit recommendations to the Council for the opening of the proceedings. The Council shall nominate him or the Commission to carry out the negotiating mandate. Council can only conclude agreements after obtaining the consent of Parliament in the following cases: association agreements; accession to the ECHR; agreements establishing a specific institutional framework by organising co-operation procedures; agreements with important budgetary implications for the Union; agreements covering fields to which either the ordinary legislative procedure applies, or the special legislative procedure where consent by Parliament is required. In other cases, Parliament will be consulted, often within a set time-limit, but the package – which was difficult for the Convention to arrive at – represents a very considerable enhancement of the Parliament's powers not only over the exclusive competence of commercial policy but also in the less charted waters of freedom, security and justice. MEPs would be expected to police their new prerogatives with some attention. Under the current Treaties, Parliament has the right of assent only over association agreements or those with important budgetary implications.[15]

The Council acts by QMV throughout this process except when concluding association agreements or technical co-operation agreements with candidate countries, or 'when the agreement covers a field for which unanimity is required for the adoption of a Union act'.[16] The Commission's mandate can be varied, or an international agreement suspended at any stage. A member state or any of the institutions may obtain an opinion of the Court of Justice about the compatibility of the agreement with the Constitution. Special arrangements are provided for international agreements concerning the exchange rate of the euro.[17]

The primary purpose of the Union's development co-operation policy is the 'reduction and, in the long term, the eradication of poverty'.[18] The policy is implemented according to European law or framework laws. For the first time, the budget of the European Development Fund is incorporated into the general EU budget, thereby further extending European Parliamentary control. The Commission can take initiatives to ensure the close co-ordination of EU policy with national policies and aid programmes. Similar EU legislation governs economic, financial and technical co-operation with third countries and the EU's disaster relief work. The Union's humanitarian aid operations are to be

[15] Article 300.3 TEC.
[16] Article III–325.8.
[17] Article III–326.
[18] Article III–316.

conducted 'in compliance with the principles of international law and with the principles of impartiality, neutrality and non-discrimination'.[19] The Constitution provides for the setting up of a new Voluntary Humanitarian Aid Corps for young Europeans.

Provision is made for the imposition of economic and financial sanctions against one or more third countries, natural or legal persons or 'non-State entities', like al'Qaeda.[20] The Council shall act by QMV on a joint proposal of Foreign Minister and Commission. Parliament will be informed.

Lastly, arrangements are made for the implementation of the new solidarity clause (Article 43) which allows a member state to call the Union in aid in the event of a terrorist attack or a natural or man-made disaster. 'The European Council shall regularly assess the threats facing the Union in order to enable the Union and its Member States to take effective action.'[21] Let us hope it does.

Complicated as all these institutional arrangements may seem, the Constitution provides mechanisms for bringing the international profile of the European Union into much sharper perspective. For the rest of the world, Europe will be easier to deal with if and when the proposals of the Constitution are implemented. Everyone will benefit from the focus brought by the Constitution to defining the Union's objectives in foreign, security and defence policy as well as in commercial policy and overseas aid and development. The Constitution is a basis for changing the dynamics of European defence by giving the Union the wherewithal to develop an autonomous military capability if it chooses to do so. Long-standing French goals with respect to European autonomy are, therefore, accomplished by the Constitution.

On the institutional front, the Constitution allows the European Parliament to become more prominent in helping to fashion and to monitor the Union's international policies. The new instrument of the double-hatted Foreign Minister, running his own joint administration, is a remarkable conception. Javier Solana, if he is confirmed in the new post, will be a powerful man. Much will depend on his ability to suppress old jealousies and divisions between Commission, Council and European Council as well as among the national diplomacies of the member states. If the Constitution and Solana succeed, Europe will have the capacity to act on the world stage. Europeans will have found their global voice, and will have something important to say.

---

[19] Article III–321.2.
[20] Article III–322.
[21] Article III–329.

CHAPTER 19

The evolving Constitution

The Constitution closes with a Part Four (Articles 437 to 448) which comprises some important general and final provisions. First of all, it is laid down that this Treaty establishing a Constitution for Europe has the effect of repealing all the earlier EU Treaties except Euratom – that is, the Treaty establishing the European Community, the Treaty on European Union, the Treaties of Amsterdam and Nice, and the five Accession Treaties.[1] In order to ensure legal continuity, it is asserted that the European Union established by this Constitutional Treaty is the successor of the European Union established by the Treaty of Maastricht and to the European Community established by the Treaty of Rome.[2] The acquis communautaire is retained. The jurisprudence of the Court remains the source of interpretation of Union law. Article 446 provides that the Constitution is established for an unlimited period.

The Constitution applies to all twenty-five member states, and to the French territories of Guadeloupe, French Guiana, Martinique, Réunion, to the Azores and Madeira (Portugal), to the Canary Islands (Spain), and to Gibraltar (UK).[3] It also applies in full to a large number of autonomous overseas places, mostly Caribbean, Atlantic or Pacific island colonies belonging to France, the Netherlands or the UK, but also including Greenland, an autonomous Danish colony.[4] The Constitution establishes special status, and partial application, to the Åland Islands (Sweden), to the Channel Islands and the Isle of Man (UK), and to the UK sovereign bases on Cyprus. The Faeroe Islands escape.

The regional union of Benelux is recognised.[5] The Convention discussed whether to permit or even encourage comparable regional unions to be formed elsewhere, for instance in the Baltic, but rejected the idea in favour of mainstream enhanced co-operation.

---

[1] Article IV–437.
[2] Article IV–438.
[3] Article IV–440 and Declaration No. 45 by Spain and the UK.
[4] These places are set out in full in Annex II of the Constitution.
[5] Article IV–441.

The final clause, Article 448, establishes that each of the twenty-one language texts is equally authentic. The question of the language regime had hovered around the Convention, not least because of the novelty (and the difficulty) of providing comprehensive simultaneous interpretation in the languages of Eastern Europe. Whereas the official languages of the Union are twenty one, including little used Irish and Maltese, the use of a smaller number of working languages is becoming normal practice within the institutions themselves.[6] The position of certain 'minority' languages, such as Basque, Catalan and Welsh, is disadvantaged. Moreover, the Republic of Cyprus has not seen fit to elevate Turkish into an official language of the Union. The principle of democratic equality will be offended if every EU citizen cannot address the institutions in his or her mother tongue.[7] A future reform of the language regime will be certainly required in order to conform with the Constitution's imperatives to respect minority rights and linguistic diversity and, in the Charter, non-discrimination on the grounds of language.[8] In recognition of this, the Constitution permits for other language versions of the Constitution to be made in response from requests by member states for authentic translations into languages that 'enjoy official status in all or part of their territory'.[9]

SIMPLIFIED REVISION PROCEDURES

Part Four offers three revision procedures: one concerning decision-making procedures, one concerning policy changes, and the third concerning amendment of the Constitution itself. All three contain a significant new role for the European Parliament. Many in the Convention, including apparently the French government, would have preferred to have been more radical; some, notably the British, less so.

The lightest revision procedure is already quite famous. The general *passerelle* or bridging clause first appeared as Article I–24.4 in the Convention's early drafts of the Constitution, and stimulated much argument. Its purpose is to allow, without the paraphernalia of an IGC, a gradual extension of QMV where unanimity is still required by the Constitution and a steady erosion of the remaining abnormal 'Council laws'. It is a major and welcome constitutional innovation. In its final version it is as follows:

---

[6] The use of Irish is reserved only for statutory purposes. The use of Maltese as a working language, requested by Malta during the accession negotiations, is hampered by the inability of the institutions to recruit Maltese interpreters.

[7] Article I–45.

[8] Articles I–2, I–3 and II–81, respectively.

[9] Article IV–448.2 and Declaration No. 29.

Article 444

Simplified revision procedure

1. Where Part III provides for the Council to act by unanimity in a given area or case, the European Council may adopt a European decision authorising the Council to act by a qualified majority in that area or in that case.

This paragraph shall not apply to decisions with military implications or those in the area of defence.

2. Where Part III provides for European laws and framework laws to be adopted by the Council in accordance with a special legislative procedure, the European Council may adopt a European decision allowing for the adoption of such European laws or framework laws in accordance with the ordinary legislative procedure.

3. Any initiative taken by the European Council on the basis of paragraphs 1 or 2 shall be notified to the national Parliaments. If a national Parliament makes known its opposition within six months of the date of such notification, the European decision referred to in paragraphs 1 or 2 shall not be adopted. In the absence of opposition, the European Council may adopt the decision.

For the adoption of the European decisions referred to in paragraphs 1 and 2, the European Council shall act by unanimity after obtaining the consent of the European Parliament, which shall be given by a majority of its component members.

Despite the fact that the *passerelle* cannot be crossed without the unanimous agreement of the heads of government, the UK insisted at the IGC on inserting the additional proviso of a veto by any one of twenty-five national parliaments. This might be thought to be an over-cautious stipulation. The insertion of a veto power to a single national parliament contrasts with the requirement in the subsidiarity Protocol that one third of national parliaments is needed to raise an objection. However, as we have noted, in order to overcome British antipathy to the general *passerelle* clause, certain sector-specific *passerelle* clauses have been included in strategic places to allow for the deployment of the same procedure but minus the reference back to national parliaments.

The second simplified revision procedure, as laid down in Article 445, is confined to Title III of Part Three concerning the internal policies of the Union in cases where competences are not shifted from member states to the Union level.[10] In this case, any member state, Commission or Parliament may submit

---

[10]   Articles III–130 to 285.

to the European Council proposals to amend an internal policy or action of the Union relating to the single market, economic and monetary policy, the area of freedom, security and justice, or any of the common policies where the EU enjoys shared or complementary competence. The European Council will decide on these amendments, acting by unanimity, after consulting the Parliament, the Commission and, where appropriate, the European Central Bank. Although this is a welcome, streamlined procedure compared to that of calling an Intergovernmental Conference to affect even minor changes to a common policy, such amendments will still need to be ratified by all member states according to their own constitutional requirements before entering into force. In some cases, national ratification may mean the holding of a referendum, which seems unnecessarily burdensome and hardly fast-track.

The significance of Article 445 should not be missed, however. In creating a softer mechanism for the revision of these common policies (where an increase in competences is not involved), the Convention and the IGC were effectively establishing a hierarchy between different parts of the Constitution. It is clearly not true, as was alleged in the French referendum campaign, that the Constitution concretised the present state of the Union for all time. In fact, it was intended to make it easier to amend the Constitution in certain important respects than it is now to amend the existing treaties in any respect whatsoever. Perhaps more should have been made of this point by the Yes campaigners. Any renegotiation of the Constitution could seek both to widen the scope of the simplified procedures and to make them more visible.[11]

THE CONVENTION HERE TO STAY

The third type of revision procedure relates to the more constitutional elements of the Constitution, including the whole of Part One, Part Two (the Charter), the remaining chapters of Part Three (citizenship, external action, the institutions, financial system and enhanced cooperation), and, of course, Part Four. Based firmly on Article 48 of the current Treaty on European Union, the 'ordinary revision procedure' is the heaviest of all.

Article 443 is noteworthy for at least three reasons. First, it would institutionalise the Convention as the normal way of drafting constitutional amendments prior to the holding of an IGC. The European Parliament had to fight hard to obtain for itself the right to confirm a decision of the European

---

[11] It is interesting to recall that Article 95 of the Treaty of Paris (1952) establishing the Coal and Steel Community allowed for minor treaty changes to be made if they secured, following a favourable opinion from the Court of Justice, a majority of three-quarters of the votes cast in the Parliament representing two-thirds of Members.

Council not to hold a Convention. Second, in another significant leap forward for MEPs, Parliament is included alongside the Commission and a member state as being able to initiate any constitutional amendment. The fact that MEPs will be able to trigger a revision of the Constitution would bring to an end the exclusively intergovernmental character of the Union's constituent process. Parliament's right of initiative coupled with the formal installation of the Convention into the Constitution is recognition, if one were needed, of the Parliament's new-found maturity as a constitutional player. And third, the new provisions admit that there might one day be a problem in accomplishing a smooth ratification of any constitutional amendment. It may be conceded that the proposal made for such a contingency – an emergency meeting of the European Council – is not a very radical constitutional step, but its implication is rather clear: no one member state (nor even a minority of one fifth of the member states) should have an automatic or absolute right to block the constitutional progress desired by the majority. The clause is as follows:

Article 443

Ordinary revision procedure

1. The government of any Member State, the European Parliament or the Commission may submit to the Council proposals for the amendment of this Treaty. These proposals shall be submitted to the European Council by the Council and the national Parliaments shall be notified.

2. If the European Council, after consulting the European Parliament and the Commission, adopts by a simple majority a decision in favour of examining the proposed amendments, the President of the European Council shall convene a Convention composed of representatives of the national Parliaments, of the Heads of State or Government of the Member States, of the European Parliament and of the Commission. The European Central Bank shall also be consulted in the case of institutional changes in the monetary area. The Convention shall examine the proposals for amendments and shall adopt by consensus a recommendation to a conference of representatives of the governments of the Member States as provided for in paragraph 3.

The European Council may decide by a simple majority, after obtaining the consent of the European Parliament, not to convene a Convention should this not be justified by the extent of the proposed amendments. In the latter case, the European Council shall define the terms of reference for a conference of representatives of the governments of the Member States.

3. A conference of representatives of the governments of the Member States shall be convened by the President of the Council for the purpose of determining by common accord the amendments to be made to this Treaty. The amendments shall enter into force after being ratified by all the Member States in accordance with their respective constitutional requirements.

4. If, two years after the signature of the treaty amending this Treaty, four fifths of the Member States have ratified it and one or more Member States have encountered difficulties in proceeding with ratification, the matter shall be referred to the European Council.

The stipulation that the European Council is to decide by simple majority to open the revision process is a useful clarification, and removes ambiguity. (Margaret Thatcher had been thwarted by her inability to veto the decisions of the European Council in Milan in 1984 and in Dublin in 1990 to open Intergovernmental Conferences.)

As in the present circumstances, future Conventions would prepare but not replace the Intergovernmental Conference. IGCs would still be subject to unanimity and their outcome still subjected to ratification according to respective constitutional requirements in all member states before entering into force. No attempt is made by the Constitution to rationalise national ratification procedures, which, as one would expect, differ enormously. In some countries a referendum is obligatory; in others it is prohibited. Some have merely advisory plebiscites; others have polls which bind the government and parliament. Some countries allow public funding of a referendum campaign, others do not. As far as parliamentary procedures are concerned, some manage with an affirmative vote by simple majority in a single chamber; others have to achieve high majority thresholds in two chambers. Belgium is the most complicated country of all: ratification of the EU Constitution requires a federal law, decrees from the regions of Flanders and Wallonia, a statutory order from the region of Brussels, decrees from the Flemish, French and German speaking communities, and an order from the joint language communities.

Neither the existing Treaty nor the Constitution provides for a final vote of consent by the European Parliament. Those who have worked to advance the constitutional role of the Parliament may regret the continuing lack of a European-level ratification procedure. MEPs could be expected to seek to rectify this omission in any renegotiation of the Constitution. Others would wish to press their previous demands for an EU-wide referendum to be held, on the same day, to assert the popular will of the European citizen on all future constitutional evolution.

CHAPTER 20

Encountering difficulties

Since the Constitution was signed on 29 October 2004, its signatory states have had a duty to refrain from acts which would defeat its object and purpose.[1] They are honour bound to use their best endeavours to bring the Constitution into force, notwithstanding that they recognised that ratification might not be plain sailing. Copying the provision that the Convention had made for the Constitution in so far as future revisions were concerned, the IGC also laid out a contingency plan for an emergency meeting of the European Council if the ratification were to be blocked by as many as five member states.[2] Declaration No. 30 stipulates that if, two years after the signature of the Constitution – that is 30 October 2006 – four fifths of the member states have ratified it and 'one or more Member States have encountered difficulties in proceeding with ratification, the matter will be referred to the European Council'. Needless to add, the difficulties which the heads of government expected they might encounter did not embrace the rejection of the Constitution by two founding member states of the Union, but by more recent, and even peripheral members. Nevertheless, the addition of Declaration No. 30 implies that, because all member states are equal under the constitutional law of the Union, all member states are expected to proceed with ratification come what may. The theory is that an upset in any one country will not be allowed to halt the collective effort to try to bring the Constitution into force – unless, of course, as many as six states falter and the threshold of four fifths needed to trigger the crisis meeting of the European Council cannot therefore be reached.

First of the twenty five to complete was the Lithuanian parliament which took everyone by surprise, including Lithuania, by ratifying the Constitution in one afternoon, on 11 November 2004 by 84 votes to 4 with 3 abstentions. The Hungarian parliament followed suit on 20 December by 322 votes to 12 with 8 abstentions. In Slovenia, on 1 February 2005, MPs voted 79 for the

---

[1] Article 18 of the Vienna Convention on the Law of Treaties.
[2] Article IV–443.4.

Constitution with 4 against and 7 abstentions. The first referendum was held in Spain on 20 February. 76.7 per cent voted Yes and only 17.2 per cent No on a turnout of 42.3 per cent, only slightly lower than that achieved at the European Parliamentary elections the previous June. The Italian Senate completed the ratification process for Italy on 6 April, with a vote of 217 against 16; earlier, on 25 January, the Camera dei Deputati had voted in favour by 436 to 28, with 5 abstentions. On 19 April, the Greek parliament backed the Constitution by 268 votes to 17, with 15 abstentions. On 11 May only one Austrian MP voted against, with 182 in favour; on 25 May the Austrian upper house voted 59 to 3 for the Constitution. Also on 11 May Slovakian MPs endorsed the Constitution by 116 votes to 27 with 4 abstentions, although the finalisation of the process is held up by a challenge from a referendum zealot in Slovakia's constitutional court. The Belgian federal parliament backed the Constitution by 118 votes to 18 with 1 abstention on 19 May: the complicated ratification process continues in Belgium and was expected to be completed shortly. The German Bundestag voted on 12 May: 568 deputies were in favour, 23 against and 2 abstained; the Bundesrat completed the process on 27 May by 66 to 3.

It should not be overlooked that the European Parliament, on 12 January, also voted by 500 to 137 with 40 abstentions to endorse the Constitution. Although the Parliament has no formal power of assent over treaty change, the expression of support by over two-thirds of MEPs was more than symbolic. For the first time the European Parliament did not qualify its acceptance of the results of an IGC by stating a long litany of regrets and objections, along with a large catalogue of demands for further reform. Instead MEPs resolved that 'this Constitution will provide a stable and lasting framework for the future development of the European Union that will allow for further enlargement while providing mechanisms for its revision when needed'.[3]

By the time the French voted, on 29 May 2005, therefore, the Constitution had already been backed by ten national parliaments and the European Parliament. France begged to differ. On a turnout of 69.3 per cent, 54.9 per cent voted No and only 45.1 per cent Yes. Not to be out done, the result of the Dutch referendum on 1 June was 61.6 per cent No, 38.4 per cent Yes, on a turnout of 62.8 per cent.

On the following day, undaunted by the French and Dutch, the Latvian parliament endorsed the Constitution by 71 to 5 votes with 6 abstentions. The Cyprus parliament went on to approve the Constitution on 30 June by 30 votes

---

[3] European Parliament Resolution (Corbett-Mendez de Vigo Report) on the Treaty establishing a Constitution for Europe, 12 January 2005, TA(2005)0004.

to 19 with 1 abstention. Malta's 65 MPs unanimously backed the Constitution on 6 July. And on 10 July, in a referendum critical to the political survival of prime minister Juncker, Luxembourg voted 56.5 per cent Yes to 43.5 per cent No, on a turnout of 87 per cent.

At the time of writing, therefore, fourteen states have effectively ratified the Constitution, and two have rejected it. The Union is still some way short of the four-fifths majority posited in Declaration No. 30. On the day after the French referendum, even before the Dutch had voted, foreign minister Jack Straw leapt to suspend the promised referendum in Britain. Since then, the Czechs, Danish, Irish, Polish and Portuguese have followed suit. The Finns and Swedes have postponed their parliamentary ratification procedures. Only the Estonians, who have also chosen the parliamentary route, apparently intend to keep going.

THE REFERENDUM TRAP

The EU's treaty revision process has already been halted twice by negative referendum decisions in Denmark (1992) and Ireland (2001). Other referendums, such as the French *petit oui* over Maastricht (1992), or votes on accession in Sweden (1994) and Malta (2003), have had narrow results. Referendums in both Denmark (2000) and Sweden (2003) have rejected the euro. And one does not forget that Norwegians twice rejected EU membership in referendums in 1972 and 1994.

Given those precedents, it may seem bizarre that Spain, France, Luxembourg, Portugal, Poland, the Czech Republic, the Netherlands and the UK opted to hold referendums even when they are not constitutionally bound to do so. There seem to have been a variety of reasons, mainly short-term expediency, why governments in those countries chose the referendum as the instrument of ratification: to overcome parliamentary opposition; to disguise divisions between or within the political parties in coalition governments; to deal a blow to an opposition party; and – as was the case with Blair's conversion to a referendum, announced on 20 April 2004 – to strengthen the government's negotiating position in the final stages of the IGC. Few referendums have been chosen in order to enhance the popular legitimacy of the Constitution itself: in fact, only the referendum in Luxembourg seems to fall into that altruistic category.

There are, of course, arguments in favour of referendums as well as against them. Political expediency is a good thing if it works in favour of a worthy project. And referendums can invoke a broad, if crude expression of public sentiment about Europe. They are a dramatic way of giving popular legitimacy to or withholding it from the European Union. In spite of the fact that the referendums are organised nationally (sometimes jealously so), and were planned to stretch out over a period of eighteen months, the campaigns could not be isolated from each other. The transnational European political parties, led by MEPs, were getting involved. A number of party and government leaders were making guest appearances in ratification campaigns in countries other than their own. Chirac campaigned alongside Zapatero in Spain, for example, and Joschka Fischer was active in the French campaign. Accordingly, the media was reporting intensively about the ratification process EU wide. It was also reporting critically, so that discordant or downright contradictory statements made about the Constitution by national leaders were picked up. Even at the time of the Spanish poll, there had begun to be a nervous anticipation about the cross-fertilisation of the politics of one member state with others, and a dawning realisation that the series of referendums might be inducing an unprecedented European dimension to political citizenship. In this sense, the referendums can be seen as a popularised extension of the élite experience of the Convention: Europe's constitutional moment prolonged and broadened.

There are also a number of weighty arguments against having referendums. Referendums on constitutions are particularly fraught because they tend to provoke simplistic answers to what are inherently complicated questions, or, worse, answers not to the difficult constitutional question at all but to other questions that interest the voters more. Referendums on European constitutions are even more esoteric, and the undeniable virtues of the EU's Constitution offered only limited insurance against a vote of dissent against something entirely domestic. The evidence is that very few of those who voted in France or the Netherlands had actually read the Constitution, and some seemed to resent the imposition of this referendum by national governments and parliaments too spineless to take the tough European and constitutional decision for themselves. Widespread public indifference to the actuality of the Constitution only served to help the far left and far right to maximise their respective votes.

The cases of France and Holland are indeed rather dispiriting. The French campaign, though vigorous, was not particularly enlightening about the Constitution. Many French seemed to believe, not entirely fancifully, that a No vote would suddenly make France more important in the general scheme of things. When asked by Eurobarometer to explain why they had voted No, a large majority blamed the Constitution for having negative effects on jobs in France. Only 18 per cent said they voted No because they opposed the government of President Chirac, and only 6 per cent because of Turkish membership. Asked to give the main motivation behind their votes (Yes and No), 32 per cent gave their opinion about the EU in general, 32 per cent the economic and social situation in France, and only 18 per cent the Constitution itself. Three-quarters of those polled believe that the Constitution is or was vital to pursue European construction.[4]

Whereas most French voters felt themselves to have been well informed about the referendum issues, Dutch voters did not. Unsurprisingly, many Dutch made up their minds only after the French No two days previously. When asked to explain why they had voted No, 32 per cent said they lacked information, 19 per cent because of a loss of national sovereignty and 14 per cent because of their opposition to the government. 13 per cent blamed the EU for being too costly for the Netherlands. With regard to the main motivation of all voters, 31 per cent gave their opinion about the EU in general, 21 per cent the Dutch economic situation, and 18 per cent (like France) the Constitution itself. Only half of Dutch voters believe the Constitution is essential for Europe. While there are still vast majorities in both countries for continuing EU membership, the Netherlands appears to be distinctly more eurosceptic than France.[5] The Dutch seemed to enjoy their referendum much less than the French. Unused to referendums, perhaps the Dutch prefer the grey areas of parliamentary discourse to the primary colours of plebiscitary democracy. Certainly, the Dutch political leadership showed little skill in campaigning for Yes.

In the aftermath of the No votes, it is interesting that in both countries the reaction has almost been completely national, and European issues have dropped out of sight. Neither Chirac nor Balkenende can justly claim a clear mandate to change the direction of their EU policies. Neither of them is asking for the Constitution to be abandoned. Equally, neither of them is prepared to put the same question on the same Constitution to their electorates for a second time. Both have been much weakened by their referendum defeats.

If there is gridlock at home in France and the Netherlands, there is not much room for manoeuvre elsewhere. Following Juncker's hard-won victory, ratification appears to have been abandoned in most of the nine member states yet to declare themselves. The problem is particularly acute in the UK, where public opinion looks set to become even more hostile to the European project in general and to the Constitution in particular. In December 2004, Eurobarometer reported that, across the EU, 68 per cent were in favour of the Constitution, with 17 per cent against and 14 per cent uncertain. Denmark and the UK showed only minority support, however. In Britain, uniquely, the trend of public opinion was in the negative direction.

[4] Flash Eurobarometer, 30–31 May 2005, European Commission.
[5] Flash Eurobarometer, 2–4 June 2005, European Commission.

THE CONSTITUTION AND PUBLIC OPINION

Eurobarometer has regularly polled public opinion on whether or not a constitution for the European Union is thought to be a good thing. Here are the results of the EU member states as a whole, and for France, Germany and the UK in particular.

YES

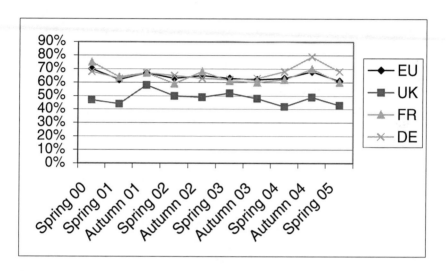

NO

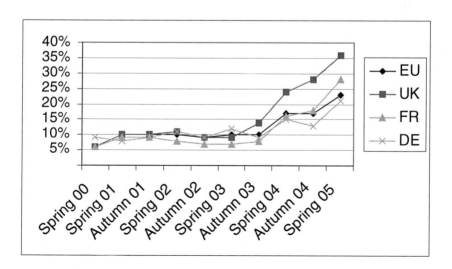

DON'T KNOW

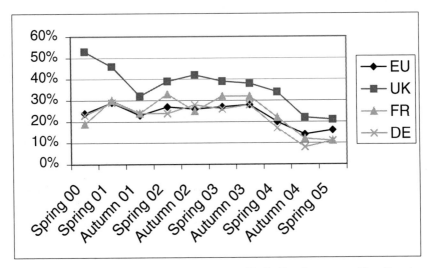

Source: Standard Eurobarometer Report, Nos 53-62; Eurobarometer First Results, No. 63.

Even had its twenty-four partner member states said Yes to the Constitution, it was far from clear that British public opinion could have been brought around to accepting it in a referendum that had been scheduled for the early summer of 2006. If the British people had said No, the UK government would have been able to wield its legal veto under Article 48 of the Treaty on European Union to block the Constitution for the rest of Europe. Some in Britain would undoubtedly have advocated this line of action. Many British, on the other hand, including prime minister Blair might well have asked themselves whether they had either the moral authority or the political credibility to veto the Constitution the rest of Europe wanted. That being the case, the UK would have found itself on the road out of full membership of the Union towards some fairly uncomfortable form of associate partnership. These considerations are not hypothetical because whatever happens next, it is still public opinion in Britain that will be the most difficult of all to persuade of the virtues of more European integration. In effect, it is not just France and the Netherlands that has found it impossible to ratify the Constitution, but Britain too. Any eventual settlement of the constitutional crisis will have to be able to satisfy a lot of people with some strikingly contrasting agendas for the future of the European Union.

PERIOD OF REFLECTION

Faced with gridlock, the European Council of 16–17 June 2005 decided on two simultaneous, but rather different, courses of action. First, in deference to those countries that had already ratified and to Jean-Claude Juncker's need to carry on with the referendum in Luxembourg on 10 July, member states which chose to do so were invited to carry on with ratification. The deadline for completion of the process was extended until mid-2007. Second, all member states were invited to mobilise a 'period of reflection' about the future of Europe involving citizens, civil society, social partners, national parliaments and political parties. The focus of the reflection would be the concerns and worries of the citizen as evinced in the referendum campaigns. The European Commission and Parliament are invited to make their contribution. The results of these national debates will be assessed by the European Council under the Austrian presidency in the first half of 2006.

The great debate should spawn reams of commentary on the state of European politics and some useful attention on the public relations policies of the EU institutions. The Commission intends a 'Plan D' – for democracy and dialogue. On past form, however, it would be all too predictable if this great public debate dwindled into nothing very much at all. The dilemma facing the Union is acute and the political will, to say nothing of the calibre of leadership, is not boundless. The debate badly needs direction and purpose. In order to provide a focus for the debate, the number of possible options will have to be narrowed down. As many as six scenarios are being canvassed of varying degrees of legality, desirability or probability, summarised as follows:

Scenario One: admit defeat

The Union abandons the Constitution and tries to make do with the Treaty of Nice, effectively saying farewell to further enlargement, the Charter, and all the promise of the Constitution in terms of improved democracy, capacity and efficacy. This would be seen, at home and abroad, as an admission of failure by this generation of Europe's leaders. In these circumstances, it would be tempting for a group of member states to attempt to deploy the provisions on enhanced cooperation in some specific policy areas. However, following the rejection of the Constitution by two founding member states, the composition of such a core group (of at least eight states) is difficult to envisage. Under the Nice rules, the scope of enhanced cooperation is limited and its value in procedural terms is questionable. It would endanger the Union's cohesion and challenge the principle of loyal cooperation. There would be complication not simplification.

Scenario Two: vote again to get the right answer

The European Council obliges France, the Netherlands and the UK to have another go at ratifying the existing text once Chirac, Balkenende and Blair are retired – presumably in 2007. This approach may be desirable but hardly seems to be possible.

Scenario Three: avoid treaty change

The European Council cherry-picks a modest number of choice bits from the Constitution and tries to implement them not by treaty amendment but by changes in rules of procedure and inter-institutional agreements or by cooking up new arrangements outside the EU structure altogether. However, even if there were unanimous agreement on this approach in general, it is unlikely that the twenty five could agree on the specifics. Although one or two ad hoc improvements could be made to the conduct of EU affairs at national level, the governance of the EU itself would be left almost untouched. Cherry-picking would be certain to antagonise the Commission and Parliament, and would have to withstand the critical scrutiny of the Court of Justice and national constitutional courts. This scenario lacks transparency and would put into reverse the drive for simplification.

Scenario Four: lower the threshold

The European Council convenes a new IGC with the sole purpose of modifying Article 48 of the existing Treaty on European Union so that the Constitution could be brought into force when ratified by fewer than all member states. Formal provision would also need to be made for second-class or associate membership of the Union. A similar proposal was vigorously opposed by most governments and many national parliaments in the Convention. Even if agreed by an IGC, such a profound change to the existing constitutional order would have to survive the test of numerous referendums. Effectively, this is the scenario of last resort.

Scenario Five: back to the old ways

The Union adopts a gradualist and piecemeal approach to treaty reform, keeping intact as many institutional provisions of the Constitution as possible but ditching the constitutional mantle. The Treaty of Nice would be amended but not replaced. There is, of course, plenty of precedent for this scenario, although none is particularly encouraging. A new Convention could be promoted to prepare the ground but it would be a demoralised affair, its usefulness would inevitably be limited, and its functions quickly ceded to a traditional IGC as each institution and member state vied with each other to protect their own pre-eminent interest. Agreement on priorities for reform would be problematic. Changes to the make-up of QMV in the Council would have to be balanced by changes in the shape and size of the Commission and Parliament. Switching from Council unanimity to QMV without extending codecision with the Parliament would merely serve to widen the democratic deficit. Turning the High Representative into Foreign Minister without making him also Vice-President of the Commission would shatter the inter-institutional balance, and as such be certain to be opposed by most of the smaller member states. In such circumstances the Commission could never be expected to support the setting up of the new external action service. So if this approach is to have any chance of success, the new package promises to be quite complex. If it is to address the Union's key institutional problems, the revised Treaty of Nice would surely need to include reforms with respect to both the formula and scope of QMV, along with codecision; the size and shape of the Commission and Parliament; the setting up of the Foreign Minister and the external action service; integration of the three pillar system; and the status of the Charter.

Under this fifth scenario the Union would try to salvage some institutional reforms by negotiating a tactical retreat from the Constitution. But, in sacrificing the Constitution's package deal, the Union would also be dismantling the impressive consensus that had been built up around it. Experience suggests that it can be more difficult to get basic agreement in the EU when tinkering with institutions than when taking bold steps. Even the suppression of the term 'constitution', while a welcome relief to some, would be a keen disappointment to others. Ad hoc treaty revision according to no long-term strategy smacks of pre-Laeken days. It would not settle the constitutional future of the Union but, on the contrary, threaten further bouts of instability. It would be bound to aggravate relations between the European Council and European Parliament, and might not go down too well with national parliaments or the media either, especially if concluded in inglorious style at a late-night, fractious and incomprehensible summit meeting. Deprived of the promise of a comprehensive constitutional settlement and of better policy making across a wider spectrum, public opinion would be justifiably suspicious. The political consequences of such a tactical retrenchment might be severe, especially in those countries where the referendum genie is out of the bottle and in those which have already ratified successfully the original, better Constitution. If national leaders and their political parties cannot win a referendum when they have the whole panoply of the Constitution in which to campaign, how will they fare when having to dress up lesser amendments?

Scenario Six: renegotiate the Constitution

Doubts about the viability of renegotiating the Treaty of Nice confirm us in our preference for renegotiating the Constitution. The goal is to remedy some problems in the existing text, remove some ambiguities, and make the whole package more appealing to public opinion. In the final two chapters of the book, therefore, we concentrate on this sixth scenario.

CHAPTER 21

A renegotiation on policy

The sudden prospect of having to renegotiate the Constitution in order to get it through the sceptical barrier of public opinion will appal many EU insiders. One of the great achievements of the last few years has been assumed to be the careful construction of a large consensus behind the comprehensive package deal which is the constitutional treaty. The realisation that that famous consensus, forged in the Convention and concluded at the IGC, is not, after all, sufficiently large to carry the Constitution into force is a bitter one. Member states which have already ratified the Constitution will be unhappy to have to annul their decision. Yes campaigners in France and the Netherlands will find it especially galling to concede victory to the Noes. Some will doubtless continue to be in denial of the political reality that the Constitution cannot enter into force unchanged. There will also be those – not least in Britain – who will settle for second best, and who will be relieved to pass on to a succeeding generation the big challenge of turning united Europe into a good constitutional democracy. The argument of unripe time is always with us, but the chances are that the Constitution will be easier to renegotiate now than at some future date when the memories of the Convention and the IGC have faded.

There are certainly risks in renegotiation. A second failure might have worse consequences than the first. It is not always easy to get people to change their minds. Re-opening a negotiation over complex elements that make up a balance of power might not lead to better solutions. Some issues in politics are intractable.

Before embarking on such an ambitious course of action, therefore, one had better be sure that judicious amendment of the constitutional treaty is not only very much worth the risk but also that it is entirely feasible. Renegotiation is only practicable if it can be agreed that the existing text should be treated as a good first draft. To determine the answer to that question should be the main task of the British presidency of the Council during the autumn of 2005. Will member states approach a renegotiation of the existing text with equanimity?

LAEKEN RE-VISITED

In order to check out the strengths and weaknesses of the constitutional project, and to learn lessons about how to rectify short-comings, the European Council could do worse than to re-visit the Laeken mandate. One recalls that the Laeken Declaration set the Convention three main goals, as follows:

- to bring citizens, and primarily the young, closer to the European design and the European institutions;
- to organise politics and the European political area in an enlarged Union;
- to develop the Union into a stabilising factor and a model in the new, multipolar world.

Ironically, the constitutional exercise has brought the citizen, even youth, abruptly closer to the EU. Lessons can certainly be learned, especially by the Commission and by national parliaments, about how to improve the public relations of any new Convention. Given that constitution-mongering does not have a great salience in the public mind, the Giscard Convention relied largely on the media, NGOs and academic critics to stimulate a wider interest. Beyond insisting on transparency of operations, the Convention did not, frankly, pay much attention to its public relations: perhaps it should have done. One could learn from that mistake, as would the media for whom the daily grind of the Convention process proved difficult to sustain high-level coverage. By contrast, the thwarted referendum campaigns were good for the media, as would be a new Convention born out of a remarkable and unexpected crisis. Even after intensive engagement in the recent referendum campaigns it is unlikely that many voters will have grasped the niceties of the ordinary legislative procedure or will be able to recite by rote the list of shared competences. But one certainly hopes that many French and Dutch citizens now know a lot more about the institutions that govern them from Brussels, and are more generally aware of the large political power and immense potential of the European Union to do good (or bad). The Convention experience prepared the ground for this shift in public awareness. In that it did its work in public and contained representatives from both government and opposition, its impact was broader than the formerly closed world of EU intergovernmental diplomacy. The precedent of the Convention was a good one, and deserves to be followed again.

Giscard d'Estaing, who succeeded beyond expectations in weaving together the intergovernmentalist and federalist strands of the argument without suppressing either, has claimed that the Convention struck the 'necessary balance between peoples, between states old and new, between institutions and between dream and reality'.[1]

ORGANISING EUROPEAN POLITICS

The second injunction of Laeken was to reorganise European politics. Our verdict on this count is broadly positive. The Constitution shifts the centre of political gravity within the European Union without destroying the basic institutional structure of Commission, Parliament, Council and Court. The Union with the basic structure of the Constitution will be more democratic, more efficient and more effective. Its system of government will be somewhat simpler and a lot clearer. Normalisation of the ordinary legislative procedure boosts the powers of the Parliament and Commission. Opening up the Council will grow its authority. Making the Charter of Fundamental Rights binding should protect and encourage European citizenship. Under the Constitution, the EU's policy decisions, and their translation into law or regulation, should be more responsive to public demand and better equipped to rise to the social, economic, technological and environmental challenges faced by Europe.

The Constitution makes the Union stronger without making the member states weaker. The European Council is installed at the top of the institutional hierarchy. National parliaments still matter, some of them very much; and they are encouraged by the Constitution to become more engaged in EU affairs. The Union wins greater competence, especially in the fields of internal and external security, but it is far from being omnipotent. The concept of post-national Europe is advanced by the Constitution, but the concept of nation-state Europe is not eliminated. The two will continue to cohabit the political market place of the EU for some generations to come, with the likelihood of greater assertiveness below the level of the state by regions.

Although its federal qualities have been accentuated under the Constitution, the European Union is not a federal state, still less a centralised super-state. The EU cannot do things that a state does, like running a budget deficit, raising an army or levying taxes autonomously. The Constitution means that the EU cannot act outside its competences or force a state to stay a member against its will. European unification does not mean European uniformity. Interdependence between member states is still the order of the day, coalescing around a common value system, with states' autonomy tempered by the obligation of loyalty to the supranational authority. The Constitution's motto 'Unity in Diversity' is, in fact, quite apt.

[1] On receiving the Charlemagne Prize in Aachen on Ascension Day 2003.

The Constitution does not answer definitively the tempting question about where the boundaries of the Union lie. Ultimately, the boundary question will be settled by Europe's success in forging a well-governed, self-governing political community, and the Constitution is a prerequisite for this. As the referendum campaigns testified, the recent enlargement has been destabilising, and the constitutional experience, if and when complete, should help the Union to overcome the shock. The Constitution is intended to demonstrate that the Union can widen and deepen at the same time. Without the Constitution, ten new member states will have been taken on board but the EU will have lost its momentum of integration and its capacity to take decisions: further enlargement will be unreasonable, even pointless.

The temptation to form a core group of certain countries is strong, especially among the euro group members otherwise frustrated by the lack of centralised fiscal and economic policies. The Constitution makes enhanced cooperation more viable by allowing core groups to use QMV in places where the rest of the Council is obliged to stick with unanimity. It facilitates its introduction in the field of judicial cooperation, and it extends the scope of differentiated integration into the area of defence.

Good constitutions can adapt serenely in the light of experience to meet changing social, economic and political necessities. We have noted the provisions in the Constitution that are evolutive, permitting the gradual adjustments to be made to the system of government without a root and branch exercise in heavy constitutional amendment.

EUROPE AS A GLOBAL PLAYER

The third mission of Laeken was to make the European Union a more effective player on the world stage. Here we can be confident that the Constitution provides for radical change, of which the Minister Vice-President, chairing the Council and running a new diplomatic administration, is the most striking illustration. The Constitution abolishes the clumsy pillar system which separates out foreign and security policy from the rest, and assumes an international legal personality for the Union as a whole. Even before the Constitution comes into force, the Union has instituted the new European Defence Agency and is preparing to set up the external action service. Despite lingering anxieties about the relationship between the Foreign Minister on the one hand and the Presidents of the European Council and of the European Commission on the other, one can be fairly confident that the Constitution would at last have provided the Union with the means to speak with one voice in international affairs.

The fascinating question not answered by the Constitution is what does the Union want to say with its single voice. Global reach carries a duty to be globally responsible and coherent. There is no lack of international challenges for which the Union must learn to prioritise. Many of those issues should not be neglected for long, but the deteriorating state of transatlantic relations has to be tackled at once and really cannot be ignored now even if Europeans sometimes give the impression that they would prefer to leave their alliance with America in a permanent state of semi-disrepair. On the other side of the Atlantic, Americans must learn more about European integration and about how to cope with a more powerful political Europe. The Constitution provides the wherewithal for the European Union to become either a credible partner of the USA or a serious rival to it. A lot depends on the outcome of this dilemma, not only for America and Europe but for the wider world, and particularly for the future of the United Nations.

Failure to have the Constitution would have ramifications worldwide. The Union would suffer a huge blow to its hard-earned political credibility. The danger is that it would cease to be a serious potential partner for either China or Russia and that the development of a genuinely multi-polar international system would be put on hold. American neo-conservatives might gloat if the Constitution is defeated, but they would be woefully misguided. Defeat for the Constitution would be a victory for those in Europe who seek to turn their faces against globalisation, who are innately hostile to America and who prefer an inward looking Fortress Europe to that postulated by the Constitution.

Overall, therefore, our verdict about the Constitution is overwhelmingly positive. It has fulfilled the Laeken goals. It is important for Europe's future. And it should be salvaged if possible. It could and should be treated as a good first draft of a final settlement that emerges, improved, after a judicious renegotiation.

THE EUROPEAN ECONOMY

The middle of the downturn in the economic cycle was an odd time to choose to hold referendums. A renegotiated Constitution could do with a little help from economic growth. The Laeken European Council did not directly pose — and the Convention did not really address — the problem of the European economy. Changes made by the Constitution to the system of economic governance of the EU are useful but minimal. Instead, European leaders have settled on the Lisbon agenda as their panacea for economic growth, but they have proved themselves inadequate at putting their prescriptions into practical effect. Many economists have analysed the problem of non-implementation, and the Commission of José Manuel Barroso has made refurbishment of the Lisbon agenda the central feature of its five year programme. But French voters, worried about being undercut by the Polish plumber and resentful of the delocalisation of factories eastwards, were untrusting of the Constitution and unmoved by the Lisbon agenda. And Dutch voters complained about how the larger members of the euro group – France, Germany and Italy – had been flouting the commonly agreed fiscal rules. Both French and Dutch voters see the promise of 'social Europe' as much-needed compensation for the austerity and competition they have experienced in the wake of the single currency and enlargement. The liberalisation implied in the on-going policy process to consolidate the EU single market, particularly in the services sector, is seen as a threat to the minimum standards of social welfare also established by the Union, and a threat that unfortunately coincides with demographic pressures on pensions and the challenges of globalisation to European competitiveness.

In the Convention there was much debate between its liberal and socialist wings about the risks of social and fiscal dumping, especially from the accession states. The final consensus maintained a good balance between liberal market economics and social welfare politics. The Constitution, as we know, strengthens recognition of the public service industries and installs the Charter, with its social rights, with binding force. It also boosts the role at EU level of trade unions. What the Constitution does not do well is to spell out clearly the economic policy objectives of the Lisbon agenda in terms of public and private investment, education, training and research – goals which, if disseminated, could not fail to appeal even to French and Dutch workers. (Article 15, for example, on the coordination of economic, employment and social policies is completely silent on what those policies might actually be.) A renegotiated Constitution could usefully include a didactic provision on the European social market economy explaining how and why the social dimension should be developed inside the framework of a regulated but liberal economy. Such a formula needs to be able to calm the exaggerated fears of the CBI as well as putting the subject beyond even the misinterpretation of the dissidents of the French socialist party.

As far as the tighter government of the economic and monetary union is concerned, the euro group aspires to ever-closer coordination of economic policy. It would be sensible for it to establish itself formally as a core group under the enhanced cooperation provisions of the Constitution. However, at present, Article 44 of the Constitution restricts enhanced cooperation to the non-exclusive competences of the Union. Monetary policy is an exclusive competence for member states whose currency is the euro. So an adjustment of the Constitution is needed here. The euro group should indicate that it intends to take advantage of the Constitution's facility of enhanced cooperation and seek to amend the Constitution accordingly. Such a signal of the euro group's political determination to move on from the budgetary confusion of the early years of the euro would command the support both of those French who want to curb the absolute independence of the European Central Bank and of those thrifty Dutch who want more fiscal discipline.

It is a paradox that so much public hostility has been created in the one area of European integration in which the Constitution made so few changes. Most of what the French centre left has objected to is not an innovation of the Constitution, but a re-statement of key aspects of the European Union such as freedom of movement of workers, freedom of establishment, and competition and state aids policy. The lack of popular understanding of what integration has involved over nearly sixty years is quite a remarkable – and depressing – phenomenon when witnessed in two *pays fondateurs*. Clearly, more sustained public information campaigning is urgently needed. A renegotiated Constitution would stimulate a further round of hot debate. A renegotiated Constitution that had made some distinct improvements to the economic governance of the Union would be very much more likely to pass.

In the meantime, the Union has to demonstrate that it has the political will to persevere with the structural reform of the European economies. Nothing is less attractive to the electorate than drift and division at the top. The European Commission, for its part, must deploy more forcefully all its available faculties, including incentives for investment and strictures for non-compliance with commonly agreed disciplines. The parties to the Constitution must not retire from their grave commitment to co-ordinate their macro and micro-economic policies just because co-ordination is difficult. The revision of the Stability and Growth Pact, the extension of the single market to the services sector (both public and private), the negotiations on the new multi-annual financial framework and the reform of the CAP or structural funds will be taking place in parallel with the renegotiation of the Constitution. They must be marshalled in aid of the Constitution and not allowed to undermine it. To reject the Constitution because of painful economic restructuring would be stupid. Fiscal discipline can be consolidated under the Constitution. Policy choices about the content of directives on services, chemicals or patents will not be affected by the Constitution. Decisions on EU spending have to be attuned to the redefinition of objectives and competences as laid down in the Constitution. Settling the negotiations over the new financial perspectives must in any case be accomplished by the end of 2006 regardless of the constitutional agenda. The fact is that economic and constitutional reforms are both necessary and mutually reinforcing. They must both be made part of the exercise which

Blair calls 'getting the politics right'. A new European consensus has to embrace common rules in economics and finance just as much as in institutional and judicial matters. There is no shortage of ideas about how to promote the linkage between economic and political integration. Romano Prodi commissioned two reports that should be early homework for those tasked with renegotiation of the Constitution. The first, entitled *An agenda for a growing Europe* and published in 2003, was by a group of independent experts led by André Sapir. The second, entitled *Building a political Europe: 50 proposals for tomorrow's Europe*, published in 2004, was the product of a round table chaired by Dominique Strauss-Kahn.

CLIMATE SECURITY

Renegotiation of the Constitution will not succeed unless the Union manages to sharpen the policy choices and, with a refreshed political agenda, to write it down well. The authors of the Constitution must focus on the big themes and relate them in more appealing language than the technical jargon one finds in much of the current Part Three. The social market economy is one such theme. Sustainable development is another.

When the Treaty of Rome was being drafted in 1956 food was still rationed across most of Europe. It was natural to make food security the central story of the new European Economic Community, with the Common Agricultural Policy its main prop. Today, terrorism aside, it is climate change that is our greatest preoccupation. In the current Constitution, environment policy is assigned two modest articles. The primary purpose of the policy is to 'contribute to the pursuit of ... preserving, protecting and improving the quality of the environment'.[2] Agriculture and fisheries, on the other hand, enjoys eight articles. The primary purpose of the CAP is 'to increase agricultural productivity by promoting technical progress and by ensuring the rational development of agricultural production and the optimum utilisation of the factors of production, in particular labour'.[3] The provisions on environment policy are twenty years old (the Single Act), while those on agriculture are fifty years old. Surely it is not beyond the collective wit of the Union to be able to re-write these key chapters of the Constitution to give climate security the greater salience, to adapt environment policy so that it reflects contemporary needs and future aspirations both domestically and globally, and to amend the CAP so that it contributes positively not only to

[2]   Article III–233.1.
[3]   Article III–227.1.

feeding Europe but also to meeting its environmental goals? (Most Green voters in France and Holland voted against the Constitution, by the way – just like the farmers.) EU policies on energy, transport and communications should also be made to conform more strictly to the imperatives of its environmental agenda.

A bold renegotiation would also seize the opportunity to assimilate Euratom, which has an anomalous position under the current Constitution. Surely there can be little justification for shirking a political debate at the EU level about the future of the civil nuclear industry.

Upgrading the importance and improving the quality of its environment policy would have an impact on all the Union's international policies, including trade, aid and development. The EU's impressive normative power has a greater stretch than its negotiating clout in international forums. Green Europe would be more influential than Fortress Europe, especially in the Union's neighbourhoods to the east and south.

Raising the threshold

A European Union with climate security at the heart of its policy stance would be well defined, especially in contradistinction to the USA. But it would also be valuable as a tool in dealing with the candidacies of countries in the Balkans and in the Black Sea region. Climate security cannot be pursued as a genuine policy goal without a market economy, good governance, the rule of law and an incorruptible judiciary. Climate security and fundamental rights are European twins, and those who seek to join the European family will have to accept paternity duty.

In addition, we have already noted how neither the Copenhagen criteria on enlargement of 1993 nor the revamped version of 2004 is to be found in the Constitution. They should be. European citizens are fellow strangers, and they have every right to know how large and how strange their political society might become in their lifetime as well as the precise conditions and pace for its expansion. A more positive story about enlargement, told in the Constitution, might also allay some of the fears of public opinion. As Tony Blair told the European Parliament in a speech on 23 June 2005, enlargement is not 'a zero sum game in which old members lose as new members gain'. Enlargement is an engine of growth, a vehicle for democracy and a projection of security. It is a good story, and should be properly told.

To recap, a renegotiation of Part Three of the Constitution should concentrate on modernising the social, economic, environmental and enlargement policies of the Union. All chapters, however, would need to be re-visited and some, like the CAP, would need to be radically re-structured. Where policy directions have been taken in the comparatively new and fast-growing field of justice and home affairs, the constitutional text should point the way. Citizens deserve to know more not only about how decisions will be taken but what they will contain. Fleshing out the policy content is particularly important where citizens' rights and livelihoods are concerned. Public confidence has to be built up, for example, in the capacity of the Union to develop a realistic common asylum and immigration policy. And the development of a sense of European identity and shared destiny has to be democratic.

CHAPTER 22

An institutional agenda

In this chapter, we look at some institutional matters which could form part of the negotiation of a revised Constitution. If renegotiation is to work, the reforms will have to be highly practicable. Whatever direction the renegotiation takes, it should not lose the pragmatic quality of the work of the earlier Convention and the IGC. Nobody will thank the leadership of the Union for imposing yet another introspective debate, however grand and reflective, if its practical results are nugatory. So the imperative of any renegotiation of the institutional package is that it further enhances the capacity of the Union to act. Those who hanker to assert more national sovereignty need not get over-excited by the prospect of renegotiation. There is no majority in Europe for a less competent Union with weaker institutions. It is noticeable that those who cling to the cliché that Europe 'should do less but do it better' have a very short agreed list of items for retrenchment, largely confined to curbing the over-regulation of the single market and to rectifying unwise spending decisions.

In the course of this book we have identified some provisions of the constitutional treaty signed on 29 October 2004 which give rise to lingering doubts or apprehension. The goal of the proposed renegotiation should be to subject the more important of those items to further examination and useful second thoughts without blasting open the whole of Pandora's famous box. The necessity to maintain or, rather, rebuild consensus is a prerequisite for the operation. Revision should only be contemplated where there is a reasonable chance of reaching agreement within a couple of years. The time is not ripe, so soon after the first Convention, to tackle some matters, such as the presidency of the European Council, where experience of how it works in practice is needed before considering what, if any improvements to make. If the Constitution, modestly renegotiated, can be brought into force in 2009, the prospect will then open up of further, incremental revision according to the provisions laid down. The present renegotiation should be limited to what it can do well and to what is necessary to do to remove some ambiguities in order to make the project less difficult to market to a sceptical public opinion. One of the things it could do, indeed, is to widen the scope of what can be revised in the future by more flexible methods, allowing for smoother evolution and allaying fears about future paralysis. The Dutch and the British have had more historical experience than the French of how good constitutions are evolutionary.

CONTENT

What, then, is our catalogue of institutional amendments which conform to the rubric of being timely, practicable, evolutive and, above all, consensual? Chastened by the referendum results in France and Holland, the Union needs to review the way it caters for constitutional change itself. It would be wise to insert, at the top of the hierarchy of norms, provision for an organic or constitutional law of the Union. The purpose of this instrument could be two-fold. First, organic laws would provide for any amendment to Part Two (the Charter) or Part Three of the Constitution and its Protocols where the distribution of competences is not affected – including institutional as well as policy matters. Second, use of organic laws could be extended to legislate for a limited number of quasi-constitutional matters such as the own resources system, the uniform electoral procedure of the Parliament, or the location of the institutions. The decision-making procedure should be heavier than the ordinary legislative procedure but lighter (and with broader scope) than the proposed 'simplified revision procedure'. For example, organic laws could be enacted by the Council acting by super QMV, following verification by the Court of Justice that competences were not affected, and with the assent of the European Parliament acting by two thirds of its component Members. The law could come into force after four fifths of national parliaments give an affirmative vote. Amendments such as these, taken together, would render Part Three distinctly subsidiary to Part One, and would silence those critics who fear perpetual stasis under the stringent amendment procedures of the current Constitution.

With respect to the general *passerelle* clause, the number of national parliaments that can exercise a veto should be raised from one to one third. This would bring the *passerelle* into line with the subsidiarity mechanism, and prevent the substitution of a government veto by a pseudo-veto of a national parliament.

As far as Parts One and Four of the Constitution are concerned, revision should adhere to the triple process of Convention, IGC and national ratification. In addition, the European Parliament would be required to give its assent. However, the agreed revision should be enabled to come into force once four fifths of member states have completed their ratification processes. As a safety valve, the Constitution's provisions on near neighbours should be expanded to accommodate the interests of a member state which, baulking at constitutional changes, chose not to retain all the duties and privileges of full EU membership but sought to remain a close associate.

No further amendment need be made to the delimitation of competence in the Constitution apart from two adjustments to make the exclusive competences less exclusive. First, the principle of subsidiarity should apply across the board to all the actions of the Union, encouraging rigour as to where and how powers are exercised. This change would enhance the authority of national parliaments, as well as regional and local government. Second, enhanced cooperation should be allowed in the areas of exclusive competence. This would facilitate the greater unity of the euro group.

The Constitution's proposal that, as from 2014, the size of the Commission should be two thirds the number of member states has been criticised as being too large (and too late). A reduction in the number to say, half, would improve efficiency and lessen the sense of exclusion for those nationalities without a current member. It would also be desirable in this context to revisit the concept of equal rotation. One cannot be sure that a college without a representative of the largest nationalities will work well.

Likewise, the size of the Court of Auditors should be cut in half in the interests of attaining the highest professional standards.

Whereas issues surrounding the presidency of the European Council and Council of Ministers fall into the category of the unripe, it should be possible to re-launch the undervalued idea of establishing a separate formation of the Council for law making. A discreet legislative chamber, open to the press and publishing its verbatim proceedings in normal parliamentary fashion, would dramatically increase the public profile and authority of the Council. It would also encourage the emergence of cabinet ministers responsible for EU affairs who would be well placed to ensure coherence within their own administrations and to be answerable to national parliaments for the European dimension of government policy. The fact that foreign ministries loathe this proposal does not make it a bad one.

It should also be possible for the renegotiation to strip out some of the over-complicating qualifications added to the original Constitution. The decision of the IGC to raise the threshold of QMV from the Convention's proposal of 50 per cent of member states representing 60 per cent of the population to 55/65 may now be regretted by the smaller states. As compensation for the loss of equal rotation in the Commission, small states could demand that the new QMV threshold becomes 50/50. Faced with the prospect of Turkey becoming the most populated member state around 2030, one would not be astonished to see this modification carry the day eventually. Simplification suggests it now.

A bold renegotiation, going well, should also be asked to review the need to retain all thirty abnormal legislative procedures, including the three 'emergency brake' clauses installed by the UK at the previous IGC. Some, of course, would switch to become organic laws. Amendments to the policy chapters – especially, as suggested above, in relation to social, economic, environmental and enlargement policies – may of themselves induce some procedural changes.

The right of individual citizens to address the Court of First Instance may still be too limited. Something more could be done to grant privileged access to the Court of Justice for regional governments with legislative powers. Refreshment of the policy content in justice and home affairs should spark a review of whether it is still appropriate for the Court of Justice to be refused jurisdiction over cross-border operations of the police and security services.

No renegotiation would be complete without taking the chance to up-date work on codification of jurisprudence. The revised Constitution should also reflect the latest institutional developments, including the provision in the 2005 Framework Agreement between Commission and Parliament concerning votes of no confidence in individual Commissioners. A significant policy advance deserving of a reference in Part Three is the European arrest warrant.

Naturally, the British, Danish and Irish will wish to exploit the opportunity given by renegotiation to reconsider whether their several opt-outs still contribute to the success of the European Union or reflect the wider concerns of their citizens.

Lastly, there will be pressure from representatives of minority language communities to revise the provisions on the use of language in the Union. Without extending the number of official languages into which everything must be translated, it should be possible to insist that every citizen can address the institutions in his or her language of choice.

PROCESS

The European Council in June 2006 is due to take a decision about if, and if so how to proceed with the Constitution. In the meantime, the period of reflection should be used to assemble a wide consensus around the need to persevere with the project. Under the Austrian presidency, the leaders should draw up a fresh mandate for a new Convention along the lines suggested here. The period of reflection should have managed to clarify the broad scope of what may be possible from the renegotiation. The new Convention could begin work, under a tight timetable, in September 2006 and deliver up a renegotiated text by June 2007. Ideally, the new IGC should be convened immediately and the Convention should stay in being for the duration of the IGC so that it is consulted about proposed further changes. Such a codecisional exercise, with constitutional texts being shuttled between Convention and IGC, would contribute to building a stronger consensus based on greater public awareness of what will be at stake. With luck, a new constitutional treaty could enter into force, following ratification in all member states, on 1 November 2009, when many of the institutional changes were in any case due to become operational. Where, as in France and Britain, governments cannot resist referendums, the European Council should at least agree to hold them all on the same day so that the lottery element of the present sorry circumstances is at least diminished. A common storyline might even be agreed. And the formerly amateurish approach to fighting referendum campaigns could usefully be dropped.

If success is to be feasible, both the content of the Constitution and the process by which it is arrived at need these modest improvements. Second thoughts can be shown to be very useful. One failure is not a humiliation. Practice can move the constitutional settlement Europe needs closer to perfection.

Given rebirth in this way, the new constitutional treaty will be democratically arrived at, socially responsible and politically credible. It should command a consensus which, while being profoundly European, would nevertheless be an example of regional integration that could be emulated in other parts of the world. Such a Constitution, which is within our reach, would widen the vision of the peoples of Europe and improve our system of government. It would put things into a post-national context, and be a timely consensus, fit to match the concerns and ambitions of a large majority of Europe's citizens. Europeans should then be capable of uniting around their first Constitution, and be proud to do so.

Index

The suffix '*tab*' after a page number denotes a table or chart within the text; '*n*' denotes a footnote at the bottom of the page.